Looking for America
on the New Jersey Turnpike

Angus Kress Gillespie
and Michael Aaron Rockland

Illustrations by Ruth Strohl-Palmer

Rutgers University Press
New Brunswick and London

Looking
for
America
on the New Jersey Turnpike

"Countin' the cars on the New Jersey Turnpike,
They've all come to look for America."
                              —Paul Simon, "America"

We gratefully acknowledge the following:

Paul Simon, "America." Copyright © 1968 by Paul Simon.

Allen Ginsberg, "Bayonne Entering NYC" and "Bayonne Turnpike to Tus-carora," in *The Fall of America, Poems 1966–1971;* "Howl," in *Howl and Other Poems;* "Don't Grow Old," in *Mind Breaths, Poems 1972–1977.* Copyright © by Allen Ginsberg. Reprinted by permission of City Lights Books.

Tom De Haven, *Jersey Luck.* Used by permission of Tom De Haven.

Bruce Springsteen, "State Trooper" and "Open All Night," from *Nebraska;* "Wreck on the Highway," from *The River.* Copyright © by Bruce Springsteen.

Joseph Cosgriff, "I Like Jersey Best." Green Monster Music. Copyright © 1981. Performed by John Pizzarelli, Jr., on LP and CD, Stash Records, New York, N.Y.

Fletcher Knebel, *Dark Horse.* Copyright © 1972 by Fletcher Knebel. Reprinted by permission of Doubleday, a division of Bantam, Doubleday, Dell Publishing Group, Inc.

James Lukach, "Milltown." Used by permission of James Lukach.

Marguerite Doernbach, "Observations." Used by permission of Marguerite Doernbach.

Dan Fogarty, "The N.J. T'Pike Blues." Used by permission of Dan Fogarty.

Gale Abrahamson, "N.J. Turnpike." Used by permission of Gale Abrahamson.

For Patricia
—M.A.R.

For Rowena
—A.K.G.

Contents

Preface

"Oh public road. . . . You express me better
than I can express myself."
—Walt Whitman, "Song of the Open Road"

From the comfortable and spacious top-floor office of the chairman of the New Jersey Turnpike Authority in New Brunswick, overlooking interchange 9, one gazes down on a scene of endless activity.[1] Elsewhere in the headquarters sensitive computers and a big board reminiscent of that in Strategic Air Command headquarters in Omaha, Nebraska, monitor traffic the length of the road, but here one actually looks at that traffic: twelve lanes of endless trucks and buses and automobiles and motorcycles. Cloverleafs circle out into the surrounding countryside; vehicles line up at the tollbooths waiting to get onto the pike; other lines of vehicles wait to get off. This is how the Turnpike looks, 24 hours a day, 365 days a year.

The scene below seems to charge Joseph "Bo" Sullivan's personal engines. "Sure I get a kick out of watching it," Sullivan says. A sometime candidate for governor, Sullivan isn't required to be in his office more than a few hours a month (Turnpike Authority chairman is an unpaid, honorary position). But he is there thirty-five hours a week, earning his living as president of a textile firm in Totowa, New Jersey. He is also a major figure in Republican state politics; in 1988, he ran the Bush presidential campaign in New Jersey. Besides the thirty-five hours a week at the Turnpike, Sullivan puts in thirty-five at his factory and twenty in politics. "I don't need much sleep, and I never watch television," he says.

Sullivan is like the Turnpike itself: a bundle of unrestricted energy. Though his knees are somewhat arthritic from injuries suffered years ago playing football for Princeton, he races around his office getting documents, lighting up cigarettes, cracking jokes. "Being chairman of the Turnpike Authority," he says, "is the best political platform there is. Other politicians running for something have to stay in their districts, but my 'district' is from the George Washington Bridge down to Deepwater. I make speeches anywhere and nobody can complain."[2]

The New Jersey Turnpike chairman is a powerful political figure. Chairmen tend to become governors; governors tend to become chairmen, as if there is a revolving door between the Authority and the Capitol. Alfred Driscoll, who served as governor when the Turnpike was built, returned to public life years later as chairman of the Turnpike Authority. Mirroring

INTERCHANGES

1 Delaware Memorial Bridge
2 Swedesboro • Chester
3 Woodbury • So. Camden
4 Camden • Philadelphia
5 Burlington • Mt Holly
6 Pennsylvania Turnpike
7 Bordentown • Trenton
7A Trenton • Shore Points
8 Hightstown • Freehold
8A Jamesburg • Cranbury
9 New Brunswick
10 Metuchen • Edison Township
11 Garden State Pkwy • Woodbridge • The Amboys
12 Carteret • Rahway
13 Elizabeth • Verrazano Bridge
13A Newark Airport • Elizabeth Seaport
14 Newark Airport
14A Bayonne
14B Jersey City
14C Holland Tunnel
15E Newark • Jersey City
15W Newark • The Oranges
16E Lincoln Tunnel • Secaucus
16W Sports Plex • Secaucus • Rutherford
18E & W George Washington Bridge

GEORGE WASHINGTON BRIDGE

NEW YORK CITY

PHILADELPHIA

PA TURNPIKE

ATLANTIC OCEAN

DELAWARE MEMORIAL BRIDGE

DELAWARE BAY

REST AREAS

A Clara Barton
B John Fenwick
C Walt Whitman
D James Fenimore Cooper
E Richard Stockton
F Woodrow Wilson
G Molly Pitcher
H Joyce Kilmer
I Grover Cleveland
J Thomas Edison
K William F. Halsey
L Alexander Hamilton
M Vince Lombardi

Driscoll's career, the Authority's first chairman, Paul Troast, ran for governor in 1953. In Fletcher Knebel's novel *Dark Horse,* Eddie Quinn, a commissioner of the Turnpike Authority, not even chairman, becomes the Democratic party's dark-horse candidate for president of the United States.[3] If you look at "Bo" Sullivan's office, you see evidence of the kind of power the chairman of the New Jersey Turnpike exercises. Covering the walls are photographs of Sullivan with Ronald Reagan, Sullivan with Gerald Ford, Sullivan with Governor Tom Kean, Sullivan with George Bush. "Yeah," he says, "the great thing about this job is that you can make a difference. What kind of shape would New Jersey be in without the Turnpike?"

The New Jersey Turnpike has certainly shaped New Jersey. While the state's geography, history, and economics made the building of the Turnpike inevitable, the Turnpike has conditioned much of New Jersey's subsequent development. Along the Turnpike is found New Jersey's population and its power. If New Jersey, as has often been suggested, is shaped like a woman, the Turnpike is her spinal column, each exit a vertebra.

One travels through the middle of the state on the Turnpike. Beginning in rural Salem County, four lanes of asphalt roll inexorably north toward the spreading suburbs of Camden. Picking up dense traffic spilling out of Philadelphia, the Turnpike widens to six lanes passing through the farms of Burlington County and on its way past the state capital, Trenton. The route then passes the state university at New Brunswick and enters the characteristic area of the Turnpike, a dense region of urbanization and industrialization—so dense that the roadway now expands to twelve lanes as, through the windshield, one gazes at bridges, factories, and oil refineries. Near Newark, the Turnpike splits in two. The westerly alignment carries traffic bound for the George Washington Bridge and New England. The original Turnpike mainline to the east carries traffic headed for the Lincoln Tunnel and New York City.

Getting the Turnpike built took enormous amounts of money. It also took political clout. Once built, the Turnpike Authority became a major force in the state with the unchallenged right to issue its own revenue bonds. In time, the Authority had its own seal, its own distinctive license plates, and its own police force. It also had its own salary schedule, outside the civil service framework. William Flanagan, at the time he retired as executive director of the Turnpike Authority in 1988, was receiving a salary nearly twice that of the governor of the state.

The Turnpike Authority even had its own laws—the regulations by which it assumed extraordinary police powers. Beyond the effective control of the state legislature and governor, the Turnpike Authority became a state within a state. And every citizen who crossed the state had to pay tribute. We examine how such a monolithic institution functions within a democratic framework.

But there is a more significant aspect to our story. Although the Turnpike is rooted in New Jersey, it is quite possibly America's most important road, certainly its widest and most traveled. In the most mobile nation on earth, where the automobile has an importance unrivaled anywhere, this is an important distinction. Therefore, we not only discuss the New Jersey Turnpike as a physical artifact but explore it as an emblem of American ideas and values. As the title of the book suggests, we use the Turnpike to look for America.

The Turnpike represents a number of American ideas and values. Built as economically as possible, with virtually no attention to aesthetics, the Turnpike is the embodiment of American pragmatism and of the triumph of function over form. Offering its patrons virtually no amenities, and with an exclusively bottom-line approach to management, the Turnpike is an unabashed shrine to American materialism. In a nation that prides itself on its level of personal freedom—and in which such freedom is often equated with the open road—the Turnpike represents a contrary American tendency toward conformity, if not repression. In a nation still very much in the thrall of an agrarian myth, the giant, machinelike Turnpike, cutting relentlessly through the Garden State, forcefully reminds America of its industrial reality.

This conflict between pastoral ideal and industrial fact is the subject of our first chapter, "The Machine in the Garden State." We then look at the physical Turnpike in Chapter 2, "Building the Pike," the economics of the Turnpike in Chapter 3, "A River of Cash," and the Turnpike as a political institution in Chapter 4, "The Authority of the Authority." Chapters 5, "Waiting for a Tow," and 6, "Road Hazards," describe what happens to motorists on the Turnpike when problems arise. In Chapter 7, "Over the Fence," we discuss the natural antagonism that exists between the expansionist Turnpike and those most directly affected, its immediate neighbors. Chapter 8, "Rest Area Culture," examines life in the Turnpike's 24-hour-a-day, 365-day-a-year oases, while Chapter 9, "So Bad, It's Good," looks at why the Turnpike, despite its ugliness, inspires so much art. In Chapter 10, "Tunnel Vision," we turn from art to aesthetics, examining what the Turnpike represents of American aesthetic ideas. Finally, in Chapter 11, "The Future of the Turnpike," we consider scenarios for the Turnpike's future.

Despite our attempt in these chapters to discover larger meanings for the Turnpike—the ideas and values of which it is emblematic—the New Jersey Turnpike is also, of course, just there, part of the landscape, and we try to describe it accurately, capture its flavor, and discuss what makes it unique among roads.

The New Jersey Turnpike is not the oldest turnpike in the country. Actually, turnpikes, which may be defined as any road charging a toll, go back to the eighteenth century in America. It is not even the first modern turnpike. That distinction belongs to the Pennsylvania Turnpike, which was opened in 1940, ten years before construction began on the New Jersey Turnpike. Nor is it the longest. The Pennsylvania Turnpike is easily twice as long.

But the New Jersey Turnpike is the busiest toll road in the nation. By the late 1980s, it was carrying 190 million vehicles and logging 4 billion vehicle miles per year.[4] The Turnpike is no doubt also the busiest thoroughfare in the world, though the Authority is reluctant to make that claim officially because reliable statistics from the rest of the world are difficult to obtain.[5]

Because the New Jersey Turnpike is so heavily used, it is very familiar to most Americans. For people from the rest of the country, it is one of the central experiences of the East Coast, along with Times Square in New York and the Liberty Bell in Philadelphia. Mention of the New Jersey Turnpike evokes powerful images of dense traffic combined with an industrial landscape and chemically fouled air.

For New Jerseyans, the Turnpike is not only a primary form of transportation; it is, perhaps, their most important common experience, the source of much of what it means to be a New Jerseyan. Because of its centrality in New Jersey life and its immensity and power, the Turnpike is representative of New Jersey, as turnpikes in such states as Massachusetts and Maryland, New York and Pennsylvania, are not.

There is a problem in viewing the Turnpike as characteristic of New Jersey, however: one is likely to gain a distorted vision of the state. Because the Turnpike passes through such an extraordinarily industrialized area, there is a tendency, especially among visitors, to see New Jersey as a place of unrelieved blight. There is blight, but it is by no means unrelieved. The Garden State has vast areas of pretty countryside, fine beaches, charming colonial towns, enormously productive farmland, and the largest deer population in the United States. It is also the ultimate suburban state, but it suffers from a negative industrial image generated in large measure by the Turnpike itself.

Part of our initial fascination with the Turnpike as the subject of a book stemmed from a reaction to the stereotype. We also found ourselves wondering, Is a gritty image of New Jersey necessarily a bad thing? Must the often bizarre landscape one sees from the northern reaches of the Turnpike be regarded as ugly? Is it not also a source of jobs and energy and wealth and production and perhaps even a curious kind of beauty?

New Jerseyans have grown accustomed to the negative imagery attached to their state. One way of coping is to concede the point and turn it into a joke. Gary Bamburak, of Bound Brook, is an entrepreneur who carries a line of T-shirts with such slogans as "New Jersey and Me . . . Going Nowhere Together," a parody of the official state tourism slogan, "New Jersey and You . . . Perfect Together." Another T-shirt's legend begins, "New Jersey Ingredients: Radon, Mosquitos, . . . High Taxes, Urban Decay, Potholes," and continues the length of the shirt without getting any more flattering.[6]

New Jerseyans have developed specific ways of dealing with out-of-state guests who make negative comments about the state based on impressions garnered from traveling the Turnpike. Jill Ross, a New Jersey newspaper editor, would tell such people, "That's why we built the New Jersey Turnpike. It's to get people like you in and out of the state as quickly as possible."[7] For some, the Turnpike may well be all they ever see of the state. "I can't believe, in this day and age, that people still believe . . . [the Turnpike is] New Jersey," says transportation commissioner Hazel Gluck. But then she concedes, "When they built the Turnpike, they didn't know they were [building] . . . a road that was going to create the image of the state."[8]

New Jersey is stuck with that image, for better or for worse. The *Princeton Packet* conducted a poll in 1988, asking its readers, "What, if you could, would you like to change" about New Jersey? Karl Light, a real estate broker, said: "Its image. People think of it as a corridor between New York and whatever's south of it. I hate the idea of the Turnpike being thought of as representative of New Jersey." Geoff Cohen, general manager of the George Street Playhouse in New Brunswick, answered the question simply: "The New Jersey Turnpike."[9]

New Jerseyans embrace their Turnpike with ambivalence. To the extent it is much used and efficient, it is appreciated. To the extent it is the source of New Jersey's negative image, it is despised. And there are those who feel these things simultaneously, such as a group of New Jerseyans working in

Washington, D.C., who decided some years ago to have a party. Nostalgic for their home state, they fastened on a tongue-in-cheek celebration of the thirtieth anniversary of the New Jersey Turnpike as their theme. The Turnpike embodied everything they both loved and hated about New Jersey.[10]

We were intrigued by accounts of this party. We, too, had strong mixed feelings about the Turnpike. From time to time we had spoken offhandedly about doing a book; the party made us give the idea more serious consideration.

Another event that inspired us was a symposium on "American Icons" at Columbia University that we attended. At this symposium, sponsored by the Center for American Culture Studies, arguments were advanced to consider Niagara Falls, the Brooklyn Bridge, and the key symbolic structures of the 1939 World's Fair as icons. It was suggested that, historically, "icon" has meant a religious object or painting, but that, in recent years, it has been broadened to include those things that represent the ideals of a people—and sometimes simply their ideas, whether or not these have religious significance.

At the symposium we asked if the New Jersey Turnpike might be considered an icon. The suggestion was greeted with laughter. Said one of the participants, "Well, it's not my kind of icon." Said another, "If the New Jersey Turnpike is an icon, anything can be an icon." Helen Harrison, art critic for the *New York Times,* joked, "The New Jersey Turnpike isn't an icon; it's the 'Twilight Zone.'"[11]

Perhaps so. Yet "Twilight Zone," referring as it does to an old television show full of supernatural occurrences, suggests that, at the very least, the Turnpike inspires strong feelings. Might the definition of "icon," already much in dispute, be broadened to include anything that bulks large in the national imagination, as surely the New Jersey Turnpike does? A recent book on New Jersey asserts that "this intimidating highway . . . stands as a 'symbol, icon, and metaphor of American culture.'"[12] Further, Linda Keller Brown has written: "If the automobile and the highway are the most fitting American metaphors, then surely the Turnpike is New Jersey's. The Turnpike conveys the popular impression of New Jersey as not really a state, or even a place, but as a corridor between the cities of New York and Philadelphia."[13] Finally, Paul Bradley has claimed, "The Turnpike is . . . our Broadway. It *is* our Brooklyn Bridge" (emphasis ours).[14]

Perhaps we reject the idea of the Turnpike as icon while accepting the Brooklyn Bridge partly because the Turnpike isn't beautiful; we do not like it. At the Columbia symposium, Jack Salzman, director of the Center for

American Culture Studies, said as partial justification for icon status for the Brooklyn Bridge, "We love the Brooklyn Bridge."

Few Americans love McDonald's golden arches, yet they are powerful symbols of our culture, if not icons. And whatever his distaste for it, the dynamo was as much an icon for Henry Adams as was the virgin.[15] Whether icon or not, the New Jersey Turnpike occupies an important place in the American imagination, and we came away from the Columbia symposium further convinced that the Turnpike was worthy of attention as a book.

We began by talking to our friends. Universally, they had strong feelings about the Turnpike—good, bad, and both. We next approached Turnpike spokesperson James Almoney. We told him candidly that we wanted to study not just the Turnpike's engineering but also its symbolism and its impact on the state's image. Almoney was visibly uncomfortable. He complained that the Turnpike does not get fair and accurate coverage from the press. He was also suspicious about a book written by a couple of "intellectuals." Too often outsiders dwell on the negative, he said.

We told him he could rely on our objectivity but shortly after made the mistake of mentioning in an offhand way that the northern stretch of the Turnpike was dirty and ugly. We had pushed the wrong button. Almoney replied testily, "It's not our fault the roadway is routed through an industrial area. We're not responsible for the surroundings; we're responsible for the roadway itself. If you will take the trouble to notice, the roadway is spotless. Our litter patrol is out every day removing the trash. Take a drive. See for yourselves if the Turnpike isn't clean as a whistle."[16]

Technically, Almoney was correct. The road itself *is* clean and well maintained. Of course, this reasoning misses the point that a road, by nearly universal agreement, is not only its pavement and shoulders but also its immediate environs. When highway awards are given out, landscaping, graceful curves, scenery, and adaptability to the environment are as much part of the judges' decision as engineering.

Nevertheless, Almoney was annoyed and angry at having to confront what he viewed as yet another inquisition. Our book was not envisioned as a muckraking attack on the Turnpike, but we had gotten off on the wrong foot. "Our critics don't like the way we do things? Okay, let's shut down the road for a day and then listen to them complain," Almoney said.

We are not suggesting that the Turnpike Authority is alone in trying to put as good a face as possible on events. Every large organization has spokespeople to look out for its interests. The Turnpike, however, which as we shall see is something of a state within a state, tends to be more defensive and self-protective than other, more open, institutions.

We should point out that the New Jersey Turnpike Authority did not support or approve our writing this book, nor did we submit our manuscript to the Authority for approval. Indeed, at first, we had difficulty getting anyone at the Turnpike Authority to talk to us. In October 1979, we asked Almoney to schedule a number of on-premises interviews with Turnpike employees. He told us he lacked authority to grant such a request and suggested we submit our request in writing to his boss, Horace A. Tani, director of Public Information. We wrote the letter.

Tani's response: "Your letter outlining the Turnpike book project you have in mind has raised some problems that cannot be overlooked in any consideration we could give your request. . . . The on-premises interviews in the various branches of our organization and with our patrons, as you request in your letter . . . would involve a continuing series of interviews . . . which the Authority could not be prepared to sustain, considering the disruption and delay to our operations and the work schedules of our operating personnel." [17]

Despite Tani's letter, he did, later on, set up a limited number of interviews. More recently, Jean Citrino Adubato, of the Turnpike public relations office, graciously set up a substantial number of interviews, and although the Turnpike people we have talked to officially have been restricted to those handpicked by the Authority, we have learned a great deal from them. Some have been quite forthcoming and candid. In addition, of course, we have had to develop our own sources of information to insure exposure to a wide range of independent views.

We interviewed dozens of Turnpike people, including present and former employees. We talked with former executive director William Flanagan and chairman of the Turnpike Authority Joseph Sullivan. We talked with Robert F. Dale and Jerry Kraft, in operations; Joseph C. Hornblower and Walter C. Bishof, in maintenance; Richard John Scott, Tim Dugan, and William Darough, in toll collection. At Troop D of the New Jersey State Police we talked with Austin O'Malley and Caesar Clay.

We also interviewed a number of people in New Jersey state government. Kemble Widmer, state geologist in the Department of Environmental Protection, provided us with helpful maps and charts. David Cohen, of the New Jersey State Historical Commission, gave us background on some of the negative imagery often associated with the New Jersey Turnpike. In the

Department of Transportation we received considerable support from former commissioner Louis Gambacinni and his then assistant Russell Mullen, who gave us access to the department's voluminous clipping files. Katy Weidner, of the Hackensack Meadowlands Development Commission, provided us with important materials on the Meadowlands, which is so vital to an understanding of Turnpike engineering and terrain.

Arthur Warren Meixner, of Fairleigh Dickinson University, kindly shared with us his doctoral dissertation on the New Jersey Turnpike Authority, which will, for many years to come, be an indispensable source for anyone interested in the Turnpike's early years and in the nature of authorities.[18]

Anyone familiar with the field of American Studies will recognize our intellectual debts to Leo Marx, John A. Kouwenhoven, and Alan Trachtenberg.[19] We try to carry on their tradition of exploring American artifacts as clues to American thought and values.

But the Turnpike is not just an artifact; it is a living social institution. Thus we draw on studies in occupational folklore for additional ideas. Notably, we have been influenced by the work of Benjamin A. Botkin, Archie Green, Robert H. Byington, Roger D. Abrahams, Robert S. McCarl, Jr., and Jack Santino. Also, not unlike Studs Terkel, we talked to people at the grassroots level to find out how they experience the Turnpike. Over the past few years, whenever we had some free time, we took a ride on the Turnpike, hung out in the rest areas, talked to truckers, engaged toll collectors in conversation; in short, we experienced the Turnpike from a perspective other than that of the patron or the employee: the perspective of the observer.

Like Erving Goffman, we have also tried in this book to analyze the institutional systems that keep the Turnpike functioning, examining in detail an institution that is normally taken for granted. In this connection, we have been inspired by Robert A. Caro's Pulitzer Prize–winning *The Power Broker: Robert Moses and the Fall of New York.*[20] Whereas Moses was the czar of New York City public works, the Turnpike is not strongly identified with a single individual. Annmarie Hauch Walsh's *Public's Business: The Politics and Practices of Government Corporations* was, therefore, equally important to us. Like Walsh, we find that "public enterprises are loaded with social and political implications," as well as with technical and financial ones; but we would go further and say that they also have broad cultural meanings.[21]

The multiple approach of *Looking for America,* its attempts to be as much experiential as analytical, may be, at once, the book's strength and weakness. The reader will find that the middle chapters of the book describe what takes place on the Turnpike, what it looks like, how it feels, whereas the opening and concluding chapters are more concerned with the Turnpike's significance. Also, wherever possible, our approach has been interdisciplinary. Thus, literature and music have been as important to us as politics and economics and engineering. We hope this makes for delight rather than confusion.

Looking for America was enormously improved by the advice of several colleagues at Rutgers, the State University of New Jersey. John Brush guided us through New Jersey geography. Richard P. McCormick advised us on the early history of the Turnpike. David Oshinsky read portions of our first drafts, giving much valuable advice.

Many other colleagues, friends, students, and former students gave us indispensable advice and shared with us their favorite Turnpike stories. Of special help were Emily Alman, Matthew Baigell, Michele Benjamin, Patty Cennelly, Joe Chapel, David Davidson, Tom De Haven, Miriam Du Bois, Jim Fisher, Nancy Gianino, Helene Grynberg, Mary Hufford, Carolyn Starr Karen, Richard Lehne, Gina Malone, Robert H. Manley, Arthur Miller, Kathleen Regiec, Catherine Sheehan, George Sternlieb, and Miriam Yucht.

Finally, we are grateful to our friend Robert Blake Truscott, who acted as "referee" when we could not agree on either a stylistic or a substantive point. We have learned that two people writing a book can be twice as challenging as one person writing a book. We are very different people. First, we have different philosophies of writing. Second, we have different political philosophies. Rob once playfully referred to us as "a mismatched pair"— a "redneck, law-and-order type" and a "knee-jerk liberal type." Still, we think *Looking for America* is richer for its dual authorship. Each chapter was written and rewritten by both of us several times, and then rewritten again in an effort to create a single voice. Usually, we were successful in reconciling our differences, but when all hope was lost, Rob Truscott came to our rescue.

Looking for America
on the New Jersey Turnpike

The Machine
in the Garden State

Chapter 1

"Some people think the Turnpike . . . is God."
—Bob Curso, shift supervisor,
Turnpike Operations Center[1]

In 1950, John Fasselly, a strawberry, asparagus, and soybean farmer, stood watching the progress of the highway. Fasselly and his wife, Gina, only one generation removed from tomato farmers in Tuscany, had saved money from his Bronx bread truck route and bought some land in New Jersey. They saved more money and bought more land. Finally, they had a real farm, 150 acres.

Until today, Fasselly hadn't believed the road would come. But now the machines had reached Hightstown, and the hot tar smell hung in the air. He could see the heat shimmering off the new road surface and feel it even a mile away where he stood in the shade of the huge oak. The leaves of the oak, as if in anticipation of what was coming over the land, were already turning inward, already wilting.

Fasselly tried not to think about it. So, the Turnpike would divide his farm in half, making it necessary to drive his tractor two miles to get to the other side. So an entrance ramp of Interchange 8 would pass one hundred feet from his house. He had no beef. The farm was a business, wasn't it? The Turnpike paid decent money. In a few years he and Gina would sell the farm altogether and move to Florida, retire early. After the Turnpike covered over the center acres of his farm, the developers would take the rest. They would put up ranch houses bordering the Turnpike. Everybody would think Fasselly's farmland was the perfect place to live. You were in the country, but you could get anywhere you wanted in no time flat.

Still, John Fasselly found the prospect unbelievable, even as he watched the far-off trucks dumping loads of steaming asphalt and heard the huge tamping machines smoothing them out. They did a whole lane of highway at a time, *ah gump, ah gump,* smacking the asphalt down and smoothing it out like cake frosting. They'd reach him next week for sure, and then twelve rows of strawberries would go under each lane of asphalt forever.

Fasselly wondered whether he hadn't made some kind of Faustian bargain with the Turnpike. Not that he had any choice. With eminent domain, they took your land one way or the other. But he wondered if he couldn't have fought them off for a while, delayed them for some months—maybe even years. At least he'd have had the satisfaction.[2]

Leo Marx might have interviewed John Fasselly. In his book *The Machine in the Garden,* Marx presents classic American individualists who enjoy a special kinship with nature, fending off an impersonal technology riding roughshod over their domains. There is Henry David Thoreau at Walden Pond, for whom "the whistle of the locomotive penetrates my woods summer and winter, sounding like the scream of a hawk sailing over some farmer's yard." There is Mark Twain's Huck and Jim, who enjoy an idyllic sojourn rafting down the Mississippi until a steamboat bears down on them: "All of a sudden she bulged out, big and scary, with a long row of wide-open furnace doors shining like red-hot teeth, and her monstrous bows and guards hanging right over us. There was a yell at us, and a jingling of bells to stop the engines, a pow-wow of cussing, and whistling of steam—and as Jim went overboard on the one side and I on the other, she come smashing straight through the raft." The train slicing through Thoreau's woods and the steamboat through Huck and Jim's raft evoke the more contemporary image of the New Jersey Turnpike moving inexorably through John Fasselly's farm.

Leo Marx's *Machine in the Garden* is subtitled *Technology and the Pastoral Ideal in America,* and the book argues that American history—the American mind—can best be understood in the contradiction between its pastoral ideal and its industrial reality, between "rural myth and technological fact."[3] Marx meant that although America is the world's greatest industrial power, it still thinks of itself as living in a state of agrarian innocence.

Marx was writing mostly about the nineteenth century and finding supporting evidence for his ideas in genteel literature. But there are also real machines in real gardens, in the past as well as today, with which he might have been concerned. That the contradiction Marx speaks of is alive and well in America is nowhere in greater evidence than in the state of New Jersey, which, despite being the most industrialized, most densely populated, and most environmentally degraded of the fifty states, insists to this day on calling itself "the Garden State." As one of us was quoted as saying in *U.S. News and World Report,* under these conditions, "to call yourself the Garden State is schizophrenia."[4]

It was in New Jersey that the machine most dramatically entered the garden, and there the two have always endeavored, however tenuously, to coexist. At Great Falls, in present-day Paterson, the Passaic River, as one eighteenth-century commentator described it, descends 70 feet "in one entire sheet, presenting a most beautiful and tremendous scene."[5] There Alexander Hamilton proposed in 1791 the creation of the nation's first manufacturing center, the Society for Useful Manufactures. Soon dozens of mills and factories, powered by water wheels, were built and flourished, including the nation's greatest locomotive works.

And New Jersey continues to demonstrate its ambivalence as between humanity's works and God's in the license plates of the state's 5 million registered vehicles. Each trumpets the words "The Garden State," their drivers blissfully unaware of the contradiction inherent in this slogan being applied to the machine that, more than any other, has made it largely untrue.

New Jersey does have many pleasant areas, and it is still something of a garden. Just as America is a major agricultural power despite, or in addition to, being a major industrial power, so New Jersey is New York's and Philadelphia's breadbasket while also being their purveyor of gasoline and chemicals. Tomatoes, peaches, blueberries, and cranberries are all major New Jersey products. Still, the overwhelming impression New Jersey makes on the visitor is of unparalleled industrialism and a debased quality of life.

"Garden State" today may express more yearning than reality, a means by which New Jerseyans apply cosmetics to their spirits, like the green-painted gravel-and-asphalt hillsides alongside the Garden State Parkway, which, from a distance, appear to be grass. It is as if New Jerseyans need to deceive themselves by painting the very symbols of their industrialism green.

New Jersey's concept of itself as a garden is largely responsible for the traditional backwardness of its politics. If one imagines oneself as living in a state of innocence—not just in a garden but in *the* garden: the Garden of Eden—it is not necessary to address glaring problems. They do not exist. Thus it was natural for New Jersey to long be the dumping ground for New York's and Philadelphia's garbage,[6] and to be the focus of much of the muckraker's efforts. New Jersey was where the monopolies and trusts came to escape the strictures of more responsible states and where Ida Tarbell and Lincoln Steffens tracked them down.

New Jersey was also where people escaped from the cities to find a place where they might live outside history, divorced from traditions and laws. New Jerseyans have thought of themselves as living not only in trans-Hudson America but in the beginning of the American West,[7] as being like Daniel Boone, who, when he could smell the smoke from the next man's chimney fire and hear his dog bark, moved deeper into the forest, away from civilization.[8]

New Jersey is the ultimate suburban state—the place where the struggle between the machine and the garden has been joined and where a compromise of sorts has been struck between competing visions of America. In New Jersey, most people live on their own land in their own houses, but just as typically, there is a toxic waste dump just over the hill from which deadly poisons leach into the surrounding terrain. "Much of the state," the authors of a recent report have written, "is already neither rural nor urban, but exhibits some of the worst characteristics of each. Many of its suburban residents experience something of the isolation, inconvenience and low levels of public service that characterize rural areas, while at the same time encountering the traffic jams, pollution, and visual blight that are typical of too many of our urban areas." [9]

For this reason, New Jersey, where the pastoral ideal flourishes despite a surfeit of evidence to the contrary, may be the most typical state in the nation. New Jersey may also be the most typical state because of its amorphous quality: it is a little of this, a little of that—not only machine and garden but hills and plain, marshes and sands, an extraordinarily diverse geography packed into a small area, with an extraordinarily diverse ethnicity and economy as well. Historian John Cunningham writes that the thing most characteristic of New Jersey is its variety: "New Jersey reflects, in miniature, much of the story of the United States." No other state provides a "better mirror on America." [10]

Typical of America is New Jersey's decentralized nature. The state has few, if any, cities that merit the name, and those it has have long been down on their heels and do not serve as true commercial or cultural magnets. Newark is not really a city so much as an untidy dormitory for the poor. Trenton is only ostensibly the state capital. The governor's mansion is in Princeton, and the current governor does not even live there. Atlantic City is the closest thing New Jersey has to an entertainment capital, but Atlantic City is nothing but a line of casinos walling out a morass of slums. A cultural center? Surely the Garden State Arts Center, located in a rural area off a Garden State Parkway exit, would not qualify.

New Jersey's vitality today is not in its cities but in the rings circling them and the corridors connecting them. Without true cities to offer a focus for New Jersey life the state's roads become what is most characteristic of it. Surely no state in the union has such an elaborate and highly developed system of roads.

This occasions much humor, often focused on the Turnpike. On television's "Saturday Night Live," actors regularly present themselves by saying, "I'm from New Jersey," with the standard retort being, "Yeah? What exit?" The comic George Carlin refers to New Jersey as "the tollbooth capital of the world." [11] One writer sees the New Jersey Turnpike as "probably the strongest impetus for the myriad jokes directed against the Garden State." [12]

New Jersey is a centrifugal state, with few forces holding it together. There is little sense of community, of belonging, except on the local level. The Turnpike, therefore, plays a unifying role. It is New Jersey's automotive Mississippi. As one writer puts it, some New Jerseyans "love it, some loathe it, and others simply accept it. The Turnpike rolls on just the same, the gray, gritty symbol of New Jersey." [13]

For many, the Turnpike and New Jersey are synonymous. And if New Jersey is the place in America where the machine is most firmly entrenched in the garden, the New Jersey Turnpike is that machine.

The Turnpike, however, says Patricia Ard, a Morristown, New Jersey attorney, "isn't a user-friendly machine." The term "user friendly" is computer language meaning hospitable, accessible, welcoming. Ard did not mean that the Turnpike is not efficient. She was referring to the institutional "feel" of the Turnpike, its ambience. By saying that the Turnpike is not user friendly, she implies that it is cold, forboding, unhealthful. As she puts it, "Even from the tone of the instructions they provide—on the toll ticket, on signs, at rest areas—you get the feeling the Turnpike regards you as unintelligent, a nuisance."

Ard continues:

> The Turnpike isn't a supportive environment. It has no time for good manners. On the Turnpike you are expected to "state your business" and get off as quickly as possible. There is no ease on the Turnpike; you're constantly reminded that you're not supposed to "loiter." There are rest areas on the Turnpike, but they aren't for resting.
>
> The Turnpike isn't an interactive environment. It's like an elevator: people keep their eyes front, don't look at one another. It's as if every car on the Turnpike has a giant bumper sticker that says, "DON'T MESS WITH ME." There's always a sense of menace about the Turnpike. [14]

Ard's comments suggest that the machinelike aspect of the Turnpike goes beyond its specific purposes. The Turnpike is an assembly line for delivering automotive vehicles from one end of New Jersey to the other, without sentiment, without amenities—cold, stark, austere, a largely lifeless environment over which humans scamper as fast as their motor vehicles, and the law, will allow.

The quality of life of patrons on the Turnpike is low. They are treated almost like vagrants. The key message is "Move on." One cannot stop on the Turnpike (it is against the law); and given the vistas offered, one would just as soon not stop. No photos are allowed—as if the Turnpike were some kind of top-secret military base. As we shall see in a later chapter, the Turnpike is something of a state within a state.

By way of contrast, Jay Appleton, a geographer at the University of Hull in England, believes public works should be designed with two paramount ingredients—besides safety and convenience and utility. They are what he calls "refuge" and "prospect."[15] By "refuge," Appleton means that public works should have built into them a sense of hospitality, of invitingness, of restfulness. More specifically, they should provide spaces where one may feel secure and quiet and contemplative. All of this is impossible on the New Jersey Turnpike. Even the rest areas, as Patricia Ard points out, are not designed for rest; they are designed to "service" people, as they service automobiles, as quickly and efficiently—and as anonymously—as possible. The Turnpike doesn't want its patrons to take a second more than necessary. Have a drink, go to the bathroom, get the car gassed up, and move on. On the northern stretches there is little grass—certainly none to sit on—no shade trees to rest under, virtually no chance for a picnic or for any of the simple pleasures and broadening experiences we normally associate with travel.

The other key word in Appleton's lexicon when discussing public projects is "prospect." By prospect he means vistas, scenery, landscape. Here, again, the impression the Turnpike makes, especially in the northern sector, is disappointing. The vistas it provides are at best boring, at worst horrible. They lack even a hint of charm. Few of the wildflowers and ornamental trees that grow alongside other major highways flourish beside the Turnpike. The Turnpike seems intentionally designed to exclude the aesthetic. Clearly, it does not conceive of itself as a linear park, as a *parkway.* It does not aspire to invite motorists out into nature, to get them to experience beauty. The Turnpike is, for the most part, an alien and alienating environment.

This is true the farther north one rides. As the Turnpike approaches New York, its pace quickens, exits become more numerous, the traffic thickens. One has the sense of machinery rushing toward some precipice. One must now drive aggressively. On the Turnpike tickets are regularly given not only for going too fast but for going too slow. Just as one may get a ticket for driving over 55, one may also get a ticket for driving under 40. One drives the Turnpike as a cog in a machine, as if one were physically part of the road.

Motorists on the Turnpike seem hermetically sealed in their vehicles. If ever road driving in America becomes automatic—one enters a magnetic highway and puts one's vehicle on automatic pilot, as some science fiction theorists project—it will probably be the New Jersey Turnpike where such a system is first put into effect. Judging from the machinelike driving, the fixed stares, the grim, unsmiling, lonely nature of the Turnpike now, we are almost there.

One wishes Edward Hopper had painted the Turnpike. He could have properly captured its anonymity, its alienation. The Turnpike is the American dream of unhindered mobility pushed to a malevolent extreme. And, ironically, the rampant individualism of the Turnpike expresses itself in its opposite. Tocqueville warned in *Democracy in America* that extreme individualism contains within it the seeds of uniformity,[16] and Philip Slater makes a similar point in his book *The Pursuit of Loneliness,*[17] where he argues that mindless mobility can be a form of slavery. Slater quotes the same lines we do on our title page,

> Countin' the cars on the New Jersey Turnpike,
> They've all come to look for America

from Paul Simon's song "America." But Slater precedes them with the line, "I'm empty and aching and I don't know why," as if the New Jersey Turnpike is especially a place of mis- (or non)communication, of loneliness, dehumanization, alienation.

This heartlessness may be more apparent to out-of-staters than it is to New Jerseyans. New Jerseyans know the diversity of the state, the many amenities it offers away from the Turnpike. But for those passing through, the Turnpike is often all they know of the state, and it has a great deal to do with the impression they have of New Jersey. "Much of New Jersey's bad image is inadvertently transmitted by the New Jersey Turnpike," says one writer.[18] Says another, the New Jersey Turnpike is "a national emblem . . . at once standing for efficiency and decay, progress and pollution."[19]

Rosemary Lyon, of the Council for the International Exchange of Scholars in Washington, says the Turnpike even "influences our foreign policy. Every time we have distinguished visitors coming to the United States who land in New York, we think about whether we can bring them down to Washington some other way because of the impression the Turnpike usually makes."[20]

Bad or otherwise, the New Jersey Turnpike's reputation far from New

Jersey is well established. Paul Sigmund, Jr., of Princeton, New Jersey, was traveling Route 101 in California south of San Francisco when he was pulled to the side by a California state patrolman. After chewing the young man out vigorously for some infraction, the officer pointed to his New Jersey license plates and said, "I'm going to let you go. You can't help yourself. You've been conditioned by driving on the New Jersey Turnpike." [21]

When Laura Kells, of Bound Brook, New Jersey, arrived in Iowa City, Iowa, to begin work as a graduate student in American Studies, she was told by fellow students and more than one professor that before completing a degree she would be required to recite in proper sequence the names of all New Jersey Turnpike rest areas. She was told this so often it did not occur to her that she was being kidded. This story illustrates the fascination the Turnpike holds for people far from New Jersey. For Kells's fellow students and her professors in Iowa, the Turnpike was not just a road. It was *the* road or, as one student put it, "road heaven." [22]

Thus, for many Americans, the New Jersey Turnpike is generic for the monster road. As one writer puts it, "No road in the nation, and perhaps the world, is quite like it." [23] This was illustrated in the advertising for Richard Pryor's 1988 film *Moving,* the comic story of one family's trials and tribulations as it moves, in connection with a job change, from New Jersey to the West. In the film there are no recognizable New Jersey sights other than quantities of automobiles with New Jersey license plates. More important, there is no footage of the New Jersey Turnpike whatsoever, nor is the Turnpike ever mentioned. Yet in all the advertising for the movie the following sentence appeared in very large type: "ON THE NEW JERSEY TURNPIKE NO ONE CAN HEAR YOU SCREAM."

From an out-of-state, national, and perhaps even international perspective, then, the New Jersey Turnpike *is* New Jersey. Although New Jerseyans may "take it for granted," says one writer, "the Turnpike, for visitors, is cause for amazement." [24] Pat Fitzgerald, of Summit, New Jersey, was in the famous Gilley's Bar outside Houston, Texas, where the movie *Urban Cowboy* takes place. "When the barmaid asked me where I was from," said Fitzgerald, "and I said New Jersey, she replied, 'I know New Jersey. I was on the Turnpike once.'" [25] From this woman's perspective, the Turnpike and New Jersey are one in the way the Rockies are characteristic of Colorado, wheat fields of Kansas, the rockbound coast of Maine.

Some New Jerseyans take exception to the idea that the Turnpike is emblematic of their state. They think the Garden State Parkway, New Jersey's other major toll road, is more typical. But the Garden State Parkway is hardly known beyond New Jersey, because most of it is outside the great North-South megalopolis corridor. Out-of-state license plates are rarely seen on the Garden State Parkway. It is used primarily by New Jerseyans to get to work or to visit friends and family or to get to the Jersey Shore. The Garden State Parkway is a local road in many ways.

Some New Jerseyans resist the idea that the Turnpike is typical of the state for other reasons. Acknowledging the Turnpike's defects, they see them as exceptions. Friends who knew we were writing this book bristled. David Cohen, of the State Historical Commission, urged us not to write the book for fear it would be "just another cheap shot" at New Jersey, "another exercise in the Jersey joke." Cohen thought the New York–based media were sufficiently antagonistic to New Jersey without two New Jerseyans and the State University Press "joining the bandwagon." [26]

But there were also New Jerseyans happy we were writing this book because of their considerable affection for the Turnpike despite, perhaps even because of, its defects. For them, the Turnpike isn't just a road; it's home. Barbara Sigmund, mayor of Princeton Borough, tells of how, when her children were young, she would promise them rides on the Turnpike as a reward. "Best behavior modification device I ever came up with," Sigmund says. [27]

There is an occasional television show in New Jersey on the CTN network called "Not Just the Turnpike," which endeavors to demonstrate the state's variety by proving there is more to New Jersey than the Turnpike. And the State Department of Tourism uses this same title, "Not Just the Turnpike," in some of its talks and literature. [28] In Randolph, New Jersey, a modern dance troupe calls itself the "Beyond the New Jersey Turnpike Dance Company." Of course, these slogans and titles prove the opposite: despite New Jersey's diversity, what is most typical of it *is* the Turnpike. Or, at the very least, if one had to pick one artifact as representative of New Jersey, it would surely be the Turnpike.

But our title, *Looking for America,* suggested by those key lines in Simon and Garfunkel's "America," very consciously means to imply that the New Jersey Turnpike is not only representative of New Jersey's condition but of America's as a whole. If one were to go looking for America—if one sought a means to understand the American mind, American values, American aesthetics—the New Jersey Turnpike would be a splendid place to begin.

What could be more typical of American values than the fact that of all the rest areas along the Turnpike honoring such famous New Jerseyans as Joyce Kilmer, Thomas Edison, and Grover Cleveland, only the rest area honoring Vince Lombardi, the famous football coach ("Winning isn't everything; it's the only thing"), has an exhibit on the honoree's life? Now, *that's* American values!

Thus, this book is not so much a history of the New Jersey Turnpike, or an account of how many tons of steel and asphalt make it up, or how many people work on it, or how many millions of automotive miles are traveled on it each year—though we will cover these subjects. This book is about what the Turnpike *means.*

But when discussing the meaning of the Turnpike a problem arises: are we discussing just the physical Turnpike itself—the 142-mile roadway of asphalt and steel? Or are we including what one sees from the Turnpike, its surroundings, that is, the Turnpike as—in the words of one writer—"a fuming gasoline alley cutting through the industrial heartland?"[29]

From the point of view of the Turnpike Authority, the Turnpike is just the roadway. In any discussion of the Turnpike's ugly surroundings with Authority employees—the sulfurous air one breathes, the blasted landscape one sees—these things do not compute. When the Turnpike's surroundings do come up in conversation with employees, they tell you that rather than being criticized, the Authority deserves credit. It has set an example by being the *cordon sanitaire* through a blighted, possibly infectious, land.

For the engineers who manage it, the Turnpike is a wonder of efficiency. It offers a product everyone wants, it is one of the safest roads in the world, and it takes in a fortune in tolls 24 hours a day, 365 days a year. For Turnpike engineers, the Turnpike is an unqualified success. Questions of aesthetics, whether on the pike or off, are simply irrelevant.

People who work at the Turnpike Authority are fond of pointing out that when someone like Charles Kuralt makes a list of the ten best highways in America, he doesn't mean best *highways;* he means best *scenery.* In response to those who think the New Jersey Turnpike is filthy, Turnpike spokespeople respond, "But that's crazy. The Turnpike is immaculate." What they mean is that the roadway of the Turnpike is very clean because of the constant litter patrols.

But just beyond the confines of the Turnpike is a landscape covered with litter of the most obnoxious sort, a landscape so ugly that billboards are perhaps its most attractive feature. It is a landscape of man-made mountains of garbage, fouled swamps, rusting, abandoned factories, and clouds of evil-smelling chemicals. And sometimes the Turnpike is directly affected by these features of the landscape, as when garbage just beyond its confines ignites, visibility is reduced to perilous proportions, and spectacular accidents occur.

Patrons, whether fairly or not, tend to hold the Turnpike responsible for its surroundings. They contemplate scenery that could have been the model for T. S. Eliot's "Wasteland," or even Dante's "Inferno," and consider it as an inextricable part of the Turnpike. The writer John McPhee, in saying that the Turnpike suggests "a gunshot wound in an infected Uncle Sam,"[30] clearly is not talking only about the roadway itself.

New Jersey has for some years now had the unfortunate nickname "Cancer Alley," because of the high rate of some cancers in the Garden State. Should the Turnpike bear this burden as well? Yes, says one writer: "There's no dismissing the hazards to health behind those sights [the sights seen while driving the Turnpike]. . . . When Dr. Irving Selikoff of Mt. Sinai Medical Center coined the term 'Cancer Alley' several years ago, he wasn't speaking about the entire state. . . . He meant the land and industries abreast of the Turnpike's northern end."[31] At the very least, many patrons of the Turnpike feel, the Turnpike Authority might have used more imagination in its choice of where to lay out the world's greatest road.

But from the Authority's point of view, placing the road through some of New Jersey's worst regions was farsighted. Other states avoid their chemical plants and oil refineries in laying down a major road, endeavoring to make a good impression. In Connecticut, for example, the Merritt Parkway avoids Bridgeport and runs through some of the state's prettiest country, thereby confirming an image of Connecticut as a pastoral New England state. The New Jersey Turnpike sees itself as, and may be, environmentally enlightened for having chosen an already blighted landscape, avoiding attractive land where it could. Indeed, the Turnpike Authority had to withstand pressure from Governor Driscoll to run the highway through the Pine Barrens, the state's largest area of untouched wilderness.[32] From the Turnpike's point of view, if a machine has to be put into a garden, why not avoid the prettiest parts of the garden?

Some patrons find a curious beauty in the Turnpike and its surroundings and celebrate the Turnpike not despite, but *because of,* its surroundings. Whether these observers are attracted to the Turnpike because it's so bad that it's good, or because they have a love-hate attraction to it, or because the Turnpike has for them a kind of reverse chic, they feel an intense loyalty to the Turnpike—its efficiency and power, its asphalt and steel, and, yes, its grim surroundings. A former student of ours has a fantasy. "When I die," she says, "I hope they bury me beside the Turnpike. Who wants to be where it's quiet? Give me noise and speed."[33]

As we shall see in Chapter 9, the Turnpike has been the inspiration for more than a little art. Songwriters, filmmakers, novelists, poets, and painters see the Turnpike as a powerful symbol of life as it is lived in America in the second half of the twentieth century—its mindless mobility, its disdain for the environment, its crushing loneliness.

These commentators on the Turnpike see it as not just awful but truly awesome. Indeed, the word *awesome* is the one we most often hear from observers and aficionados of the Turnpike, especially when describing the northern reaches of the highway, which are most distinctive and which we will be concentrating on in this book.

The word *awesome* certainly means impressive, but it also connotes something with extraordinary, if not supernatural, properties. State troopers on the Turnpike, who sometimes refer to it as "the Black Dragon," do not mean this term disparagingly but, rather, as celebratory of the Turnpike's raw power. Ayn Rand, in her novels, exulted in the "ring of sacred fires" near New York, a clear reference to the refinery flares along the New Jersey Turnpike.[34]

In an article in *New Jersey Monthly* discussing unusual New Jersey tourist attractions, Patrick Sarver celebrated what he called the "Landscape from Hell":

> Just south of Exit 13 on the Turnpike is a view that is, well, breathtaking. If Hieronymus Bosch, the fifteenth-century Flemish painter, had glimpsed this view of the Elizabeth oil refineries, he might have had a better model for his famous vision of Hades. As far as the eye can see, flames perform a *dance macabre* above ghostly white holding tanks. Skeletal towers rise against a perpetually leaden sky. Steam hisses angrily from miles of black pipes. Corroded drums stand like sentries at the edge of Morses Creek. It is a world of twisted metal and high-tension wire, in which any green, growing thing would be an intrusion. If you find yourself traveling north on the Turnpike, pull off to the shoulder just before the sign directing you to the Goethals Bridge and take in the view. Watch out for the big rigs, though, which will rattle your windows as they thunder by. Also notice the guardrail, crumpled by numerous impacts and stained by auto paint. It is testimony, perhaps, to the legion of aesthetically sensitive drivers who have come upon this hideous landscape and literally lost all control.[35]

Celebrating the Turnpike in another way, *New Jersey Monthly* has a soapbox feature that appears on the last page of each issue called "Exit Ramp."

Those who celebrate the Turnpike seem particularly taken with it at night. Judy Muller, writing in the *New York Times* Sunday magazine section, in an article about nighttime commuting, says: "Only the New Jersey Turnpike welcomes the nighttime commuter with open arms. . . . From the oil refineries of Linden and Elizabeth to the marshes of Secaucus, the only interesting piece of topography is a large hill, which, as it turns out, is made of garbage. But at night, that hill has a most commanding silhouette. Even those foulest of New Jersey landmarks, the refineries, are transformed by darkness into twinkling dragons with tongues of fire." [36]

And so, part of the Turnpike's appeal, for some, is precisely the nighttime drama of its world-class ugliness. In its northern stretches—with Newark Airport on one side, Port Elizabeth on the other; with the flames of the refineries and huge tank farms of petroleum; with planes roaring in one after another, so close one is sure a Lockheed Tri-Star is going to land on the roof of one's automobile; with the giant cranes of the container shipping port seeming to stalk across the land on their long legs like Martian war machines in *War of the Worlds*—one is impressed almost to speechlessness by the sheer, raw power of this technological landscape. Hideous, yes. But theater that rivals anything on Broadway ten miles to the northeast.

It is as if Hollywood had been asked to devise the perfect backdrop to the monster road, a road where the law forbids stopping, where the air sears one's lungs, where machines dwarf and humble nature and human beings. This is the ultimate technological landscape. Here is where you come to see the twentieth century. This is where we would lead a Martian if we had to choose one place, one artifact, to explain our civilization. For here the machine is not only in the garden; the garden has been obliterated, has disappeared. Here the machine *is* the garden.

Building the Pike

Chapter

2

"It was obvious that U.S. Route 1 just couldn't handle the anticipated traffic and that we needed a new artery and we didn't have the money to build a free highway, and so we proposed a toll road."

—Alfred E. Driscoll,
Governor of New Jersey, 1947–1954[1]

Near Newark Airport is one of the New Jersey Turnpike's best-kept secrets: a small traffic bridge marked "OFFICIAL VEHICLES ONLY." This little bridge is at the heart of one of the world's most heavily industrialized areas. The most frequent users of this bridge are state police cruisers, which U-turn over the twelve lanes of traffic. Another occasional user of the bridge is the official photographer for the Turnpike, Alexander Oleck. If you were allowed on the bridge you would immediately know why Oleck loves the place.

Looking north from the bridge one sees an amazing panorama of transportation. It looks like a sixth-grade geography lesson brought to life. To your right is the vast Port Elizabeth, with the huge blue cranes of the Maersk Lines, painted with white stars on a blue field. The port is the largest containerized freight facility in the United States. With the Maersk cranes, a few men can unload an entire ship in twenty-four hours, a job that used to take a large crew of men several weeks under the old break-bulk system.

Closer to you are the Conrail freight yards. Long trains of black tank cars with mysterious white markings on their sides, such as ACLX, NATX, and UTLX, pull in and out, each preceded by three or four blue Conrail diesel locomotives. There are other trains, almost as long, their many-colored rows of boxcars exciting the imagination with their logos—Missouri-Kansas-Texas Railroad Company, the Southern Railway, the Chesapeake and Ohio, the Richmond, Fredericksburg, and Potomac.

Over to your left, off in the distance, are the hangars and terminals of Newark Airport. Much closer, you see a whole line of buff-colored Continental Airlines jets waiting to take off. A sharply angled red-and-white shield protects the passing automobiles and trucks from the jet blast. A large radar antenna, revolving briskly, takes in the busy air traffic. A jet roars in for a landing overhead. It touches down with a loud thump, rubber tires smoking, engines roaring in reverse.

On that bridge, you feel you are at the center of a civilization. The whole scene is difficult to take in at once because there is so much going on. Everything is so crammed in, it looks unreal, like a model railroad layout. Some mad hobbyist has jammed everything he can buy onto a four-by-eight piece of plywood to show off his miniature trains, planes, and boats.

And cars, trucks, and buses, of course. Under your feet twelve lanes of traffic rumble by. The diesel exhaust wafts up in black plumes of smoke.

This is an exciting place to be. There may be no more exciting on the globe. It is the epicenter of what historian John Cunningham has called the "Vital Corridor."[2] The term describes the strip cutting across the waist of New Jersey, which runs between the Hudson and the Delaware rivers. With the great ports of New York and Philadelphia on either end, New Jersey's destiny as a corridor state was inevitable.

The corridor, lying across the state, is mostly flat. In the northern stretches it is tidal marshland, consisting of mud and marsh vegetation—cordgrass, thatch grass, and salt hay—good breeding grounds for muskrats and mosquitoes. In the more upland stretches, the corridor varies between 100 and 400 feet above sea level.[3]

At first, European settlers used the gentle trails the Indians had carved across the corridor. Later, the trails were expanded for stagecoaches. The toughest part of the stagecoach trip was the stretch of corridor between Newark and New York, where the badly kept roadway went through a marshy area of soft and easily rutted terrain. An 1804 guidebook explained: "This is an artificial road, over the great cedar swamp, made of logs, laid across the road, close together, of three or four layers, and covered with sods and earth dug up on each side, to form a ditch, for keeping the road dry: over this is laid gravel; but it is brought from considerable distance, and at great expense, and the road is in many places unpleasant. It continues about three miles to the Hackensack river, over which is a bridge, similar to that over the Passaic, where tolls are collected."[4]

If the eighteenth century was the era of the stagecoach, the twentieth century has been the era of the automobile. Today, in addition to the Turnpike, there are three major highways in the corridor: U.S. Route 1, state Route 130, and Interstate 295.

But it would not be until the second half of the twentieth century that the superhighway dominated the corridor. And the Turnpike was built here not by whim, but by necessity. No matter where you are going on the eastern seaboard, you must traverse the corridor and, if so, you are likely to use the New Jersey Turnpike. This is *the* way to get from New York to Philadelphia. It is also the way to get from Boston to Washington, since New Jersey is the key link in the chain of the eastern megalopolis.

Ever since colonial days, New Jersey had been the corridor state. But by the 1940s, getting across the state was becoming difficult. Automobile traffic had gradually increased; the state was choking on traffic. For years there had been talk about putting a superhighway across New Jersey. But, meanwhile, World War II had to be fought and won.

Now the war was over and there was no reason why the highway could not be built. In addition, the need for it was greater than ever. New Jerseyans were spreading out; everyone was moving to the suburbs. With the end of the war there was a restless longing for normalcy, expressed so well in the 1946 film *The Best Years of Our Lives.*[5] "Normalcy" seemed to be represented by picture windows, barbecues, patios, power lawn mowers, and plentiful gasoline, which cost only 15 cents a gallon. But to live this suburban life-style, rapid automobile commuting was a necessity.[6]

Building the New Jersey Turnpike required a plan of great magnitude, a great deal of money, a devoted leader, and a sympathetic public. Through a fortunate circumstance of history, such a leader appeared at just the right moment in New Jersey's political life.

If the Turnpike had a father, he was Alfred E. Driscoll. Driscoll, a man of forceful personality, was an extremely effective politician. He was a strong Republican governor who enjoyed the support of a Republican legislature, which meant he was able to move most of his programs forward with little difficulty. In his first inaugural address to the legislature on January 21, 1947, Driscoll launched his plan for the Turnpike.[7]

If the New Jersey Turnpike was to be built, Driscoll had to promote the idea with the state legislature. Quietly, he pointed out the possibilities for patronage in contracts to be awarded and jobs to be given out. His image as a reformer notwithstanding, Driscoll knew how the system worked. Drawings and mathematical symbols were fine for explaining the idea to civil engineers, but first he had to show people in the business community that there was money in it for them. And before that, he had to show the politicians that there were deals in it for them.

Even popular governors in the best of times cannot get everything they want. They have to set priorities. For Driscoll, nothing was more important than the Turnpike. Once the legislation was passed and the commissioners appointed, Driscoll delegated the project to the best and most trusted managers he could find.

The 1948 legislation that set up the Turnpike Authority called for the governor to appoint three nonsalaried commissioners, subject to the approval of the state senate, to oversee the project. The legislation implied that the commissioners would be prominent, public-spirited citizens who had the time and interest to devote to a major undertaking.

Early in 1949 the governor named his commissioners. Paul L. Troast was to be chairman; George F. Smith was to be vice-chairman; and Maxwell Lester, Jr., was to be treasurer. Smith was chairman of the giant Johnson and Johnson pharmaceutical corporation at the time and well known for his involvement with hospital and civic projects. He was to become valuable for his management and labor relations expertise. Lester, who came from a wealthy background, was a partner in a Wall Street investment firm. His contribution was mainly in financial management and (most important) marketing the bonds.[8]

Governor Driscoll's selection of Paul Troast to be the first chairman of the Turnpike commissioners was an inspired choice. A silver-haired man with bright blue eyes, always dressed conservatively, Troast had no formal college education and no technical background, but he did have considerable management experience in both the public and private sectors. And by 1949 Troast had sufficient personal wealth that he could shoulder this public burden.

Early on he acquired a reputation as a man who got things done. In 1927 he was named secretary-treasurer for the Passaic Consolidated Water Company, which was charged with the responsibility of getting water from the Wanaque Reservoir to Paterson, Passaic, and Clifton. With Arthur S. Mahony, then Clifton city engineer, Troast founded the Mahony-Troast Construction Company in 1928, which became one of the largest construction firms in the nation. Troast was not a charismatic leader; he was, instead, a strong, solid, business-oriented administrator.[9] So the Turnpike project was conceived by a politician and supervised by a manager.

Earlier civil engineering projects in America had produced heroes. When we think of the Brooklyn Bridge, we think of John Augustus Roebling.[10] When we think of the Panama Canal, we think of George Goethals.[11] The New Jersey Turnpike was different. The Turnpike had no engineer heroes as such. There were no pioneering developments comparable to the suspension bridge or horrible risks to be taken comparable to caisson disease. The Turnpike project had none of the uncertainty of outcome associated with earlier big projects. From a civil engineering viewpoint, the Turnpike was a big job, but one involving largely routine techniques.

The commissioners held their first meeting on March 31, 1949. In April 1949 they began to communicate with nationally recognized firms in highway engineering to work up basic studies on the suggested routes. The commissioners spent the first few months with engineers preparing and reviewing these preliminary studies. There was a great deal of paperwork, but the project was a highway engineer's dream come true. The commissioners instructed the engineers to prepare design standards with a view toward maximum capacity and safety. Afterward, the engineers would determine the costs of construction, operation, and maintenance.

A few employees were hired as early as 1949, and they had a great sense of mission and high morale. They started calling themselves "the forty-niners," a term reminiscent of the California Gold Rush of one hundred years earlier. Lillian M. Schwartz, the Turnpike's first employee, was secretary to Paul Troast during those hectic early months. Years later she was to be called "the First Lady of the Turnpike" and "the Original Forty-niner."

Approaching her ninetieth birthday when we talked with her, she remembered the period vividly. The Turnpike Authority was assigned a three-room suite in the statehouse in Trenton, directly across the hall from the senate chamber. The suite included the room where Woodrow Wilson served tea when he was governor. Governor Driscoll's office was around the corner, where he could keep an eye on the work of the Turnpike commissioners. Schwartz recalled that one of the first things Paul Troast did was to put up a sign on the office door reading:

THE TURNPIKE MUST BE DONE
BY NOVEMBER FIFTY-ONE!

There was a real sense of urgency in those days for a number of reasons. The crush of traffic was real. The prestige of the administration rested on building the Turnpike quickly and well. Finally, the interest of the bonds would start accumulating the moment they were sold.

Lillian Schwartz recalled that the commissioners' meetings with consulting engineers would start at seven in the morning, and work would continue straight through until seven in the evening. There was no lunch break. Sandwiches were served right at the conference table. At first, Schwartz tried to take down their deliberations verbatim, but this soon proved hopeless. She just took down their decisions. Even so, it was grueling work. After working a twelve-hour day taking notes, she would go home, eat dinner, and go to sleep. Then she would get up at 4:00 A.M. to type up her notes so that the commissioners would have complete reports of their decisions by the start of business that morning. "I was so tired, I was ready to cry," she says today.[12]

In addition to conducting preliminary studies, the commissioners had to begin the process of building a permanent organization. During 1949 a number of key appointments were made. General W. W. Wanamaker, a retired career officer from the Army Corps of Engineers, was named executive director, and Charles M. Noble was made chief engineer. Then Henry E. Rose was put in charge of public information, Thomas R. Lowrie in charge of land acquisition. These crucial, early days were also significant in terms of appointments not made. Not a single landscape architect was hired.

Once the top appointments were made, it was up to General Wanamaker to recruit his own management people. Though some of these executives were recruited from university placement bureaus, so many were the general's old army friends that state legislators objected that he was practicing his own form of patronage.[13]

During these early months of 1949, basic decisions about the Turnpike had to be made. The early reports make fascinating reading, not only for what was said, but also for what was not said. There was a commitment to build "by far the best and most modern highway . . . and yet avoid any extravagance."[14]

The design vocabulary communicated safety and convenience without a hint of luxury or indulgence. After all, the bond market had to be convinced that this was a hardheaded, practical, straightforward, businesslike enterprise.

It made sense for the planners to cultivate the bond market by developing sensible and modest plans. But they went far beyond this requirement. In fact everything on the Turnpike was designed so as not to appear ostentatious. Even in their designing of a bridge (usually the civil engineer's masterpiece) the engineers hid their work from the motorist. All of the structure was underneath the roadway. This passion for anonymity and emphasis on a team approach were part of the spirit of the 1950s, discussed in such books as *The Organization Man* and *The Lonely Crowd.*[15]

As an artifact, the Turnpike tells us that its builders were not imbued with the Protestant ethic but with the social ethic. They were consummate team players. They lived quiet lives under the protection of large engineering firms. Like characters in *The Man in the Gray Flannel Suit,* these bureaucrat engineers put a premium on smoothing out differences. The idea of these practical, hardworking, shirt-sleeves workers was not to make waves, to get the job done—but only after consensus had been reached.[16]

The spirit behind building the Turnpike can be compared to that of the U.S. Navy's famous Seabees in World War II. Only a few years earlier, the Construction Battalions, or CBs, had been out in the Pacific building advanced bases for the Navy in the war against the Japanese. The motto: "Can do." Another slogan attributed to them was "The difficult we can do overnight; the impossible takes a little longer." Their work was indispensable in the amphibious "island-hopping" war. At Guadalcanal, the Seabees made Henderson Field ready for flight missions in five days, even in the face of repeated Japanese assaults.[17] Many of the Turnpike contractors were veterans, and they readily identified with that World War II spirit of getting the job done quickly, no matter what.

One of the key early decisions was to divide the project into seven sections, each a separate and simultaneous construction project. Dividing the Turnpike into seven sections was undoubtedly borrowed from the World War II–era task force approach to problem solving.

Directing the building of the Turnpike was like managing an army. But Paul Troast was, as a leader, less like George Patton, more like Dwight Eisenhower, a man who knew how to work with other people, knew how to manage, knew how to organize, direct, and lead. He saw building the Turnpike as basically a management problem. The first of more than eighty major construction contracts was awarded in December 1949, of which fifty-five were for over a million dollars. Fifty prime contractors used equipment with a total value of $45 million. Paul Troast and General Wanamaker, working closely together, directed the efforts of some seven hundred engineers and ten thousand workers.[18]

In these pre-environmentally conscious times, the focus was strictly on getting the job done. Today, the state has difficulty building a jughandle in twenty-one months. The paperwork, hearings, and clearances alone take that long. But in the early 1950s there was a good deal more respect for efficiency for its own sake, for getting the job done, whatever the obstacles.

Historian William L. O'Neill has called this period the "Years of Confidence." People believed in progress, that they were building a better world for the future. O'Neill explains: "Fifteen years of depression and war had left the country in a rundown state. The infrastructure of roads, telephone and power lines, generating stations, and the like needed to be expanded or rebuilt. . . . There was no lack of things to be done, nor, as it turned out, of willing hands to do them."[19]

In constructing the Turnpike, Troast enjoyed one of those brief periods in American history when there was a political consensus for his work. Nearly everyone at the time believed in the inevitability of progress and, therefore, in the necessity for the roadway. At the time no one seemed to question this can-do attitude. The war years had given Americans a sense of common sacrifice. They read Sunday supplement features about the future, and they believed the future was theirs. Such articles referred to the New Jersey Turnpike as "tomorrow's highway built today."[20]

At the time, no one questioned the need to pay for the road through the sale of bonds. Because New Jersey is a corridor connecting New York and Philadelphia, the state had frightful traffic problems. But the State Highway Department had only some $30 million per year available for new state highway construction, and parts of the Turnpike, particularly in the northern section of the state, cost as much as $8 million per mile. Under these circumstances, the financing of the Turnpike could be accomplished only through bonds. Two hundred twenty-five million dollars of thirty-five-year bonds bearing 3.25 percent interest were issued, at the time the largest bond issue ever for a toll highway.[21]

When the original bonds were issued, promoters of the Turnpike justified the economic feasibility of the project by saying it would pay for itself. Though estimated revenue was barely enough to pay the interest for the first year of operation, the revenue was expected to double in the first five years and to be sufficient to pay off the debt completely in twenty-five to thirty-five years. Of course, these were just projections. No one was sure the road's income was going to meet them.

The commissioners were busy in 1950 and 1951 drumming up business for the road around the state, addressing civic and service organizations and showing slides illustrating the benefits of the new roadway. In anticipation of the opening of the Turnpike, the Authority's new public information department was busy preparing press releases and media campaigns so as to maximize traffic quickly.[22]

The Turnpike turned out to be more profitable than its designers ever dreamed. But the profits were not used to pay off the bonds and close the tollbooths. Instead, the Turnpike Authority kept coming up with new projects and new bond issues. Critics of public authorities in general and of the New Jersey Turnpike in particular charge that this is a regular pattern: once an authority is set up, its bureaucracy becomes self-perpetuating through new bond issues.[23]

A key problem that had to be solved early was the alignment of the roadway. Alignment decisions were partly technical, partly economic, and very political. In broad outline, the alignment was already spelled out in Governor Driscoll's original plan and in the enabling legislation. Everyone knew the Turnpike had to run from the George Washington Bridge to the Delaware Memorial Bridge. But there were many details to be worked out. How could the new road serve, but not disrupt, such cities as Newark, Elizabeth, New Brunswick, Trenton, and Camden? How could it best serve the populous areas of Bergen, Hudson, and Passaic counties adjacent to its northern terminus?[24]

There was a political consensus that the New Jersey Turnpike was necessary and desirable. But when it came down to the specifics of the road's alignment, some people stood to lose a great deal. Certainly the hardest hit was the city of Elizabeth, which fought the project fiercely. The city objected because the elevated construction would create a wall separating the city into two sections. The Turnpike planned to push through the most depressed areas of Elizabeth, where property values were lowest. The homes of 450 families would have to be condemned. The city knew this would make property values plummet even more. Not only was the proposed Turnpike unattractive and objectionable from an aesthetic standpoint, but city officials argued that the dark underpasses would become high-crime zones. There was a major political fight.

The city of Elizabeth did offer an alternative route along the waterfront, which would avoid disrupting residential neighborhoods. But it would have disturbed eleven major companies and twenty smaller ones. One of the major companies was Singer Sewing Machine, which threatened to leave the city altogether if the waterfront route was adopted.[25]

In fairness to the Turnpike Authority, the State Highway Department had studied a route through Elizabeth years earlier in developing plans for state Route 100 (which was never built because the Turnpike took its place) and had reached much the same conclusion: there was no place else to go. At that particular stretch, there is a railroad on one side and Route 1 on the other. The planners were further constrained by water here and the airport there.[26] Looking at a map, one might sympathize with the Turnpike Authority. But if today one visits the residents of Fourth Street, who live next to the Turnpike, it makes one wonder. Vibrations from the highway rattle the windows and walls of their homes. In the summer, when their windows are open, they sleep fitfully.

If some would lose drastically through building the Turnpike, others stood to experience major personal gain. One of the most difficult and complicated problems facing the Authority in 1950 was the acquisition of some thirty-four hundred parcels of real estate. Each of the section engineers was responsible for the preparation of property maps that defined the lands to be acquired. The original estimate of cost for the acquisition of real estate had been $10,145,000. This estimate had been prepared by experienced appraisers who surveyed the route of the Turnpike. The appraisers were instructed to establish "liberal cost estimates based on their experience and acquaintance with local conditions." Yet when Enoch R. Needles, consulting engineer, tallied up the revised estimates in 1952, the total land acquisition costs were about $7.5 million above the original figure.[27] In more recent years, New Jerseyans have speculated about personal fortunes made in Turnpike land transactions.

But the generation that built the New Jersey Turnpike did not think about such matters. Years earlier, Huey Long in Louisiana had proved that the people will overlook the fine details as long as the road gets built. Whatever the public thought about the Turnpike, the engineers who built it expressed the same kind of pride and enthusiasm about their roads as the engineers of Louisiana had expressed back in the 1930s. Summing things up, Needles wrote in 1952:

> The New Jersey Turnpike is a magnificent public undertaking. Its construction will affect the movements of many, many millions of motorists in coming years. The effects of its building will be nationwide rather than statewide. A very large number of civil engineers may claim honor and gratification for having been identified with its construction. In planning and building, we have performed a real service on behalf of our fellow men. Projects like the New Jersey Turnpike make us very proud to be called civil engineers.[28]

One of the reasons the engineers were so proud was that the new road would save time. According to George W. Burpee, one of the original consulting engineers, the estimated time saved by the Turnpike over its full length was one hour and ten minutes for a passenger car and one and a half hours for a truck. So, from the start, the Turnpike sold time and convenience. Burpee also pointed out that the savings in time and distance were not the same over all sections. South of the Raritan River the general highway system offered much greater competition than it did north of it. In fact, this is still true today, nearly forty years later. The greatest congestion and the greatest possibility of time savings were always north of New Brunswick, and this situation was recognized in the toll schedule adopted.

The initial toll rates proposed for the New Jersey Turnpike for passenger cars were only slightly more than one cent per mile for the 83 miles at the southern end, between the Delaware Memorial Bridge and New Brunswick, but the rates jumped to nearly three and a half cents per mile on the northern 35 miles between New Brunswick and the George Washington Bridge because of the greater congestion and the difficulties in building there.[29]

Before actual construction of the New Jersey Turnpike could begin, the engineers had to come up with a standardized design. Since the roadway had been carved up into seven more or less autonomous sections for construction, the engineers needed a set of uniform standards to follow. For example, the designers determined that the Turnpike should be a limited-access express highway with interchanges considerable distances apart. They also decided to have wide, stabilized shoulders on both sides of the traffic lanes, extra wide traffic lanes, and grades as moderate as possible.

The design speed for the southern section, below the Raritan River, was 75 mph and for the northern section, 60 to 70 mph. For the average motorist in 1952, this really was the miracle road. The motorist could cross the Delaware Memorial Bridge, barrel up through the marshland of Salem County, and tick off the mile markers faster than one a minute. For most people, this was an entirely new driving experience. Historian Richard P. McCormick, in a letter to us, wrote: "I well recall my first trip up the Turnpike. I had bought a used car in Baltimore in 1952 and drove it up to New Brunswick. I was amazed at the paucity of traffic and thrilled by the speed I could make on America's finest highway." [30]

To make this kind of speed possible, the engineers had to build to particular specifications. The maximum allowable grade was 3 percent. The minimum radius for curves was 3,000 feet. The pavement lanes were 12 feet wide. In addition to these design standards for the roadway, there were design specifications for bridges and storm-drainage structures. The list went on and on, creating conditions under which motorists could drive safely at high speeds. The whole idea was for patrons to enjoy sustained uniform speed and freedom from delays. [31]

According to Charles M. Noble, who was chief engineer for the Turnpike Authority at the time, it was anticipated that, by November 1951, interest charges on bonds issued for the construction of the Turnpike would total $48,000 per day. The large sums at stake were a powerful incentive to rapid progress. Noble decided to push the work through in two working seasons, with grading and bridge foundations in the first, and paving and superstructures in the second. Noble's program required that plans and construction proceed simultaneously along the entire length of the Turnpike. [32]

As these plans unfolded in 1950, the Second World War seemed remote. In New Jersey everyone seemed to have a job and an automobile. On Sunday mornings, you could read newspaper feature stories about how they were building the "Miracle Turnpike." Then on Sunday morning, June 25, 1950, there were front-page stories about a strange war that had begun during the night in a faraway place called Korea. Catching the Turnpike at the beginning of its first construction season, the war created enormous problems. Engineers had a hard time getting materials. Costs went up. The army took key seasoned workers off to war. Chief engineer Noble wrote: "At times it appeared that these obstacles would be insurmountable. If the original schedules had not been set up on the basis of an early start, and allowance made for some leeway in construction time, the program would have been much more seriously affected." [33]

Even if there had been no Korean War, there was still one important natural obstacle to be faced—the muddy marshes of northern New Jersey, the same marshes that had plagued the stagecoaches of the nineteenth century. They were still there. The Turnpike had to place heavy structures on top of this mud. This was a threat not only to the schedule, but to the whole project.

In the 1950s, despite modern advances, the muddy marshes were still the most challenging area for engineers. The mud threatened a long section at the northern end of the Turnpike that was routed over the New Jersey meadows. This route had been chosen to avoid heavily built-up industrial and residential areas in Newark. Geologically, the meadows are made up of mud and silt with a high water content, varying in depth from a few feet to as far down as 250 feet. Where the mud is only 5 or 6 feet deep, the solution is simple. Excavate and fill with crushed stone, raising the roadbed above the water table. But what do you do when the mud is deep?

Fortunately, there was a solution. The general principle was to use a great deal of sand as a wick to draw off the excess water. Specifically, they sank multiple caissons down to a firm stratum, filled them with sand, and then covered them and the surrounding areas with blankets of sand. Gradually and continuously, the water would be drawn up through the caissons of sand and gently distributed to the sand blanket, from which it drained off into the adjacent meadows. [34]

Another aspect of civil engineering that deserves mention was the problem of creating structures to overpass and underpass streams of water, railroad tracks, local streets, pipelines, and other utilities. This problem was especially significant on the northern section of the Turnpike that crosses through densely developed industrial sections of Elizabeth and Newark. The most interesting of the structures built there are the bridges required to cross two major rivers—the Passaic and the Hackensack.

At the time they were built, these two bridges were the longest of their type. The total length of the Passaic River Bridge is 6,955 feet; that of the Hackensack River Bridge, 5,623 feet. Their respective costs of construction were $13.7 and $9.5 million. It is noteworthy that both bridges were completed and ready for traffic in about two years, a remarkably short period of time. [35]

Although the Turnpike's bridges over the Passaic and the Hackensack are certainly not in the same league as such American classics as the George Washington and Golden Gate bridges, they are an important part of Turnpike history. Since both rivers are navigable at the point of the Turnpike's crossing, the bridges had to be built with provisions for maintaining the width of the channel and substantial vertical clearances.

Early on, the engineers decided on simplicity of form. In a report, one of them wrote that "unnecessary architectural embellishments were avoided."[36] This low-key approach resulted in placing all of the carrying structure below the floor of the bridges. Photographs and architectural drawings reveal both bridges to be handsome structures, but one cannot appreciate this beauty from the Turnpike itself. On the plus side, this design does provide an unobstructed view for vehicles passing over the bridges. On the negative side, the bridges are so understated travelers can easily sail across each of them and never realize they have crossed a river.

Contrast this experience with that of crossing over the George Washington Bridge. Passing beneath the majestic steel towers is like walking down the nave of a cathedral. It is virtually impossible to cross the George Washington Bridge and not be impressed. Yet thousands of people cross the Hackensack and Passaic rivers every day completely unaware. There are not even signs indicating the rivers being crossed. We asked a senior Turnpike official about this and were told that signs are a bad idea since they are a distraction. The Turnpike, in other words, does not see itself as a purveyor of scenery, architecture, or geography. It moves traffic. Period.

The New Jersey Turnpike bridges not only represent an interesting solution to a number of complicated problems; they also embody a set of beliefs characteristic of an age. In the 1950s, we believed in progress so much that technology was allowed to overcome, if not obliterate, nature. Progress meant the total eclipse of nature. The rivers were taken for granted. There was no appreciation of the place of rivers in history and as part of the environment. The Turnpike's bridges over these two important rivers are monuments to America's disregard of the landscape.

In a letter to us, historian James Fisher wrote: "The highway dominates the landscape so totally that the motorist is unaware of the Passaic and Hackensack Rivers. I usually miss them myself. It's difficult to obscure major features of the landscape altogether, but the Turnpike manages it."[37] What Fisher describes is the total triumph of the built environment over the natural environment.

Other states may celebrate their great rivers, but not New Jersey. The Passaic and Hackensack rivers have been, in effect, erased by the Turnpike. The two great rivers that provide the waters of the Jersey meadows are geologically still there. They meander lazily underneath the Turnpike's bridges unnoticed. True, at this point, as they are about to empty into Newark Bay, they are sick streams, poisoned with the waste of New Jersey's industry. Along the banks of the Hackensack, there were once Dutch settlers and, later, George Washington's army camped there. But on the Turnpike, nothing marks the Hackensack River. Along the banks of the Passaic in Paterson, the poets William Carlos Williams and Allen Ginsberg lived and worked. But on the Turnpike, nothing marks the Passaic River.

Another aspect of constructing the bridges was dealing with the obstruction posed by the Pulaski Skyway, which links Newark and New York, just south of the Passaic River. The Pulaski Skyway is a fantastic engineering structure named for Polish General Casimir Pulaski (c. 1748–1779) who led patriot troops to a number of victories in the American Revolution. The structure is made of a delicate latticework of black steel, resembling an elaborate construction made by a child prodigy from an erector set. It has been called "America's first cosmic road."[38] At the intersection with the Turnpike, it is an elevated structure about 90 feet high.

The engineers faced a tough choice: whether to pass under or over the Pulaski Skyway. If they went over, they would have to elevate the Turnpike high above the ground, an expensive undertaking. If they went under the skyway, costs would be lower, but then the Turnpike would clear the river by only 110 feet at the channel lines, a tight squeeze for shipping. Somewhat reluctantly, the decision was made to go with the lower elevation. Whatever the merits of this choice, Turnpike motorists enjoy a rare sight as they speed just under the fantastic black steel tracery of the Pulaski Skyway. This convergence of the Turnpike and the Pulaski has got to be one of American engineering's great shrines.

If bridge building is the most spectacular aspect of road building, then paving may be the least. Still, while doing the preliminary research for this book, we often played a game with friends who claimed to know the New Jersey Turnpike well. We would ask them a simple question: "Is the Turnpike made out of concrete or asphalt?" Many people who had driven the road frequently could not remember. The failure of people to note the pavement points out a fundamental fact about their perceptions of the Turnpike: what they largely notice, as suggested in the previous chapter, are the surroundings, not the road itself. The Turnpike is experienced as a passage through an environment, not a passage over a roadway.

One of the engineers involved with the project, John R. Deitz, has written about the paving decision. The first meeting of the engineering firms involved was held in October 1949. According to Deitz, "The question uppermost in everyone's mind at that time was whether the Turnpike would be white or black. A very preliminary discussion indicated that if the thirty engineers present were each to select a type, there would be thirty pavements, no two of which would be identical." [39]

The ground rules were to pick a pavement that would stand up best under extremely heavy truck loads and that would give good and economical service for the life of the Turnpike bonds. An extensive review of the literature was conducted. Understandably, the deliberations were followed closely by the Portland Cement Association and the Asphalt Institute. Like most important decisions in life, there was no clear-cut answer. Each type had its advantages and disadvantages. In the jargon of the profession, the concrete road was called "rigid pavement" and the asphalt road was called "flexible pavement."

What do you do when you cannot decide something? You appoint a committee. The Turnpike's committee did not actually make a decision either. Instead, it presented a list of four options: (1) pave with concrete; (2) pave with asphalt; (3) pave with both; or (4) take bids for both materials, choosing the least expensive. In the end, the Turnpike Authority decided on the fourth choice—to take bids. Flexible asphalt 12 inches thick was adopted on the basis of bid price, some $5 million lower than that for rigid concrete pavement 10 inches thick. [40]

Once the land had been acquired and the design specifications worked out, actual construction began full blast with the tremendous job of moving 52 million cubic yards of earth. [41] In constructing the road, engineers deviated little from conventional methods. What made the project unique was its scale and its speed. No one had ever tried to push through a civil engineering project this big quite so fast. A number of familiar factors once again made this possible: a political consensus that ironed over the wrinkles of dissent and a can-do attitude among the work force, many of whom, from General Wanamaker on down through the ranks, were veterans.

As soon as the paving was complete, along came workers to put in guardrails, traffic signs, and electrical lighting. Time was of the essence. Every day spent building the road meant that much more in interest costs on the bonds. Every day saved in building the road meant that the Authority could start collecting tolls faster. Sooner than anyone expected, it was time to apply the lane stripes. They were placed in 25-foot dashes with 25-foot skips by automatic spray machines. Like a chef putting the final touches on an entrée, the machine dropped glass beads in the paint as it was applied to provide reflection for night driving.

The design and building of the service facilities was the last step. Concessionaires could have erected their own buildings. This is exactly what had been done on the Pennsylvania and Maine turnpikes. Such a scheme would have reduced the initial capital investment by the Authority, but in the long run it was more profitable for the Turnpike Authority to have direct ownership.

There is much to praise about the design of Turnpike service facilities in terms of safety in comparison with other East Coast facilities. In Delaware and Maryland, one has to squeeze into the left lane, otherwise known as the fast or passing lane, in order to enter the facilities. Returning to the highway, one has the terrifying experience of merging into the fast lane. The reason this is done in Delaware and Maryland is to save money; the same facility serves both northbound and southbound traffic. But this arrangement is dangerous. On the New Jersey Turnpike, the engineers agreed to make the rest areas "half-sites" (a word coined for the purpose). These half-sites were to be paired on opposite sides of the road. The traveler would thus always use the slow lane for exit and entry. An attempt was also made to place the sites on high ground for visibility. This design feature made the deceleration of vehicles turning into the rest area and the acceleration of vehicles entering the Turnpike much easier.[42]

If we look at the building of the New Jersey Turnpike in theatrical terms, it is a play in four acts. Act One is the politics of the Turnpike. Act Two is its economics. Act Three deals with the construction of the Turnpike. Now we are ready for Act Four, placing the Turnpike into service. We begin this last act with the opening festivities.

The inauguration of the Turnpike was a public drama, with Governor Driscoll heading a motorcade from Trenton to Hightstown, where a dedication ceremony took place on November 30, 1951, even though not all sections of the Turnpike were complete. A platform had been erected and draped with bunting. High school bands played. The guest list had been drawn up carefully so as not to overlook construction company executives and political office holders on every level.[43]

Said Governor Driscoll: "The Turnpike has permitted New Jersey to emerge from behind the billboards, the hot dog stands, and the junkyards. Motorists can now see the beauty of the real New Jersey."[44] Reading Driscoll's speech today, it seems charged with irony. Today, the view along the Turnpike is universally regarded as anything but beautiful. New Jerseyans see beauty in their state despite the Turnpike, not because of it.

A further irony, of course, was that *beauty* had never been part of the design plan at all. True, there are no hot dog stands; but billboards and junkyards are very much in evidence.[45] It made a nice speech, but Driscoll's words had almost nothing to do with the actual appearance of the Turnpike then or now.

The November 30, 1951, festivities began at 9:30 A.M., with a buffet breakfast in the War Memorial Building in Trenton. Paul Troast's secretary, Lillian Schwartz, and his wife, Eleanor, had been up since 4:00 A.M. supervising the place settings and making sure guests were seated according to protocol. One of the important guests was Howard Johnson, the restaurateur and original Turnpike concessionaire. Howard Johnson himself supervised every detail of the breakfast to make sure it was flawless. He brought in the top people from his organization to make it a meal to remember.

After breakfast, the official procession motored to Hightstown, now Exit 8. The mile-long motorcade of buses and cars then went on to New Brunswick for an inspection of the Turnpike Authority's brand-new administration building, which replaced the temporary offices in the state capitol. From its hilltop site, the new building had a commanding view of a long stretch of the Turnpike. Eight-tenths of a mile north of the building, the party stopped at the Raritan River for ribbon-cutting ceremonies. Lillian Schwartz was to produce the scissors at just the right moment.

The bridge over the Raritan was named in memory of Marine Sergeant John A. Basilone of Raritan Borough. Basilone, a gunnery sergeant, won the Congressional Medal of Honor on Guadalcanal. He was killed later on Iwo Jima in the western Pacific. In a touching ceremony, Salvatore Basilone, the hero's father, and other members of his family unveiled a plaque honoring the marine.[46]

After the ceremonies, 93 miles of the $250 million highway were open to motorists between Woodbridge in Middlesex County and Deepwater in Salem County, the southern terminus. A 53-mile section from Deepwater to Bordentown had already been placed in service on November 5. Sixteen additional miles between Woodbridge and Newark were opened in December 1951, and the final 9-mile link to the George Washington Bridge was opened in January 1952.[47]

At first, when the Turnpike was opened, a sense of euphoria prevailed. There was state pride when the Turnpike received nationwide attention in such magazines as *Business Week, Fortune, Nation's Business, Popular Science, Saturday Evening Post,* and *Time.* The real estate industry and the chamber of commerce hailed the Turnpike as an expansion of opportunity and as a boon to commerce. It was another fulfillment of the American Dream. The Turnpike was tangible evidence of the success of the American Way of Life.

This period of euphoria and approval was short-lived. The 1950s had begun with a national consensus that more housing was needed; but, by the end of the decade, there was a chorus of criticism about the housing that had sprung up in the suburbs. Critical articles began appearing in prominent national magazines. Sociologist David Popenoe, who has surveyed this literature, sums it up: "A move to the suburbs was alleged to foster conformity, hyperactivity, anti-individualism, conservatism, momism, dullness and boredom, and status seeking, as well as a host of specific psychological and social ills including alcoholism, sexual promiscuity, and mental illness." [48]

The New Jersey Turnpike was not immune to the growing criticism of suburban life. Architects, city planners, aestheticians, and designers described the Turnpike as an excrescence on the landscape. It was too straight, too boring, too ugly. Other states had beautiful and scenic freeways that skirted their blighted industrial cities. Why did New Jersey choose a route that looked upon oil refineries and junkyards? Pity the poor commuter who was subjected to all this ugliness on a daily basis.

The New Jersey Turnpike was conceived in the postwar urgency of the late 1940s and built in record speed in the early 1950s by bureaucrat-engineers. The engineers did their job well: they followed the political mandate of the day—to build the road as quickly and cheaply and safely as possible. The struggle to produce the road has largely been forgotten, but the road itself, wider than ever, is still in place.

It is a reflection of its times. The administration in Trenton may have been aesthetically unimaginative, but the Turnpike was exactly what the people wanted. The stolid engineers, in the absence of artistic leadership from Trenton, built a road that mirrored their own taste and values. The roadway was utterly straight and boring and bleak, but it was somehow magnificent. It conveyed an image of strength and permanence and stability. It enhanced the citizenry's sense of well-being. In its day, the New Jersey Turnpike seemed just right.

With the luxury of hindsight, we can regret the failure and shortsightedness of the Turnpike commissioners in not including landscape architects on the team. At the same time, however, we can appreciate the Turnpike as a living embodiment, a museum really, of the prevailing values of the era in which it was built. This was the era when diners served blue-plate specials, when cars had lots of chrome, when suburbanites put pink flamingos on their front lawns. Many of the artifacts of the 1950s—the Hula-Hoop, the Davy Crockett coonskin cap, and the bomb shelter—have faded from the American scene, but the New Jersey Turnpike is still very much with us.

In the 1950s, when it was first completed, the Turnpike seemed to be delivering on the promise of the 1939 World's Fair. It was truly the Highway of Tomorrow. The New Jersey salesman who worked in Manhattan could easily get home in time for dinner in his own car. People liked the Turnpike. With fresh memories of earlier congestion, people did not mind paying a small toll for the privilege of driving on a road where one could travel 70 miles per hour.

But in the 1960s and 1970s there was a negative reaction. In an era of environmentalism and protest, the Turnpike was seen as a despoiler of the landscape. What had once seemed like progress now seemed like ruthlessness. The Authority's ambitious widening schemes ruined neighborhoods with more asphalt, more noise, and more noxious fumes. Motorists and editorial writers wondered aloud why other states had free interstate highways, whereas New Jersey seemed to be stuck with a permanent toll road.

In the 1980s, there has been a coming to terms with the Turnpike. The people of New Jersey are accustomed to it. An entire generation has grown up with it, taking it for granted as a part of the landscape. Although it is no longer seen as marvelous, neither is it seen as evil.

The Turnpike Authority has also realized that there are limits to the highway's growth. It now takes for granted that the Turnpike is fixed at 142 miles in all, covering 117.5 miles of mainline, plus two extensions totaling 14 miles, as well as a northern alternate spur of 10 miles. The most dramatic limitation came in 1980 when then Governor Brendan Byrne decided not to push through with a proposed spur to Tom's River, close to the Jersey shore. The era of unlimited growth had come to an end, and the Turnpike reluctantly accepted the fact that future growth will be modest, largely restricted to widening. Even so, the Turnpike would still be able to collect tolls—day after day, year after year—which is the subject of our next chapter.

A River of Cash

Chapter

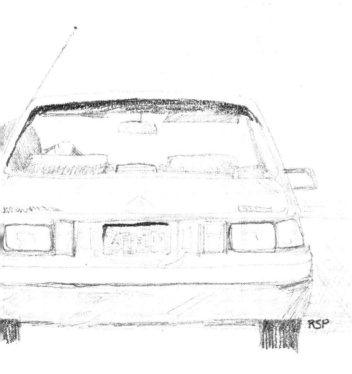

I hope the Good Lord blesses
All whom I have come to know,
May you enjoy good health and happiness.
Just keep raking in the dough.
                —Written by Samuel B. Meli,
            toll collector, on the occasion of
                        his retirement[1]

In collecting money, the Turnpike Authority generates a veritable river of cash. In the late 1980s the Turnpike Authority was collecting $182 million per year in toll revenues. To collect this money requires a small army of toll collectors, all of whom must themselves be paid. In addition, there have to be elaborate checks and controls to make sure proper accounts are maintained. A large share of the Turnpike's operating expenses goes for toll collection. To collect that $182 million in tolls, the Turnpike spends $38 million (or about 21 percent) for toll collection.[2]

The river of cash starts with a trickle—one patron at a time, one transaction at a time. The New Jersey Turnpike's 142-mile roadway network includes some twenty-seven interchanges, each with several toll lanes.[3] And this is a 24-hour-a-day, 7-day-a-week, 365-day-a-year operation. So if each toll booth is a little dribble or little trickle of cash, then each toll plaza may be seen as a stream or tributary. By the time all the revenues from all the plazas are gathered, we have a flood tide. Arthur Warren Meixner of Fairleigh Dickinson University writes: "The Turnpike has been a phenomenal fiscal success."[4]

The people on the front lines are the toll collectors. One may not meet other Turnpike employees, but it is impossible to escape the toll collector. We talked with half a dozen toll collectors ranging in rank from trainees to supervisors. These interviews were not in their booths, but in Turnpike Authority headquarters in New Brunswick and at the toll collector training facility in Milltown.

The toll collectors we talked to were pleased to speak with us and surprised to learn that someone was interested in their stories. We learned a great deal about their career patterns and their life-styles. They were open and candid about why they took the job and what it has meant to them.

Today there is no typical toll collector. A collector may be male or female, black or white, young or old. Since 1968, the toll collectors have been unionized, giving the job certain rules and protections. But it was not always this way. Originally, these nonunion jobs were given mostly to white males with political connections. These good, steady jobs were tied to the political patronage system. Chairman Paul Troast felt that it was politically wise to solicit nominees for jobs from the state senate in recognition of its favorable legislative treatment of the Authority. Nearly all collector positions were filled by asking senators for recommendations.[5]

The typical toll collector of the early days had a certain background. He was likely to be from a white ethnic blue-collar family. As often as not he was a high school graduate with some military service. He probably went to an inner-city parochial school and at one point aspired to become a policeman or fireman.

When our typical candidate finished military service, he returned home to New Jersey. He wanted to get married, so he needed a job right away. Like anybody else, he looked around to see what he could get. Although he might have preferred to become a police officer, being a toll collector was not a bad alternative. He could still enjoy some of the prestige of wearing a uniform and a badge; he could enjoy steady work with good benefits and a pension plan.

It is a truism that where there is political power, jobs are sure to follow. And the Turnpike is a big employer. The humble tollbooth is often the passport to a suburban home. If you persist in one job and in one place year after year, eventually you will have the down payment to move out of the city to a place with nice lawns and good schools. The sons of toll collectors become doctors, lawyers, professors, and technicians. For some people the Turnpike is not a road; it is an avenue of social mobility.

To be happy as a toll collector, one has to adjust to a repetitious job in a basically paramilitary organization. This may have been easier in the early days of the Turnpike, when many employees were veterans of either World War II or the Korean War. The career advancement path and titles are parallel to the police and military system—collector (or private?), sergeant, lieutenant, captain.

The actual work done by sergeants and lieutenants and captains is supervisory and managerial, but these managers carry military rank and wear insignia appropriate to their rank. Collectors collect the tolls. Sergeants supervise a particular toll plaza during a particular shift. Lieutenants serve as assistant chiefs of a section, or geographical division, of the Turnpike. Captains serve as section chiefs. People holding the various ranks expect to be addressed by their titles, even if there is a certain puzzlement to the outsider when confronted with all the military panoply in an organization not devoted to combat.

The toll management staff follows a classical pyramidal hierarchy. There are 818 collectors, 105 sergeants, 26 lieutenants, and 6 captains. For each rank, the eligible candidate takes a management test. If he passes the test, he is placed on a list for promotion.[6]

For someone from a working-class background, being a toll taker is a good job—steady, secure, and lucrative. Those who fit in best generally have an ingrained sense of law and order and respect for authority. The arrangement is good for the Turnpike and the toll collector. The Turnpike Authority gets its revenue; the collector gets a job that is practically guaranteed for life. There are no layoffs on the Turnpike. It is a recession-proof job.

Still, toll collectors must hold onto their jobs through steady and honest work. At the start of an eight-hour shift, collectors are given a certain amount of change. During their shift, the computer terminals located in their booths keeps track of the tickets and of the amount of cash required for those tickets. At the same time, the treadles buried in the lanes are relentlessly counting the number of axles that pass by. At the end of their shift, the collectors must "bank out." This is a process of counting the money in the presence of a sergeant, who must verify the count. Collectors have to account for all the money collected, plus the amount of money they were originally given as change. Some collectors come out to the penny every time. Others are a couple of dollars over or under. This is not a big deal. But someone who is five dollars or more short every time is watched carefully. Since the system is virtually foolproof, only a fool would try to cheat. Why jeopardize a good job for a few dollars?

And it is a good job. At the time this is written, starting wages for new collectors are $9.13 per hour, plus shift differentials and overtime. The starting base pay can be calculated at over $20,000 per year. Veteran collectors, where traffic volume is extraordinarily heavy, can make up to $50,000, $60,000, even $70,000 per year if they are willing to put in the hours.[7]

Because of sickness or other absences, an ambitious collector can put in a great deal of overtime. Since the Turnpike is open twenty-four hours a day, somebody has to be there to collect the tolls. Under union agreement, one can only work sixteen hours at a time, except for extreme emergencies such as snowstorms when replacements cannot get to work. But if one works enough sixteen-hour days, the money starts to add up. Overtime is paid at time and a half. Working on holidays, one is paid for the holiday (which would be paid anyway even if the employee stayed home), plus time and a half for the overtime (which is the regular overtime compensation rate). This adds up, in effect, to two and a half times base pay.

What of the work itself: is it demanding? Well, there is more to the job than one may think. On barrier toll roads such as the Garden State Parkway everyone is charged the same thing, say, a quarter or a dime. But on the New Jersey Turnpike, there are six classifications of vehicles and seventeen different places of origin, so the collector must cope with a great many variables. In addition, one must work quickly to keep up with the flow of traffic. There is also the paperwork of documenting irregular transactions. Finally, the toll collector has to be alert for flimflam and toll evasion scams. Probably every collector has been flimflammed a few times. If you get fooled often, at the very least you lose face with your supervisor; eventually, you might lose your job.

Patrons sometimes imagine that anyone could walk in off the street and become a toll collector immediately, as easily as becoming a cashier in a diner. But experience has shown otherwise. During a strike of toll collectors in 1959, the Authority staffed the toll plazas with inexperienced supervisory personnel. To keep things simple, the complicated ticket system was suspended. Instead toll charges were set at a flat rate of 25 cents per passenger vehicle and 50 cents for trucks and buses. Under these circumstances, the Authority was able to collect only 40 cents of the usual toll dollar.[8]

Each booth on the Turnpike has what looks like a cash register. It is actually a small tabulator linked to a large computer. This computerized system was installed in 1980 and is quite remarkable. The system monitors traffic flow by keeping track of the actual axle count for each booth. Tolls are tied to the number of axles on a given vehicle. A three-axle truck pays more than a two-axle truck, and so on. The bigger the vehicle, the higher the toll. As mentioned before, every tollbooth has a treadle—a counting device embedded in the roadway. The treadle records the number of axles that pass during a given shift, so each toll collector has to account for every axle that goes through his or her booth.

Most transactions are routine, but what if the motorist presents a ticket that is wet or mutilated? Since such a ticket might jam the machine, the collector must make up a substitute ticket that is color-coded green. What if a motorist loses the ticket? Now that Turnpike toll tickets, like so much else in American life, have been miniaturized, they can easily blow out of the car as one streams along with the windows open in the summertime. Or they can get mixed up with items in the glove compartment. Anxiety about losing that little ticket runs high among Turnpike patrons.

Actually, the Turnpike is quite benign with regard to lost tickets. Just as it says on the toll ticket, "IF TICKET LOST, HIGHEST TOLL FOR CLASS CHARGED." This is done, no questions asked. If the patron has a good excuse or a good explanation for a lost ticket, the collector cannot reduce the toll, but the plaza supervisor can.

An interesting situation presents itself if the motorist enters at either extreme of the Turnpike, Exit 1 or Exits 18E or 18W. In such a case, the toll for a lost ticket will be no more than it would have been had you not lost your ticket. Which means that if one has a perverse hankering for a souvenir Turnpike toll ticket, this can be accomplished at little or no cost. Toll collectors will admonish patrons to "destroy the ticket if you find it." This is to insure that the ticket is not used in the future, possibly mixing up the computers. But if there are beer can collectors, why not Turnpike toll ticket collectors?

Collectors must be prepared to deal with problems as quickly as they present themselves, so that traffic does not get backed up. In collector training sessions, one of which we attended, instructors try to cover every conceivable irregularity so that nothing will take the new collector by surprise. What if the vehicle is a police car, fire engine, or ambulance? Upon entry, such vehicles are issued special nonrevenue tickets.

Sometimes in the course of a shift, a collector may be busy with a whole chain of transactions, one right after another. Then the collector may notice a gap or space and a vehicle lurking 30 yards back, waiting for the car ahead to clear the gate. An experienced collector knows what to expect: a toll evader. The malefactor will accelerate rapidly and zoom through the opening without surrendering the ticket or handing over the money. If the collector gets the license plate of the vehicle, in a few days the miscreant will receive a $35 ticket for toll evasion.

Actually, dashing through a tollbooth to avoid a toll is stupid. Because of a little-known loophole in New Jersey law, a better choice is available to the toll evader. If you simply pull up to the tollbooth, hand over the ticket, and drive off without paying, you cannot be charged with anything serious. Some do this and even smile and tell the toll collector, "Have a nice day!" Technically, you are still liable for the toll itself, but cannot be fined for toll evasion since you respected the stop order at the tollbooth and surrendered the ticket.

The best thing to do if you find yourself at a toll plaza without money is to tell the truth. This occurs every day. The toll collector calls the sergeant in the toll plaza office. You pull over, go into the office, and fill out a form. Officially you are a "patron without funds." You sign a statement: "I ACKNOWLEDGE MY OBLIGATION FOR PAYMENT OF *TOLL DUE* THE NEW JERSEY TURNPIKE AUTHORITY AND AM AWARE OF N.J. LAW R.S. 27:23–25 CONCERNING NON-PAYMENT OF TOLLS."[9]

Nevertheless, anyone who rides the Turnpike must wonder what would happen if you reached a tollbooth and found yourself without funds. Do you go to jail? Is your car held in escrow while you go off on foot to seek $1.50? Do you get some kind of summons or is your name entered in a heartless computer from which it will emerge only after years of spirit-breaking red tape?

Treatment of the patron who is embarrassed by lack of funds is benign, though a bit complicated. Recently, a patron found himself at Exit 18W with nothing in his wallet. He had run out the door and grabbed his wallet, not checking to see if there was anything in it. His wife, he later learned, had "borrowed" his cash and forgotten to say anything.

Imagine his horror, after being in line behind ten other cars, when he reached the tollbooth—there were now a similar number of cars behind him—and discovered nothing in his pocket and a $1.50 toll facing him. In a great sweat he confessed his impecunity to the toll collector. "No money . . . Can't believe it . . . I could swear there was money in here." The toll collector holds up his hand for the explanations to stop. He speaks on the radio to someone: "Got a no funds."

The answer crackles back: "Point of entrance?"

"Nine."

"Okay."

The toll collector comes out of the booth and stands in front of the car, writing down the license plate number. Returning to the booth, he says, "Okay, pull to the side up ahead, take your driver's license and registration, and go downstairs."

"Downstairs where?"

"Over there."

"Over where?" The toll collector has pointed vaguely in the direction of the next tollbooth, in whose lane an eighteen-wheeler coughed. Later, a staircase is discovered just the other side of the toll lane where the truck stood. Indeed, staircases heading underground are in front of every third tollbooth.

Parking just beyond the booths is simple, but walking back to the staircase is not pleasant. All those drivers in all those automobiles in all those toll lanes seem to be staring. A person on foot in this place is an alien life form.

Reaching the relative safety of the staircase surround, the patron descends what has to be one of the narrowest staircases anywhere, at the bottom of which is an extraordinarily narrow aluminum door. The sense is one of utter claustrophobia. Where does this door lead? Through the looking glass? The other side of the door does not evoke *Alice in Wonderland* but, rather, an intercontinental ballistic missile silo deep under the ground in a farmer's field in North Dakota, invisible even from nearby roads but capable of launching lethal horror into the skies.

Our patron finds himself in a long, dimly lit tunnel, everything dull gray, with invisible equipment whirring and a cacophony of barely audible voices and music. At first, the source of these sounds is impossible to locate. Then it becomes clear. He is underneath the tollbooths, and the sounds emerge from the ductwork that rises along the wall to each booth, providing heat to them in the winter. Up above are the eighteen tollbooths at Exit 18W, and this football-field-length tunnel connects them underground.

The toll collector has said simply to go downstairs, but there is nothing downstairs but the tunnel.

"Hello, anyone home?"

No response.

"Where do I go?"

Silence.

There is nothing to do but walk the length of the tunnel—but in which direction? In both directions the corridor looks like it leads to a gas chamber. Voices respond from the ductwork, but the patron recognizes them now as emanating from KISS radio in the booth above or from a crying child unjustly awakened in her carseat by the sudden halting of her parents' car after a hundred miles of the reassuring whir of rubber tires skimming over asphalt.

One end of the tunnel proves to be a dead end. Reversing course, he passes a number of small rooms. A locker room. Toilets. But still no response to his shouted queries about where to go. Just that grimy underground world and endless tunnel.

At last his cry of "Anyone home?" is greeted by "Yes. What do you want?" The answer comes from the end of the tunnel.

"I don't have money for my toll."

"Up here."

Sure enough, at the end of the tunnel is another staircase—a broad one this time—and it leads up into an office that overlooks all eighteen tollbooths. Inside are television monitors and radios. The sergeant on duty is talking to a toll collector: "Right, yes, okay, do it."

On the dutch door of the office a sign says: "NO TOLL COLLECTORS BEYOND THIS POINT. TURN IN CASH DRAWERS FROM OTHER SIDE OF DOOR." The patron's driving license and registration go over this same dutch door.

They are returned with a form. "Sign here," the sergeant says. After signing the patron receives a copy of the form and a business reply envelope addressed to the New Jersey Turnpike Authority in New Brunswick. The form says he has three days to send in the toll—money order or check. Easy enough to do.

Down in the tunnel again, he knows this time which direction to walk. But which staircase to take back up into the light? Maybe the last one. The last one would leave one with the smallest number of toll lanes to cross to one's car.

But before heading for the last staircase it seems only prudent to the patron to avail himself of the toilet, which, along with some grim locker rooms, is just off the corridor. On the wall of the men's room are the usual things. "To get laid, call Betty Sue"—that sort of thing. But one wag has written something more substantive:

> Fly like a butterfly
> Sting like a bee
> You only get
> What the patrons don't see.

What this means isn't clear. Do toll collectors (or, perhaps, the toll collector who wrote this graffito) skim a little money from time to time from unsuspecting patrons? Maybe flimflam between patrons and toll collectors is employed both ways. Toll collectors cannot easily cheat the Authority, so maybe patrons are fair game. There is no way to know.[10]

As suggested earlier, patrons are not always honest. A common trick truckers sometimes try on neophyte toll collectors is the "request for directions" gambit. The rogue trucker pulls into a tollgate and, instead of producing a ticket, presents a bill of lading. The trick is to get the collector so involved in providing directions to the address on the bill of lading that he or she forgets to ask for either the ticket or the toll. Usually the collector will realize the mistake shortly after the trucker pulls away. But by then it is too late. The collector will be in a jam because the treadle count at the end of the shift will reveal the error, and truck tolls are costly.

The most elaborate scam we ever heard of involved five truckers. They all drove car transports. Once a week, always at the same time, they would exit at Port Newark. Five in a row, they would pay their toll. One day they arrived, as usual, and the first trucker paid his toll with a twenty-dollar bill. So did the second truck, and the third, and so on. Finally the fifth truck pulled up and handed over a five-dollar bill for the toll. When the collector offered change for a five, the trucker protested, "I gave you a twenty-dollar bill."

"No, it was a five-dollar bill," the collector replied.

"It was a twenty-dollar bill and I can prove it."

"How?"

"I know I gave you a twenty dollar bill because my wife had written *bread and milk* on it. Just check your drawer."

Sure enough, the top twenty-dollar bill did have *bread and milk* written on it. Puzzled, the toll collector made change for the twenty-dollar bill. By the end of the day, the collector realized he had been taken. The *fourth* trucker, of course, had given him the marked bill. The truckers had fooled the collector.[11]

Veteran collectors have to be alert to all kinds of tricks and schemes that wily motorists try to pull. At the same time, they have been known to help out motorists who leave themselves vulnerable to trickery. For example, as reported in the Turnpike newsletter, motorist M. R. Hammer of Leonia drove through Interchange 14 on his way to the Newark Airport. "I was preoccupied and handed the Toll Collector a $20 bill and drove away. When I realized my mistake, I came back. (The change was significant for the completion of my trip.) . . .

"I would especially like to mention that the Collector not only had my change set aside, but he had also identified my car and was taking steps to see the money was returned. Alexander Cook, Badge Number 203, was both thoughtful and considerate."[12]

Understandably, the Turnpike Authority is proud of collector Cook. There was, however, another episode a few years back that did not make the Turnpike newsletter. A group of toll collectors conspired to defraud the Turnpike. Anytime you create a river of cash, there will be a temptation to divert a small stream. These crooked collectors stole a large number of entry tickets from a nearby toll plaza. To anyone else, a bunch of entry tickets represents just so much cardboard; but to a clever collector they are valuable indeed. When a patron would pass through the collector's booth and surrender a legitimate entry card from a distant point, the collector would collect the toll shown on the legitimate card and pass the motorist on. After the motorist left, he would feed the machine a stolen card from the nearby toll plaza, put the lesser toll in the till, and pocket the difference. Eventually the collectors were caught and dismissed.[13]

Now the Turnpike Authority maintains strict inventory controls on entry cards, so this loophole is apparently plugged. The entire system is engineered to make cheating nearly impossible by giving the collector as little room for initiative and innovation as possible. The treadle counts the axles and the computer tallies the tolls. The money is counted at the beginning of the shift and at the end of the shift. Of course, there is a catch: collectors feel like cogs in a machine. Predictably, this feeling affects their attitude and behavior, as we shall see.

Whatever the reputation of Turnpike toll collectors for honesty, when it comes to courtesy, their reputation is less than excellent. As far back as 1975 we felt strongly enough about the discourtesy of some toll collectors to write to then Governor Brendan Byrne. At the time, we had no idea how little control over the Turnpike the governor exercises. Our letter included these remarks:

> I have had the occasion several times to drive up into New England. I was pleasantly surprised when toll takers of the turnpike in Connecticut and Massachusetts almost universally said "Thank you" or engaged in some conversation. It seemed so in contrast to the silence—almost a surliness—which one experiences from the toll takers on the Turnpike here in our own State.
>
> In addition to the warmth or human factor, I would wager that there is a safety factor as well. A bit of conversation at a toll booth, especially at night, would, I should think, tend to wake up the sleepy or half-mesmerized by boredom traveler.
>
> I know this is a small matter—but it is these small matters which characterize a community and substantially add to or subtract from the quality of life.[14]

The governor did not reply. Our letter was directed to the Turnpike Authority, and Robert E. Ramsen, director of Toll Collections, responded:

> I would like to take this opportunity to advise that the over seven hundred men and women of this department have an excellent record of assistance to the motoring public. Hundreds of commendation letters have been received from patrons citing instances covering the spectrum from simple directions to the use by a collector of his uniform jacket to put out a fire that had engulfed a patron. One of our highlights during 1974 was to receive a commendation from New Jersey's own Senator Harrison Williams who commended an employee for his valuable assistance.
>
> In the same manner that we have a majority of pluses we, as any organization, have a minority of minuses. It is these individuals that we try to improve through communications, training, and when all else fails, stern disciplinary action. Even here we have had a fair margin of success but as we feel this is still not totally satisfactory, we will go on trying.
>
> It is our policy to fully investigate all letters received with regard to employees and we deeply appreciate your comments in this matter. The New Jersey Turnpike is very proud of its performance and has, and always will, make safety and service its major goals.[15]

What was galling about this letter was that it was utterly unresponsive to the issue we had raised. We were not making a complaint: we were making a suggestion. Our idea was that perhaps the Authority could promote courtesy, or at the very least encourage the use of the expression "Thank you." In his letter Ramsen supplied examples of how toll collectors had rendered assistance to motorists. We have no doubt these examples were accurate and commendable. We were not questioning the humanity of the collectors; we were merely questioning their routine failure to say "Thank you."

An ironic note in Ramsen's letter was his happy reference to receiving a commendation from "New Jersey's own Senator Harrison Williams." Williams has, of course, since gone to jail for his role in the Abscam affair. In any event, we were so discouraged by Ramsen's unresponsive reply, we set the whole matter aside for a year and a half. But on November 16, 1976, we wrote to Governor Byrne again, enclosing a copy of Ramsen's letter and pointing to its self-serving nature. A week later, we again heard from Ramsen. This letter was also unresponsive to the actual issue we had raised—the failure to say "Thank you." The letter did offer a rather draconian remedy:

> In reply to your most recent correspondence we can only add that the situation regarding these "minus" employees has improved to some degree, and will continue to improve. A blanket condemnation of the Authority's operating personnel is most unfair since you have based your conclusions upon your contact with a very small percentage of our over seven hundred toll collection force.
>
> Our operating procedures and Union Agreement with our employees provides that we may take disciplinary action against employees who fail to carry out their duties satisfactorily. However, these provisions also provide that the accused employee must have a hearing and that this employee, or a representative of his choosing, whether legal or union, has the right to examine the complainant's statements during the proceedings of a hearing. Therefore, we request that you supply us with specific details such as dates, locations, and the individual identification of the persons involved. As the result of this positive information we will institute immediate action as provided under our regulations.[16]

By now the whole correspondence was taking on the tone of theater of the absurd. The New Jersey Turnpike Authority seemed to have no mechanism for dealing with a suggestion. The Authority kept insisting we were making a complaint.

And the remedy to our "complaint"? If we went through a tollgate, surrendered the ticket, paid the toll, and failed to hear "Thank you" from the collector, we could get the badge number of the employee and note the date, time, and location. Then we could write the Authority, which would schedule a hearing in the Administration Building in New Brunswick. Then we could take off from work, attend the hearing, be cross-examined by the employee's attorney, and try to persuade the hearing officer to discipline the collector for not saying "Thank you." Though we were sincerely interested in promoting a better image for New Jersey, this procedure was an unwieldy method for achieving our objective. We might hope to hear a collector say "Thank you," but we would hardly want to get him fired for failing to do so. We again decided to drop the matter.

Ten years went by. We devoted ourselves to issues of less consequence and with a greater chance of success. But then, in early 1986, we were asked by the editors at *New Jersey Monthly* magazine to do a short essay on some aspect of the state's image. Did we have a topic to suggest? We did. Our article appeared as an "Exit Ramp," the soapbox feature that appears on the last page of every issue of the magazine. We tried to recapitulate the story of a decade before:

> Do you know what gripes me about the New Jersey Turnpike? It's not that it smells. Or that there's a state trooper lurking behind every concrete abutment. Or that there isn't a tree on the North Jersey stretch. What really riles me is that, as I exit, this person takes my money without saying "Thank you."
>
> If he says anything at all, it's an insult. Like the time I drove from Exit 9 to Exit 8A and all I had was a $20 bill. This guy glowers at me and says, "What do you think I'm running here, a bank?"
>
> Up in his booth, the toll taker acts as if it's his Turnpike and you're lucky to ride on it. He's occupied by weightier matters than you and your toll. There's Frank Sinatra singing "My Way" on the radio. There's the telephone. Who *do* toll takers talk to on the phone? The way they treat you, it must be the governor asking, "How's business?"
>
> To put a little humanity into our transaction, I occasionally swallow my pride and say "Thank you" to the toll taker. Usually, there's no reaction. Either he thinks I'm crazy or he can't hear me over Sinatra. Sometimes he nods in a lordly manner. Sometimes he says, "You're welcome." But I never heard a toll taker say, "You shouldn't be thanking *me*. I should be thanking *you*." [17]

The column continued in this vein, part grousing and part just gentle satire. Now usually, when we do one of these essays, that's pretty much the end of it. Maybe a few colleagues around the office water cooler politely murmur some vague words of praise. But this piece stirred up an unusual amount of commentary. Letters piled up in the magazine's offices, and the editors published a number of them. On the one hand, it was gratifying to see a letter such as the one written by Sheldon W. Wernick of Harrison: "The article 'Unhappy Motoring' was terrific. You reported on the big gripe that my wife and I have had for years but never had the time or the ambition to sit down and write about it. It is truly amazing that only on the New Jersey Turnpike can one find toll collectors who are doing you a favor when they collect your money." [18]

Of course, it is always gratifying to see your own good sense and judgment confirmed by your readers. On the other hand, the satisfaction in reading Wernick's letter was quickly offset by a letter from James Mustillo of Bayonne, himself a toll collector. Mustillo mustered some strong counterarguments:

> I'm writing in response to the article concerning the New Jersey Turnpike toll collectors. I am a toll collector, and being nasty as I am, I'll try to make this a polite reply.
>
> I'm not going to imply that all collectors are polite, because people are people and everyone has problems. But I thought the generalization that all collectors are rude was childish. . . . Moreover, a person under stress or quite often treated in a demeaning fashion can't always be polite. . . .
>
> Let's examine what collectors deal with besides "listening to Sinatra" or "talking on the phone." There are drivers who slam money in our hands, give us slugs and Chuck E. Cheese tokens, curse at us, spit from buses, and of course, blame us for every traffic jam and all the construction that ever took place on the Turnpike. I even had a woman give me a ticket that her daughter had thrown up on. Not to mention the fumes and the noise. I could go on and on. . . .
>
> *Thank you,* and happy motoring. [19]

Here, at last, was a response from a Turnpike employee that demanded respect. It was from a rank-and-file collector, not from management. The letters from the director of Toll Collection had ignored our suggestion. Ramsen's bureaucratic prose had ducked the issue, but James Mustillo was confronting the issue head-on. Here was an honest working man who had suffered indignities at the hands of motorists. Quite possibly the toll collector was victim, not villain. He was squeezed from the top by a production-oriented, paramilitary bureaucracy that gave him no room to budge and from the bottom by a rude, cursing, spitting public. The problem we had been brooding over for ten years was taking on a new dimension.

Mustillo's letter chastened us a bit. Nevertheless, only one week after reading it, we stopped at Exit 9 to pay a toll in the wee hours of the morning. There was one car ahead of us. It was pulled a bit to the right in the lane, not as close to the tollbooth as it should have been. Whether this was by design or not, it was impossible to determine. What was clear was that the toll collector, in his lit-up booth, was ignoring the patron.

Finally, we tooted our horn to alert the patron and the toll collector that we wished to pay our toll and be on our way. At this point, the toll collector reached out for the patron's money. As the patron pulled away and we put our own car in gear and inched forward, and as far to the left as possible, the toll collector yelled after the patron, "So long, asshole!"

Perhaps the patron was drunk or had been abusive. We had no way of knowing. But the toll collector's response, the response of a public servant to a citizen whose toll pays his salary, was inappropriate to say the least.

The courtesy problem at the Turnpike is, no doubt, related to the problem of courtesy in the Greater New York area in general and, perhaps, in any congested area. Nevertheless, the discourtesy of New Jersey toll collectors seems particularly bad and may be related to the Turnpike Authority's priorities. Every large organization has its own personality, its own unofficial rules of conduct, and its own priorities. The first priority of the Turnpike seems to be to protect the revenue, and this is done, as we have suggested, in an almost military manner. The second priority seems to be safety; there is a genuine concern to make the roadway as safe as possible. The third priority seems to be neatness. To see this for yourself, try to spot litter as you drive along the Turnpike. You may find some, but it is difficult. The litter patrol picks up trash as fast as motorists discard it. At the bottom of the list of priorities, seemingly, is courtesy. We certainly do not think it should be at the top; but we do not think it should be at the bottom either.

Large bureaucracies are rarely adept at solving problems of human engineering. These problems are not very satisfying to work on because there are too many variables and because success is difficult to measure. To put this in concrete terms, compare the litter problem with the "thank you" problem. The presence or absence of litter is more or less an objective fact. Either the roadway is clean or it is not. Litter patrol crews can measure their output: so many truckloads of trash per day. Compare this with monitoring courtesy at the tollbooth. How would one go about it? Would one use television screens to check up on the toll collectors? Would one use supervisory personnel in unmarked cars to check up on people? The whole idea of monitoring courtesy is distasteful. It conjours up an image of some Orwellian fascist state. Collectors would understandably resent such Big Brotherism.

Still, something could be done. The courtesy issue is ultimately of vital importance to the Turnpike Authority. If the issue is allowed to fester unattended, eventually there could be a taxpayer's revolt. It has already happened elsewhere. People tend to resent paying tolls in the first place, especially in a country where there are so many free interstate highways and especially on a highway on which there long ago existed a public expectation that the bonds would be paid off and the tolls cease.

People also complain bitterly about the frustrating stop-and-go delays created by the toll collection process.[20] Indeed, not only is the motorist's time consumed in toll collection; it also wastes gasoline and contributes to air pollution. Even more unsettling is the realization that stopping cars to collect tolls creates a safety hazard. Toll plazas invariably set up a situation that invites collisions. Toll road authorities understandably try to downplay this problem, but such accidents are not unusual.

Since toll plaza accidents are seldom fatal, they tend not to get much publicity. But to the victims, these accidents are painful and costly. Worst of all, such accidents are unnecessary and preventable. Take the case of Marvin and Lillian Israel of Princeton, New Jersey. They were on their way to New York City on September 24, 1987, looking forward to a family celebration of Rosh Hashanah (the Jewish New Year). In their car, a 1984 Honda Accord hatchback, was a cake baked especially for the occasion. Neither the cake nor the Israels ever made it to the party. While waiting in line at a tollbooth at Turnpike Exit 14C, they were rear-ended by a big Buick with California plates. The driver of the Buick said her brakes failed. An ambulance took the Israels to Jersey City Medical Center. Lillian Israel suffered chest injuries; Marvin Israel suffered leg injuries. The car was a total loss.[21]

This little story is hardly a headline grabber. But for the family who suffered the physical pain, the property loss, and the disruption in their lives, it was not a minor episode. Take the same story, with variations in the details, and multiply it many times over, and one realizes the hazards to which every patron is subjected. Under these circumstances, the courtesy issue takes on renewed importance. When motorists stop to pay tolls, they not only are inconvenienced by the time delay and the monetary cost, but are also (in a very real statistical sense) risking their lives. At the very least, the collector, whose salary is being paid by the motorist, should be polite.

Once we sat in the office of a senior Turnpike official who proudly went through ten years of annual reports, showing us examples of Turnpike improvements. After a while, we noticed a pattern: many of the improvements were devoted to widening toll plazas, adding tollbooths, improving ramp approaches to toll plazas, and so on. These improvements were costly.

We asked why they were necessary. He told us that the improvements re-duced accidents at toll plazas. We said, "Wouldn't it be best just to remove the tollbooths altogether?" He said, "Yes, but we cannot run the road with-out collecting a user's fee."[22]

Of course, there is no easy solution, no panacea, no magic bullet. If, how-ever, it is really necessary to collect tolls, then the process should be made as safe and as pleasant as possible. Employees of an official quasi-monopoly can easily forget to be polite. In the face of this problem, the Turnpike Authority could do worse than borrow a page from the book written by the U.S. Postal Service, another quasi-monopoly. The Postal Service is far from perfect, but it does at least have a widely praised program to deal with the courtesy issue.

The Postal Service, realizing it had a problem in public relations, devel-oped a policy statement and a program to remake its image. Though prob-lems still occur, complaints have been reduced. They developed a "Postal Pledge to Customers" that reads, in part:

- We are dependent on you.
- You are the purpose of our work.
- You do us a favor when you call. Our purpose is to serve you.
- You are people who bring us your needs. It is our job to fill those needs.
- You deserve the most courteous and attentive treatment we can give you.[23]

Clearly, to have a customer-service policy is not necessarily to have em-ployees follow it. But at least in the case of the Postal Service, they do have such a policy. It is an excellent first step.

Someday New Jersey may, as Connecticut did in 1985, remove the toll-booths from the Turnpike; but it is not likely to be soon. The present ar-rangement is too comfortable. Collecting the tolls not only brings in money to pay for the maintenance of the road, it also brings in money to pay the toll collectors. Meanwhile the mighty river of cash just keeps flowing. The nickels and the dimes and the quarters, not to mention the dollar bills, keep trickling into the tollbooths.[24]

The money keeps flowing day and night without stopping. Twenty-four hours a day, 7 days a week, 365 days a year the river flows—$15 million every month, $182 million a year, more than $1 million for each of its 142 miles. The collection of tolls is usually justified by pointing to the high cost of maintenance and operation. But more money is spent on toll collection every year ($38 million) than on maintenance, repair, replacement, and re-construction ($29 million).[25]

Nevertheless, day after day the toll revenues flow from South Jersey up to New Brunswick. Up from the Delaware Memorial Bridge, from Swedesboro and Chester, from Woodbridge and Camden, from Burlington and Mount Holly. The money flows up from Bordentown and Trenton, from Hightstown and Freehold, from Jamesburg and Cranbury to New Brunswick.[26]

And day after day the money flows from northern New Jersey down to New Brunswick. It flows down from the vicinity of the George Washington Bridge and Lincoln Tunnel. Down from Newark and the Oranges, from Jersey City and Bayonne, from Newark Airport and Elizabeth Seaport. Down from Carteret and Rahway, down from Edison and the Amboys, this river of cash flows into New Brunswick to the headquarters of the New Jersey Turnpike Authority.[27]

The Authority
of the Authority

Chapter

4

"There's the right way, the wrong way, and the
Turnpike way."
                              —Retired state trooper[1]

We have learned how the New Jersey Turnpike Authority goes about collecting $182 million per year in tolls. We turn our attention now to the political nature of this successful public authority. We will look at how the Turnpike Authority as an institution has been shaped by forty years of wielding virtually unchecked authority.

The political nature of the Turnpike is built into its charter, under which it was organized outside the regular state government chain of command. There is a positive side to this arrangement, one the Authority is quick to point out. In one of its public relations pamphlets, the Turnpike asks, "Is taxpayers' money used to build, operate, and maintain New Jersey Turnpike projects?"

Not too surprisingly, the answer is a reassuring no. "No taxpayer's money is used by the Turnpike Authority for any purpose whatsoever. The New Jersey Turnpike is self-sufficient. Its revenues are derived from tolls and concession revenues. . . . *The State's taxpayers in no way contribute to the Turnpike's financial structure*" (emphasis in original).[2]

This sounds wonderful. What, then, is the problem? Simply this: with financial independence from the state comes political independence from the state. All state agencies are ultimately accountable to the voters or their elected representatives; this is the way democracy is supposed to work. But independent authorities are not accountable to elected officials on a day-to-day basis. Put bluntly, independent authorities are not democratic. Authorities go to great lengths to disguise this basic truth, but sometimes they are careless.

Such was the case when the executive director of the Turnpike Authority, William J. Flanagan, was allowed to retire in February 1988 with a bonus above pension of $343,541 in sick and vacation time accumulated over the years in a job that everyone sees as a patronage position. Years earlier, Flanagan had served as Hudson County sheriff and as chief strategist of that county's Democratic organization. He had been very helpful to Richard J. Hughes in the gubernatorial contest of 1961. Hughes, in turn, made Flanagan executive director of the Turnpike in 1962.[3] To appreciate fully the resentment generated by Flanagan's bonus, it is helpful to know that ordinary state employees are limited to $15,000 in such benefits at the time of retirement.[4]

The press blasted Flanagan's retirement riches. In a hard-hitting editorial, the *Bergen Record* quoted Flanagan as saying, "I believe it's a fair policy." The editors had a ready rebuttal for what it considered an overly comfortable arrangement. "Of course, he thinks it's fair," they said. "It's the rest of us, the drivers whose quarters and dollars are supporting him so lavishly, who think it's unfair. Not to mention unjustified, arrogant, and wasteful." The editors took the old-fashioned position that sick days were to help out employees who were actually sick. Flanagan argued that the Turnpike's policy discourages absenteeism. The editors replied, "We can think of a better, and cheaper, way to discourage absenteeism. That's by firing anybody who takes sick days when he's not sick."[5]

Flanagan's benefit package attracted so much adverse criticism that, in May 1988, the New Jersey Turnpike Authority changed the retirement rules so that executives could no longer bank sick time and retire with hundreds of thousands of dollars. The policy change was intended to limit the Authority's seventy to eighty executives to cashing in no more than $15,000 in unused benefits at the time of retirement.[6]

This quick move to cap sick-leave accumulations should have been a coup for the Turnpike Authority. Instead, it resulted in yet another embarrassment. Learning about the upcoming rule change, the Turnpike's personnel director quit without warning four days before the new cap was instituted. Valeria Jean Dalesandro, who had accumulated $250,000 in sick and vacation days, retired on a Friday; the rules were changed the following Tuesday. Predictably, the media covered this scandal with relish.[7]

These repeated embarrassments are serious business for the Turnpike. Eventually, if enough such incidents occur, the legislature could be provoked into taking action. Even though intervention would be costly and difficult, the independent Authority could conceivably be brought under the yoke of state control.

Even before the Flanagan retirement fiasco, his high salary itself had attracted criticism. In the early years, the Turnpike Authority felt an obligation to limit the salary of its executive director so that it would not exceed the salary of the governor. In 1949, the salary of the governor was $20,000 per year, and the Authority paid General Wanamaker, its executive director, $18,000. In 1954, the governor's salary rose to $30,000, and General Wanamaker was paid $29,500. As the years went by, however, the custom of linking the two salaries was abandoned, to the enormous benefit of the executive director.[8]

The *Bergen Record,* in an editorial in early 1988, questioned the need for the executive director of the Turnpike to make $144,989 a year when the governor was making only $85,000. The editors went on to point out that the executive director is responsible for only a relatively few miles of highway, whereas the head of the Department of Transportation is responsible for 2,316 miles of roads and bridges. The editors then placed much of the blame on Governor Kean for lax supervision. The governor's spokesperson answered that it was impossible for the governor to go over Authority budgets item by item.

The *Record* responded: "Of course not. But someone should be minding the store." The salary of the executive director of the Turnpike, the *Record* asserted, was an example of "outrageous waste." With no real supervision, the Turnpike Authority was "running amok."[9]

Underlying much of the criticism of the Authority was basic skepticism about the wisdom of its expansion projects. In February 1988, the *Record* ran an editorial attacking the Turnpike's $2 billion program to widen the highway from southern Middlesex County to within a few miles of the George Washington Bridge. The editors were especially upset that the Turnpike had gone public with its plans before the state Department of Transportation, the Department of Environmental Protection, or New Jersey Transit (the state mass transit agency) had a chance to review the documents even hastily. The editors concluded that the Turnpike Authority "should be abolished," its commissioners "sent packing, their debts assumed by the state, and their affairs taken over by the Department of Transportation."[10] Joseph F. Sullivan, in the *New York Times,* echoed this sentiment when he wrote that "the years of unfettered independence" for the Turnpike appear to be over.[11]

Criticism continued to snowball. The widely respected *Trenton Times,* which keeps a close eye on state government, joined the chorus calling for the abolition of independent highway authorities in the state. The lead editorial in its May 20, 1988, issue began: "The case gets stronger for New Jersey to phase out its independent toll-road authorities and put the roads under the control of the Department of Transportation." The editorial said there is "something inherent in these authorities, which deal in huge amounts of public money and are insulated from accountability to the voters, that leads one to believe that new excesses will eventually follow."[12]

The very day this editorial appeared, we discussed it with a senior Turnpike official who asked not to be identified. Understandably, he was furious about the editorial. "Okay," he said. "Let's send the toll collectors home tomorrow. Let's open up all the tollbooths and make it a free road. Let's turn the keys to the Control Center over to the Department of Transportation. Do you have any idea what would happen? You would have 142 miles of chaos, that's what would happen."

He has a point. The Turnpike Authority does a good job in operations, traffic control, accident management, maintenance, and the handling of hazardous materials incidents. The Authority has accumulated forty years of expertise in doing its job well. Its engineers are well respected in their profession. Highway officials from other countries regularly study the Turnpike.

The idea of abolishing the Authority seems unlikely to go very far in the near future. Several governors, including the present one, Tom Kean, have suggested it would be counterproductive. Years of successful toll collection, combined with a good safety record and high bond ratings, argue against a major change in the immediate future. The 1988 furor did, however, dramatize to citizens and elected officials around the state how very different the Turnpike is from other agencies of government.

The Turnpike Authority may continue indefinitely, but it will have to develop the political skills that are part of being more accountable, something it shows little inclination to do. Certainly, with a public far more sophisticated than that of the late 1940s and early 1950s, a public that has experienced Vietnam, Watergate, and the Iran-Contra scandal, cosmetic solutions will not suffice. For the Turnpike Authority to survive as an institution, it will have to drop the paramilitary image it acquired in the immediate post–World War II era and work hard to remake itself into a more sensitive, consumer-oriented enterprise. The Authority will have to stop thinking of the Turnpike as *its* Turnpike and begin to think of it as belonging to the public.

The Turnpike may remain an independent authority, but it will have to rein in the arrogance that has been fostered by its virtual political and economic independence. This arrogance, as we shall see, has trickled down to Turnpike employees on every level, including, most notably, some of the state police who patrol the Turnpike.

Whether accurate or not, the perception has existed for some time that one enjoys a somewhat reduced level of rights on the Turnpike. A former student of ours writes:

> The state troopers on the Turnpike were known as bigots/rednecks/civil rights violators—at least that was the consensus where I worked at Howard Johnson's (remember the era?: 1970–1973) on the Pike. Hippies in a van or blacks in anything had a much higher chance of being pulled over and searched and

harassed than your average citizen. One story I heard was that a black man was pulled over for a broken taillight, and was told to get out of the car and be searched and let them search his car. He refused, citing his civil rights, and the officers yanked him out, frisked him, and beat him up, ending by locking him in their trunk and driving him to a rest area, where he was let go minus his wallet and severely beat up. Well, they picked on the wrong guy—he was an attorney for the ACLU! Who promptly sued them. I heard the outcome was a couple of week's suspension for the officers involved.[13]

Of course, this letter reflects a particular time period and is based on hearsay. Furthermore, events similar to those described could and did occur in places other than the New Jersey Turnpike. Nevertheless, many New Jerseyans perceive the Turnpike as a place where anyone who does not fit a squeaky-clean image is especially likely to be harassed. A New Jersey sociologist tells of a criminology class she was teaching in which one of her students was a state police officer. He candidly admitted that blacks and hippies *are* often stopped on the Turnpike on some pretext. "But that's because the numbers are there," he said. "There's a good chance we're going to find drugs or a weapon or something."[14]

Turnpike Authority chairman Joseph Sullivan confirmed that what he calls "profile arrests" are a problem with which he is contending. "It's true," he says.

> Sometimes a trooper stops somebody because he's black or Hispanic or "looks suspicious" and he's a perfectly good citizen. I'm trying to stop this. At the same time, there's a war going on out there on the Pike. Especially over drugs. You have a twenty-four-year-old trooper out there, and somebody's shot at one of his buddies, and so he's seeing certain people and imagining, "Yeah, that guy's bound to be one of the drug runners and he's probably armed," and, so, you end up with an altercation and maybe even an arrest that's based on nothing but a profile.[15]

One wonders whether there is anything about the Turnpike and the state police on the Turnpike that engenders this behavior more than in other places. What of the administrative structure of an institution that issues its own bonds and rules and regulations? What of the physical nature of an institution that is fenced off from the rest of New Jersey? Is the Turnpike, in short, a state within a state?

There would seem to be some evidence to that effect. In May 1988, two state troopers exhausted appeals of their convictions in connection with the death of a motorist on the Turnpike in 1982. Trooper Harry Messerlian had been charged with beating to death Joseph Topolosky after arresting him for drunk driving on the Turnpike in Elizabeth. Evidence at Messerlian's trial showed he beat Topolosky with a metal flashlight after Topolosky, who was handcuffed in the rear of Messerlian's cruiser, kicked out a rear window. Another trooper, chief investigator Henry Wolkowski, was charged with participating in a coverup of Messerlian's crime. Wolkowski interviewed three eyewitnesses who saw Messerlian strike Topolosky repeatedly in the face and head with the flashlight. Wolkowski's reports, however, did not mention these eyewitness accounts. As we write this, nine other state troopers face possible charges in the coverup.

At the time of Topolosky's death, the Internal Affairs Division of the state police completely exonerated Messerlian. And based on their findings, the state attorney general's office found no grounds to convene a grand jury or to bring charges. There the matter may have remained, except that the victim's family persisted in their complaints and finally got federal law enforcement officials to intervene on the grounds that Topolosky's civil rights had been violated. Wrote Edward Martone, executive director of the New Jersey chapter of the American Civil Liberties Union: "When will State Police Superintendent Col. Clinton Pagano and Attorney General Edwards begin the process of investigating and reforming the method by which the state's law enforcement community regulates and investigates itself? . . . Officers Messerlian and Wolkowski came very close to going unpunished for a murder and its coverup."[16]

The Messerlian and Wolkowski cases represent the first time in state police history that troopers have been found guilty of a duty-related homicide. Is there any significance that this took place on the Turnpike? There may well be, given the closed, paramilitary world of the Turnpike and the particular relationship that exists between the Turnpike and the state police. This arrangement may engender a somewhat more casual appreciation of citizens' rights than is found elsewhere. We wouldn't go so far as to suggest that there is an unholy alliance between the Turnpike Authority and the state police, but there are aspects of their relationship more than a little reminiscent of that which existed between the steel companies and the Pinkertons at the dawn of the American labor movement. To put it another way, do the state police work for the people or for "the company"?

One is manifestly aware of the closeness of the Turnpike–state police relationship at Authority headquarters, where one finds the Operations Center of the Turnpike in a large room surrounded by state police offices. The New Jersey Civil Liberties Union (NJCLU) is concerned whether something in the relationship between the Turnpike and the state police engenders abuses. The NJCLU wondered why $650,000 of public funds were spent on Messerlian and Wolkowski's legal defense. Said NJCLU executive director Martone: "What should have happened all along is that the troopers should have paid for their own defense and, if acquitted, applied to the state for reimbursement. . . . I'm not sure other state employees would have gotten the same kind of service out of their government these troopers did." [17]

At the present time, the NJCLU is conducting a study of state police misconduct throughout New Jersey. Attorney Eric Neisser, legal director of the NJCLU, says initial evidence indicates that complaints about state police far outweigh complaints about local police, that "the state police are the most serious violators of civil rights among police forces in the state." In addition, says Neisser, an "inordinate number of the complaints about state police concern the Turnpike."

Neisser wonders whether there is something in the nature of police work on the Turnpike that engenders misconduct. "Maybe it's because they're just staked out watching traffic all day. It's boring. There's nobody to talk to. So, when they see an out-of-state license plate and a 'suspicious-looking' person, they come on real strong and overbearing because they're eager to bust somebody and feel useful and get some credit." [18]

New Brunswick attorney Arthur Miller feels the lack of a constituency leads to abuses of power among state police officers on the Turnpike. "Other police," he says,

> even state police off the Pike, have constituencies. They relate to people on a day-to-day basis. They go into stores, they meet people. They see people as human and people see them as human. A kind of natural relationship develops. And they're less likely to abuse the public because, for one thing, everyone knows everyone else. But on the Turnpike everyone is just passing through. And the state police there don't relate to anyone. They haven't as much of a sense that they're there to serve the people, so a psychology develops that maybe it's the other way around. There are fewer social controls on Turnpike police, so abuse of power is more likely to occur.

Miller feels something in the nature of authorities spawns abuses of power. "Authorities," he says,

> don't have to run for office. They're hybrids, products of the legislature which creates a quasi-governmental institution which isn't, like the executive branch, under the governor's control. The governor is responsive to the people, and everyone under the governor has got to be sensitive to public desires and needs.

> But the Turnpike isn't under the governor, so it isn't as sensitive to the public's needs. So there's this attitude at the Turnpike Authority that the Turnpike is *its* Turnpike, not the people's Turnpike. And then the Authority aids and abets the state police on the Turnpike because the state police are working for them. They're keeping everything neat and clean and antiseptic. The Authority appreciates the state police and the state police appreciates the Authority, only it's possible the people's welfare isn't being served by this arrangement.[19]

The Turnpike is patrolled by one of five troops that make up the New Jersey state police. The 185-member Troop D is assigned entirely to the Turnpike. Indeed, its salaries and expenses are paid out of Turnpike revenues, and its headquarters and lockup adjoin the Turnpike Authority's headquarters at Exit 9.

Of course this close relationship is beneficial to coordination on the world's most traveled road. In 1987, nearly 190 million vehicles traveled 4 billion miles, with an accident rate of 123.0 and a fatality rate of 0.65 per 100 million miles traveled, one of the lowest in the country. State police patrols issued 75,521 summonses and made 746 drinking driver arrests. They assisted almost 80,000 disabled motorists and initiated 1,732 first aid and fire calls.

On Friday, November 20, 1987, a slow day by Turnpike standards, 15 persons were picked up for carrying drugs, knives, rifles, and pistols. One man was arrested for carrying a *nunchaku* (two hardwood sticks joined by a chain). And there were 218 flat tires, overheated radiators, dead batteries, abandoned cars, and one hijacking.[20] Says state police Captain Thomas Carr, "The Turnpike is really a large city, presenting every kind of law enforcement challenge that an urban center presents. It just happens to be . . . long."[21] Echoing Carr's imagery was a newspaper article on the Turnpike some years ago titled "City On Wheels";[22] similarly, Turnpike Authority Chairman Joseph "Bo" Sullivan likens himself to a big city mayor, with two thousand employees on the payroll, including Troop D of the state police.[23]

For the Turnpike Authority, coordination between the Authority and the state police—having the state police under its control—is essential. Coordination makes it possible to do things that might not be possible elsewhere, and many of these things are good. For example, the Turnpike is justly proud that it is one of the only places in America where speeding foreign diplomats are stopped and castigated.

As recently retired executive director of the Turnpike William Flanagan tells the story: "You'd have these diplomats traveling the Turnpike at 100 miles an hour and a trooper would stop them, but there was nothing he could do because of diplomatic immunity. So I said, 'From now on, when these jokers get stopped, the first time they get a warning; the second time they get escorted off the Pike and told they cannot use it anymore. Maybe we can't give them tickets, but we can sure keep them off our Pike." Flanagan, known as "Mr. Turnpike" for the thirty years he served as executive director, tells of being called down to the State Department in Washington and told "You can't do this," and replying "We can too do this, and we're going to do it."

And to this day, The New Jersey Turnpike is one of the few places in America where foreign diplomats do not enjoy special privileges. Some may see the Turnpike as authoritarian here, but many New Jerseyans are pleased with what Flanagan calls the "Robin Hood" way the Turnpike has dealt with insensitive foreign diplomats.[24]

State police officers have been especially effective in interdicting narcotics along the Turnpike, one of whose current nicknames is "Cocaine Alley." It is along the Turnpike that most narcotics bound for New York City are transported. "Cocaine Alley" is also used to describe the specific stretch of the Turnpike just north of the Delaware Memorial Bridge, where most narcotics arrests take place. State trooper William Sweeney says, however: "I would consider the whole New Jersey Turnpike to be Cocaine Alley." [25] In 1987, 300 pounds of cocaine, with a street value of $7.5 million, were seized on the Turnpike. Nearly two-thirds of the 1,977 people arrested on the Turnpike in 1987 were charged with drug-related offenses.

And the figures continue to rise. In March 1988 alone, the state police made 635 narcotics arrests, almost equal to the 698 narcotics arrests made for the first three months of 1987. And total drug arrests in 1987 were almost double those in 1986. "Our intelligence indicates that traffickers tell their people to avoid New Jersey," a spokesperson for the state police says,[26] but the corridor state is the direct route to New York. "This is the gateway," trooper Randy Martin says, "and the majority of drugs come up from the south and they run right through here. It's a wonder they don't avoid the Turnpike, although it is the fastest route." Recently a narcotics trafficker was intercepted with specific instructions in the trunk of his car not to use the Turnpike.[27]

The connection between the Turnpike and drugs also has its lighter side in the popular imagination, or at least it had before the current national obsession with drugs. The 1970s song "(The Texas Kid's) Retirement Run," performed by fiddler and singer Alvin Crow, is about a Texan who drives his truck up to New Jersey full of bales of marijuana. A few verses should suffice:

> He tucked his head beneath a Stetson as he left Laredo behind
> He had to stop in Galveston to bid his sweet Corrina goodbye.
> She said, "Baby, baby, please don't go with that evil load out of Mexico."
> He said, "Don't worry, darling, you daddy's been living right."
>
> And there was eighteen wheels rolling heavy out of Galveston
> To the cold Atlantic seaboard from the hot, hot Texas sun.
> Well, he ain't stopping nowhere along that road.
> He's running heavy with that overweight contraband gold.
> That Texas kid is making his retirement run.
>
> It was big black Firestones rolling across the wide concrete.
> He turned off the Jersey Turnpike in order to the buyer's street.
> Then he met his man and made his deal.
> He slipped from behind the big semi's wheels.
> And on the way back to Galveston, he leaned back on the jalousy.[28]

Mary Hufford, a folklorist, tells a story that connects the Turnpike with drugs during a less drug-obsessed time:

> There were a whole group of hippies, and they were going to drive the distance between Camden and New York on the New Jersey Turnpike. Before they took the trip they dropped acid. So they were driving along and they dropped acid, and all of a sudden it occurred to them that they just were not with it enough for one person to drive, so what they did was to divide the labor of driving up and they assigned tasks to people.
>
> There were five people, so one person was in charge of steering, one person was in charge of the brake, one person was in charge of the gas pedal, one person was in charge of the windshield wipers, and one person was in charge of the radio. And then, all of a sudden . . . they saw this flashing light approaching from behind, and they realized "Oh, my God! We forgot to have somebody watch the speedometer."
>
> So they stopped the car and this cop came up, this huge state trooper looking like a bear in the fog. He looks in the window and he says, "Do you know how fast you were going?"
>
> One of the hippies stammered feebly, "Sixty?"
>
> Says the state policeman, "You were going five miles an hour."[29]

Of course, in the present drug environment this song and tale seem almost antique. Today, with the so-called "War on Drugs" in full flower, violence and guns seem inextricably bound to drugs, as much on the Turnpike as elsewhere. In the first three months of 1987, 184 weapons arrests took place on the New Jersey Turnpike; in 1988, there were 323 in the same period. Says Captain Thomas Gallagher, spokesperson for the New Jersey state police, weapons arrests are a "ripple effect" of the increased arrests for drugs.[30]

Thus, despite their excesses, the state police invite sympathy for the enormous burden they carry in fighting crime on a highway that in the popular imagination is synonymous with crime. When Teamster boss Jimmy Hoffa disappeared and was presumably murdered in 1975, one place speculation placed his body was a New Jersey Turnpike bridge abutment; another was a garbage dump alongside the Pike. And the state police themselves have more than once been the victims of violence on the Turnpike. Several state troopers have been viciously murdered in the course of their work on the Pike, most prominently Werner Forester, who, in 1973, was shot and killed by Black Liberation Army activist Joanne Chesimard near Exit 9. Trooper James Harper was also seriously wounded in that incident, which attracted and continues to attract national attention. Chesimard escaped from the State Correctional Institution for Women in Clinton, New Jersey, in 1979. More recently, she has been in the news since she was discovered living in Cuba.

Regardless of the danger, considerable esprit exists among state police officers of Troop D (or "Dog Troop," as they call themselves), who patrol the Turnpike. No one directly out of the state police academy is assigned to the Turnpike, since duty there is considered too demanding for a neophyte. A good number of troopers on Turnpike duty at any particular time are volunteers because, as trooper Austin O'Malley feels, "there's so much going on, so much to do."[31] And adds Caesar "Woody" Clay, a black trooper who has, by preference, been on Turnpike duty for several years, "Working on the Turnpike—well, it's like a family. I've made a lot of friends here. I know all the toll takers and maintenance people. We all joke with each other."[32]

Duty on the Turnpike is not always dangerous or particularly demanding. Sometimes, like duty anywhere, it can be amusing. Trooper Randy Martin was heading north when he came upon a young man and woman parked in the breakdown lane and chasing each other around the car, with traffic whizzing by inches from them. "'A lover's spat,' Martin says animatedly. 'Right in the middle of the Turnpike. Can you believe it?' It sounds, Martin is told, like he also serves the public as a babysitter. 'You're not just a babysitter,' he says, 'you're everything out here. You're a father figure, of course you're a policeman, and sometimes, I hate to say it, you wind up being a judge.'"[33]

We interviewed trooper Austin O'Malley in depth. Since he was assigned to us by the Turnpike Authority for this interview, we do not know how typical he is of state police officers. Born in 1953, O'Malley has had several years of duty on the Turnpike and is a volunteer. He had sixteen years of Catholic education. He was an altar boy, played basketball in school. In his spare time he moonlights on construction jobs to make extra money. He has had a steady girl friend for several years but is unmarried.

O'Malley, a college graduate, is well-spoken. When asked whether he thought the pendulum of civil rights had swung so far as to make law enforcement work unrewarding, O'Malley said that, yes, he was hampered in his work but, at the same time, "the American Constitution is all about checks and balances." O'Malley allowed as how there were fools to be found in every profession including the state police and that one of the main challenges of his job is to remain professional and, yet, treat the public "the way I would like to be treated if I was them." O'Malley patrols the central section of the Turnpike, from Interchange 7A to just north of Interchange 12. This section is closest to his home in Spotswood, New Jersey. Usually, O'Malley goes home after a shift on the pike but occasionally, when he has a P.M. shift followed by an A.M. shift, especially when delayed filling out forms in connection with accidents and arrests, he will stay overnight in the state police barracks.

We asked O'Malley what his most unusual recent experience on the pike has been. "That's easy," he replied.

> I stopped a guy speeding on the Pike. Nicely dressed guy. Good manners. A real gentleman. He's a real estate dealer in Fort Lauderdale. Couldn't have been nicer about the ticket. Said he was sorry to have been speeding, wouldn't do it again—that sort of thing. And, while I'm talking to him, I notice this little case on the seat next to him. I ask him what's in it. Mind you, he doesn't have to answer me. I don't have a right to know. I was more curious than anything else. The guy opens it up and shows it to me.
>
> Inside there's some cocaine. At least, I thought it was cocaine. I ask him if he has any more. He says, "Yes," and takes me back to the trunk and opens it and, sure enough, there's three pounds of cocaine in the trunk. Mind you, even when I find cocaine in the car I don't have the right to search his trunk, but he's being as cooperative as can be. Couldn't figure it out. And then it finally dawns on me: I've been watching too much "Miami Vice." This guy doesn't look like anyone on that program so I can't really believe he's a cocaine dealer. But, of course, he is! Shows you what stereotypes are all about.

We also asked O'Malley what his most memorable experiences on the Pike were when he started. "That's also easy," he said.

Twenty minutes into my very first day on the job a drunk drove into the back of a truck which was on the shoulder—the truck driver was changing a tire—and the guy in the car was instantly killed. So, twenty minutes into the job I had a death to deal with.

Then the very next night, at 1 A.M., near Interchange 8, two more people were killed. This man and his wife were killed and sixteen other people were injured. The Turnpike was closed completely northbound for two hours. I remember both of those experiences because they happened immediately after I started.

But that wasn't all. A week after, I was on day shift and there was this van with North Carolina license plates on the shoulder and these four guys standing around with a bad tire. I stopped to see if they needed help. I came up on them real cautiously because this was just after another trooper, Carlos Negron, was killed. He'd stopped for the same reason: a van by the side of the Pike that had run out of gas. They pumped seven or eight bullets into Carlos.

Well, while I'm talking to these guys I notice a sawed-off shotgun peeking out from under the seat. So I humor these guys, ask them if they want a service truck or what and, meanwhile, try to pretend I haven't seen the shotgun. There's four of them, and maybe they're all armed. Despite what the public may think, I don't have a big red "S" painted on my shirt.

Only when another trooper arrived did O'Malley go into action. "All right, everyone on the ground, spread 'em," O'Malley suddenly demanded. O'Malley and the other trooper found two more concealed weapons on the men on the ground.

These guys insisted they were going hunting and fishing and visiting relatives up north, but there were no clothes in the van—just some extra pairs of sneakers and some beepers. Later it was concluded these guys were probably planning a bank robbery in New York.

But the really neat thing is that while we've got these four guys on the ground and are finding the other two guns, my mother, believe it or not, comes by on the Pike with my sister and my two nieces. They're on their way to the Meadowlands—the Ice Capades—and they see me and they wave. They had no idea what I was doing.

Anyway, all of this happened during my first eight days on the job, so maybe you get some idea of what we're dealing with here. It's a little of everything, and you meet some really nice people, but there are also some really bad people on the Turnpike. If you came over to headquarters and took a look at the lockup, any time of day or night, you'd find it's full.

No doubt O'Malley is correct. Crime abounds on the Turnpike, and the lockup at headquarters is unusually busy. But is everyone in there jailed for good reason? Not everyone, as we shall see. We're not sure, finally, who is more typical of state troopers on the Turnpike, thoughtful, intelligent people like Austin O'Malley or convicted murderers like Harry Messerlian.

The norm is probably somewhere in between. But the question remains: is there something about the Turnpike–state police relationship that fosters aberrant behavior? To answer that question, let us examine the case of David Levinson.

"VIRGINIA JOURNALIST GUILTY OF TAKING TURNPIKE PHOTOS" ran the headline in a New Jersey newspaper.[34] The reference was to David Levinson, then forty-two, of Newport News, Virginia, a professor at Thomas Nelson Community College in Hampton, Virginia, and a professional photographer. Levinson was traveling south on the New Jersey Turnpike with his wife on August 8, 1986, in the vicinity of Edison. He observed a state police car traveling rapidly backward on the right-hand shoulder of the Turnpike. The police cruiser went out of control, its rear end entering onto the Turnpike itself, causing a four-car collision that occurred just in front of Levinson and that he narrowly avoided. Levinson pulled onto the left shoulder and got out to try to aid the victims of the crash.

A short time later, Levinson found himself in the Troop D lockup, his ankles shackled together. From their car, his wife, Beverly, had observed him being pushed into a state police vehicle but did not know where he was being taken or why, nor would any of the state police now on the scene tell her anything. She also did not know where in New Jersey she was, and there she was stranded on the shoulder of the Turnpike, with cars whizzing by. Eventually, she made her way to Troop D headquarters, where she was first told her husband was not there. She was then told that whether he was there or not was none of her business. Finally, when she demanded to see him, she was threatened with arrest. Beverly and David Levinson are in absolute agreement on one thing as far as their independent experience of the events of August 8, 1986, is concerned: "The New Jersey state police are fascists."[35]

At his November 17, 1986, trial in municipal court in Edison, Levinson, who had never before been arrested, was charged with resisting arrest, obstructing the administration of the law, walking on the Turnpike roadway, and taking pictures of the Turnpike. Eventually, he was found not guilty of the first three charges. He was found guilty of the fourth, taking pictures on the Turnpike, and fined $50 plus $15 court costs. He was convicted under Turnpike regulation NJAC 19:19-1.6k, which reads: "No person shall be permitted to take photographs or motion pictures on the New Jersey Turnpike except as authorized by the Authority."

We might mention that the regulation on photography has affected the book you are presently reading, especially in our choice of art. We originally wanted to ask a distinguished art photographer—ironically, someone like David Levinson—to do a series of studies of the Turnpike. We learned to our dismay that this was against the law. The Turnpike was willing to provide us, free of charge, with *its* photographs—but these were slick and self-serving and, in any case, not art. We were in a quandary as to what to do.

Eventually, for the jacket of this book we discovered a painter, Marguerite Doernbach, who was fascinated by the Turnpike and had painted it on several occasions—usually not from life but in imaginative recreation. We were also able to find Ruth Strohl-Palmer, an illustrator, who surreptitiously took snapshots out her car window while being chauffeured by her husband and, later, created drawings based on them. The reader should understand that we have a particular sympathy for David Levinson's case based on our own experience and, perhaps, should accept our recounting of it with reserve.

In any case, why was David Levinson taking pictures on the Turnpike and what was he taking pictures of?

When Levinson got out of his car to aid the victims of the accident, he soon saw that other state troopers who had arrived at the scene were involved in an obvious coverup of their colleague's role in causing the accident. When Levinson mentioned to trooper Russell Fleming that the accident had been caused by the out-of-control state police car (thinking Fleming would want Levinson's testimony as an independent eyewitness), Fleming became irate and said that the accident had to have been caused by the vehicle that struck the police car, a van driven by Ronald Speicher, a postmaster from Far Rockaway, New York.

Levinson, thinking simple justice demanded that he document the accident, went back to his car, withdrew his expensive Hasselbad camera, and began taking pictures of the scene, something he believed was the duty of a responsible citizen—for insurance purposes if nothing else. Fleming and another state trooper, Sergeant Miele, shouted to him, "No pictures!" Levinson, unaware that Turnpike regulations prohibit picture taking, assumed this was a further effort at coverup. He kept taking pictures.

At his trial, Levinson would say that he had no idea it was illegal to take pictures on the Turnpike, that he could not be expected to be familiar with this obscure regulation, not being a New Jerseyan. He was found guilty under the reasoning that ignorance of the law is no excuse. We have, however, asked dozens of students in our classes, almost all New Jerseyans and regular Turnpike drivers, if they are familiar with the photography ban and have not found one who is. Said one student: "Who says you can't take pictures? What is the Turnpike, a top-secret military installation?"

Before becoming familiar with the Levinson case we, who as the writers of this book might be expected to have some special knowledge of Turnpike regulations, had never heard of this prohibition either. Turnpike regulations, we have discovered, are posted at all entrances on metal signs. Since there are so many regulations, however, the print is small. One would have to stop one's car in traffic, get out, and peruse this sign carefully and at length to discover NJAC 19:19-1.6k, almost like searching for a passage in the Lord's Prayer engraved on the head of a pin. Even if one managed it, one's automobile would probably be demolished in the process.

Levinson, as we have suggested, had no idea troopers Fleming and Miele were ordering him not to take pictures because of Turnpike regulations— assuming this was their intent, which, given the circumstances, seems doubtful. Whatever Fleming's and Miele's intentions, Levinson was struck by the fact that the state troopers seemed more interested in stopping him from taking pictures of the accident than in attending to its victims. In any case, Levinson, standing on what he believed to be his First Amendment rights, stated emphatically to the troopers, "You can't stop me from taking pictures."

The Turnpike's prohibition on picture taking is not entirely unreasonable. After all, motorists stopping to take pictures wherever they wish could present a considerable hazard on a high-speed, high-volume road. Nevertheless, on what other road is such a regulation applied or enforced so strictly? Written as it is, the regulation forbids passengers in cars from pointing cameras out windows and even people in rest areas from taking pictures, and neither of these activities is in any way obstructive of safe travel on the Turnpike. Besides, although safety is certainly an important consideration, so is freedom of expression.

The American Civil Liberties Union interested itself in Levinson's case almost from the start. Arthur Miller, the attorney assigned by the NJCLU to David Levinson, prepared a brief appealing Levinson's conviction on the charge of taking pictures, arguing that NJAC 19:19-1.6k is "unconstitutionally vague and broad" and is "a clear prior restraint on First Amendment rights." Miller's argument was that the regulation is "arbitrary and capricious and exceeds the authority granted by the legislature" to the New Jersey Turnpike Authority in its enabling legislation.[36]

When Levinson was found guilty of the photography charge in Edison

Municipal Court, Levinson and Miller appealed to the Superior Court of Middlesex County, where they again lost. Then Miller filed a brief in the Appellate Division of the state courts. In this brief, Miller argued: "Appellant was arrested because he was taking photographs of an accident in which the State Police were involved—and not because he was an obstruction or hazard to anyone." Miller also argued that since the exhibition of photographs is a protected First Amendment right, the taking of pictures also is protected under the First Amendment. Said Miller in the brief, "The taking of pictures is as much a part of the right of expression through photography as the taking of notes or the writing of essays is a part of the freedom to distribute literature." [37]

Luckily, Miller and Levinson were not alone in their quest. Melvin Vogel, driver of one of the other cars involved in the accident, said to Levinson, "What is New Jersey, some kind of totalitarian state?" This occurred when the state police were demanding that Levinson turn over his film, just before he was arrested. Vogel suggested that Levinson get a receipt. This suggestion angered the state troopers. When Levinson refused to turn over his film without a receipt, he was pushed, placed under arrest, handcuffed, and shoved into Fleming's patrol car.

But first, as a struggle was going on over Levinson's camera, his film rolled onto the ground unseen by the two state troopers and was picked up by Ronald Speicher, driver of the van. The film was not exposed and so, eventually, Levinson obtained prints of the pictures he had taken, and these pictures were reproduced in Miller's brief. According to Levinson, both Speicher and Vogel are "conservative guys." Nevertheless, they saw Levinson's treatment at the hands of the state police as in violation of his rights and as part of a coverup, and they were zealous in helping Miller prepare Levinson's case.

Aid for Levinson's case came from other, totally unexpected quarters. *Popular Photography* magazine ran a story on the Levinson case, which focused national attention on it. The article began: "If Moses and his contemporaries owned cameras, there might well be an 11th commandment: Thou shalt not photograph without a permit." Accompanying the article, a drawing shows a photographer and his camera in a jail cell. [38]

An article also appeared in the *New Jersey Law Journal,* the official publication of New Jersey's legal community; it was titled, "The Turnpike and the Constitution." Wrote Robert Seidenstein: "One would think that Levinson was photographing a Soviet secret police break-up of a peaceful demonstration in Moscow or South African forces beating up a few blacks in Soweto." And, continued Seidenstein: "This may not seem like the most important constitutional case ever to come down the pike. But put yourself in Levinson's place and try not to be upset. In many respects, we have a system of constitutional rights precisely to guard against such indignities being heaped upon ordinary citizens."

The *New Jersey Law Journal* article described what apparently happened on the shoulder of the Turnpike that day in August 1986, and its aftermath, and asked: "Can this really happen? One has to admit that it is a possibility. After all, a year ago a trooper was convicted in federal court in Trenton in connection with the beating death of a drunken motorist. Another member of the state police was guilty of conspiring to cover up the beating." [39]

The reference was to the Topolosky case. A year after the *New Jersey Law Journal* article appeared, troopers Messerlian and Wolkowski began serving their terms for the death of Joseph Topolosky and the coverup, ten years for Messerlian, one year for Wolkowski. One can now say with some certainty that, yes, it can happen, that the Turnpike may indeed be something of a state within a state where ordinary citizens may not enjoy the same rights they enjoy elsewhere. On the Turnpike, apparently, the authority of the Authority, while not absolute, is very broad indeed.

But at least in the Topolosky case, justice was served. [40] And it was served eventually in the Levinson case as well. In May 1988, the Appellate Division of the New Jersey Superior Court found David Levinson not guilty of violating the law when he took pictures at the scene of the accident in 1986. Although the court did not rule on the First Amendment aspects of the case, it found that Turnpike Authority regulations exceed the authority granted the Turnpike in the enabling legislation creating the Turnpike. The prohibition of all picture taking was simply too broad. So David Levinson won his case.

That Levinson and Miller had to fight it so long and hard, however, is to be regretted. Levinson repeatedly had to travel back and forth from Virginia to New Jersey at his own expense on a matter that, for him, had become an issue of absolute principle. And Arthur Miller worked for months on the Levinson case pro bono.

Says Miller: "Why would the Turnpike even think of banning photography on the Turnpike? Were they really thinking of safety when this regulation was passed? Or was this simply out of a desire to control, to say, 'This is our Turnpike, and we'll tell you what you can do and what you can't do?'" Although heartened by the results of the case, Miller isn't sure the Turnpike has learned very much. The NJCLU has assigned him another Turnpike case on which he has just begun work. A middle-class black man and his wife were stopped on the Turnpike, searched, harassed, arrested for possession of a pocketknife, and finally allowed to proceed on their way without any apologies offered and without having a clue as to why they had been stopped in the first place. "Here we go again," Miller says.[41]

Waiting for a Tow

Chapter 5

"People don't realize something about the New Jersey Turnpike. Once you're out there, you're on a private road."
—Mark DiGiovanni,
Guaranteed Motor Towing Service[1]

The New Jersey Turnpike Authority is, as our last chapter suggested, interested in controlling its domain in every aspect. It even has rules and regulations on what motorists may and may not do in the event of mechanical breakdowns.

All motorists worry about breakdowns. How much more, then, do they worry about breakdowns on the New Jersey Turnpike? On the Turnpike an inoperable car is not only frustrating; it is a distinct embarrassment. Unlike other highways, there is no possibility of privacy. Everyone whizzes by and looks at you on the paved, fenced in, barren shoulder. You are stranded in an alien and dangerous world where it seems help will never arrive. What actually happens when one breaks down on the Turnpike?

Back in January 1952, the New Jersey Turnpike had only been open one hour when Pete DiGiovanni got his first call for towing service. In a sense, it was not the first call: he had been called a couple of times the year before to pull out contractors' bulldozers that had stuck in the mud in the Milltown and East Brunswick areas. Pete loves to say that Guaranteed Motor Towing Service was on the Pike even before the Turnpike was built.

When Pete's father, Frank DiGiovanni, left Italy and came to New Brunswick early in the century, he first joined the Roman Catholic parish of St. Peter's Church. Then he went into the automotive business. In time he had six sons, and they all went into various aspects of the automotive business—auto body, parts, sales, repairs, and towing. Pete went into the tow truck business. By the time the Turnpike was being built, Pete's company, Guaranteed, was well established.

In everyday life we think of a towing service as something provided by our friendly, neighborhood gas station. They probably have one or two three-quarter ton pickup trucks modified to serve as wreckers. All garage owners have to do is paint their name and telephone number on the side of the truck and they're in the towing business. But the companies sanctioned by the New Jersey Turnpike are of an entirely different order of magnitude. Towing on the Turnpike is big business. Guaranteed Motor Towing Service has a fleet of nearly twenty tow trucks. Most of these are flatbed tow trucks, which have numerous advantages over conventional tow trucks. In a severe wreck, the rear wheels are often completely destroyed, crushed, or burned—making a conventional tow difficult or impossible.

The industry has a saying: "If you leave with a flatbed, you'd better come back with the wreck or else!" Guaranteed was among the first in the United States to pioneer the use of flatbed trucks in the late 1950s and early 1960s. In those days, the concept was so new that one had to build the trucks on one's own. Heavy demands made by the Turnpike led the DiGiovannis to custom-build the first ones used in New Jersey. Today they are standard equipment and can be bought straight from the factory.

In addition to its flatbed trucks, Guaranteed has eight heavy-duty trucks and two lowboys. Lowboys are giant 60-foot tractor-trailers with 48-foot flatbeds suitable for picking up disabled, but upright, buses and trucks. The most spectacular tow trucks, however, are the heavy-duty ones. These monsters are tow trucks for trucks. If the New Jersey Turnpike is the Mississippi River of American roads, then surely these huge trucks are its tugboats. All heavy-duty tow trucks are big, but Guaranteed has two of the biggest in the entire world.

Originally built for the U.S. Navy as salvage and recovery vehicles for retrieving damaged aircraft and rockets, these behemoths of the highway were constructed on chassis made by Oshkosh of Wisconsin. They are truly impressive. Behind the massive glistening chrome grillwork in the front is an engine big enough to power a small oceangoing minesweeper. The driver sits high up in a cab that is surmounted by immense chrome-plated airhorns and spotlights, not to mention numerous yellow marker lights. These are serious trucks.

Whereas the average heavy-duty tow truck weighs in at a modest 18,000 pounds, these massive vehicles weigh 50,000 pounds. They can pick up an overturned, loaded tractor-trailer and put it back on the road, rightside up. In a recent New Jersey Turnpike incident, Guaranteed was able in forty-three minutes from the initial call to right a disabled and overturned tractor-trailer and tow it away. Speed was important since the southbound roadway had been completely blocked off by the accident. When the tractor-trailer rolled over, it blocked the left shoulder, the left lane, the center lane, the right lane, and part of the right shoulder. The only traffic that was moving was skirting by, partly on the right shoulder and partly on the grass. In similar instances, Guaranteed has hooked up an Oshkosh heavy-duty tow truck and dragged a disabled tractor-trailer beyond the shoulder to the grass, in order to let the traffic flow by. They dealt with the wreck after the traffic volume was reduced. This was the procedure of choice at 7:50 A.M. on a weekday in the midst of New York City-bound rush-hour traffic.

In the early days of the New Jersey Turnpike, towing companies were engaged on an informal basis. The state police had an idea of who was already in the business, and they called them as needed. Nowadays, given the heavy traffic volume, the arrangements are more formal. Signed contracts divide the Turnpike into zones of responsibility. For example, Guaranteed Motor is one of the companies assigned the northbound stretch from Exit 8 at milepost 67 to Exit 9 at milepost 83 and southbound from Exit 11 at milepost 91 to Exit 9 at milepost 83. Guaranteed's zone supplies enough business for three different companies. In peak periods, such as during a snowstorm, there is more than enough business.[2]

If a patron suffers a breakdown, what should he or she do? The answer is printed in capital letters on the toll ticket: "PARK DISABLED VEHICLE / ON RIGHT SHOULDER / STAY WITH VEHICLE / AND AWAIT POLICE AID." There is only one problem: no one reads the ticket. We talked with dozens of patrons who travel the Turnpike frequently, and none of them was aware of the ticket's directive. Motorists are unaware partly because they are supposed to watch the road, not read their tickets. Thus many motorists break down and do not know what to do. They certainly do not know that, in theory, they can be arrested for going off to seek aid, since walking on the Turnpike shoulder is illegal. When the system, as the Turnpike Authority envisions it, is working, a state trooper should be along in a few minutes to size up the problem. If the patron needs assistance, the trooper will radio the dispatcher, who will call one of the towing companies, who will come out and either get the patron going or provide a tow.

But if breakdown procedures are entirely logical and reasonable, very few Turnpike patrons know what they are. In an informal survey of thirty-five Rutgers University students enrolled in a course on New Jersey, we found not a single one who knew exactly what the procedures were. All of them had a driver's license and all had driven the New Jersey Turnpike. If our admittedly unscientific survey is at all representative, most people in New Jersey have little idea of how things work on the Turnpike in the event of a breakdown.

We presented each student with the same theoretical problem: "You're driving along the New Jersey Turnpike, the car is overheating, and you pull onto the shoulder. What would you do next?" The answers varied greatly.[3]

In general, the women favored waiting for help. Jeanette Rosario said, "I would sit in my car and wait for someone to help me." She had no idea who might help or what the procedure might be.

Most of the women expressed some concern for their safety. They felt that being with a disabled vehicle put them in a particularly vulnerable position. Melanie Goeller said: "I never take the Turnpike because there's no place where you can call, say, a business or something. Lord knows who would come up and pretend to help you! Being a girl alone, it's a lot different, I think."

Some of the women thought they could rely on their looks to extricate themselves from this hypothetical predicament. Roxanne Guzman explained: "I know cops aren't going to help me. So I'd wait for a guy or some guys to pass by. I'd stand next to my car and I'd just wait there. Some guy is *bound* to pull over!"

Most of the men we talked to preferred to take some kind of direct action. Peter Lugar said, "If I was close to an exit, I would walk and try to find a phone." Howard Lubert echoed this idea, saying, "Depending on how close I was to a telephone or the nearest exit, I would attempt to get either a mechanic or maybe a police officer or maybe a tow truck. If I was close enough, I would walk, otherwise I would hitch."

In the same vein, Sergio Cruz answered, "I carry flares, so the first thing I would do would be to put out flares. I would lift my hood and put out a handkerchief on either my antenna or the handle of my car. If I was close to a rest stop that had a phone, I would probably walk to it. I would get a local tower from my area to come out to the Turnpike."

After giving everyone a chance to respond to the hypothetical situation, we told the class the "correct" procedure as outlined on every toll ticket. Most of the students were indignant. "How are you supposed to know what to do?" they asked. "It's explained on the ticket," we replied. "That's dumb. Who reads the ticket? You're supposed to keep your eyes on the road!" Some students said friends had indeed followed the rules when they had breakdowns and waited two or three hours before help arrived.

The official procedures sound businesslike and straightforward, but there are psychological aspects to breakdowns that are not immediately apparent. Most people associate their cars with freedom of movement. When their cars won't move, they feel edgy, anxious, and betrayed. Typically, motorists have a destination, a purpose for their trip. A parent is expected home for dinner. An employee is supposed to show up for work. A salesperson has a client to call on. A lover has a rendezvous. These people are already in a bad mood by the time the tow truck operator shows up.

Besides, the towing industry in general has a bad reputation. Rightly or wrongly, most people think of tow truck operators as "rip-off artists." We asked Pete DiGiovanni about the problem. He told us: "It's a rough business. You work real hard, and people don't appreciate nothing you do for them. The patron is all excited and mad that he's broke down. You gotta calm him down. Customers are mistrustful nowadays. It ain't like it was years ago. All these damn lawyers and whatnot are telling the people that everybody's screwing everybody else, especially in the automobile business. You gotta prove it to them they're not getting screwed. The bad part is that some people in the business *are* screwing people. You see it, but what can you do? So people think you're just trying to make a fast buck."[4]

Pete's son, Mark DiGiovanni, the third generation in the business, explained further: "There are some people that are so mistrustful, especially on the Turnpike, that before you even get out of your truck, they're starting to attack you, before you have a chance to prove yourself to them. They're so scared something awful is going to happen to them. We've had people stand right in front of the truck and say, 'Don't touch my car.' There are times you can spend almost an hour on the side of the road arguing. You have to phone the state police. They won't argue with the trooper. No one is going to argue with someone with a nine millimeter on his side. But as soon as the trooper goes, they start arguing again."[5]

The Turnpike is both a good place and a bad place to have a breakdown. Bad because of the volume of traffic and the general sense motorists have, assuming they can get to the shoulder, that they are terribly exposed and vulnerable. Good because they will probably not have to wait long for help, assuming they haven't started walking down the highway seeking it. The roadway is constantly under patrol by state troopers. Unless the troopers are tied up with drug arrests and the accompanying paperwork, the hapless motorist should be spotted quickly. The trooper can then radio a tow garage, and (except in a heavy snowstorm) help will be on the way almost immediately.

The Turnpike Authority insures that the consumer is not at the mercy of the towing company. Allowable charges are fixed by contract. For example, at the time this is written, the standard service call for a passenger car is $40.00 plus $2.00 per mile to get the car off the Turnpike. If the motorist opts to return with the tower to the tower's garage, there is no charge for the mileage from the exit to that garage. If, however, the motorist wants the car taken to any other point, the tow becomes private from the Turnpike exit. On this portion of the tow, the fees are negotiable. Unfortunately, some garages do take advantage of the situation.

To take the disabled car to a reliable garage is in the towing company's best interest, and most do. This helps to limit complaints that come back to the Turnpike Authority, which might jeopardize the tower's valuable Turnpike contract. Motorists who know how to fix their own cars are sometimes towed to a nearby shopping plaza with a parts store. The scenario is less simple on nights and weekends. At these times, a quick fix is very difficult and the vehicle is typically placed in storage. Drivers with adequate funds can then be taken to a train station or taxi stand so they can be on their way. Drivers without funds can phone a family member or friend for a ride.

Truck breakdowns on the Turnpike also are usually handled in a routine manner. Truck drivers working for large companies such as UPS or Roadway are usually relaxed about such incidents. The drivers have an agreement with their employers that includes a breakdown pay rate. Problems arise with the independent trucker. Imagine you are a trucker driving your own $125,000 Peterbilt and carrying a load of frozen meat. If you suffer a breakdown, you stand to lose a fortune. You will be under a great deal of stress to deliver your cargo quickly.

You will probably want to leave your truck by the side of the road, get parts, and make repairs right on the site. This is pretty much standard procedure elsewhere. On the New Jersey Turnpike, however, motorists are, by regulation, allowed only two hours to complete repairs. The reason given for this regulation is safety. The Turnpike Authority figures a vehicle sitting on the shoulder is an accident waiting to happen. On the face of it, the regulation is reasonable; but independent truckers seldom see it that way, especially since they are accustomed to leaving a rig on the shoulder everywhere else, including, for example, the Pennsylvania Turnpike, where they could leave one for a couple of weeks if necessary.

Thus, in the case of the independent trucker, tow truck operators often find themselves in the uncomfortable position of rendering an unwanted service. Independent truckers resent both the tow truck operator and the New Jersey Turnpike Authority. In their view, the Turnpike is high-handed and the tow truck operator is arrogant. Both seem to be conspiring to rob them of their livelihood.

Most of the time those whose vehicles have broken down on the Turnpike accept the towing service offered. But what if patrons want to call their own towing service or an automobile club? They will find themselves up against a stone wall of Authority objections. Such people understandably become very angry and frustrated. Take the case, for example, of Mr. and Mrs. Charles R. Beeber of Jamesburg, New Jersey. Mrs. Beeber was so enraged by the treatment she and her husband received that she wrote a letter about the experience to the *New Brunswick Home News:*

I am angry about being victimized by the New Jersey Turnpike personnel, the Automobile Association of America and a state trooper Aug. 16 at the Exit 10 toll plaza when we had car trouble. Since we have AAA coverage, we phoned the Edison office (little did we know they were not allowed on the Turnpike) and told them where we were. They sent a tow truck. While we were being hooked up, a sergeant in the observation booth came out, told us which booth to go through and went back into the building. When we got to the booth, I paid the toll for our car. The collector wanted $2.80 from our tow truck driver, who said he did not have any money. I offered to pay so we could be on our way to the garage. At that point, the toll collector told us to pull over to the side, saying they had called the state police because AAA trucks are not allowed there. The trooper arrived (siren on), got out of the car and said, "Drop that car."

Words were exchanged. They all went to see the sergeant and when they came out, the trooper said, "Drop that car or I'll fine you $1,000." The tow truck driver said, "All I wanted to do was to help these people." He then dropped the car and left. The trooper called the Turnpike tow truck, and we finally left two hours and 20 minutes later.

My point is: AAA should have told us it is not allowed on the Turnpike. The sergeant, instead of telling us which booth to go through, should have sent the AAA trucker on his way before he hooked us up. And the trooper should have given the guy a warning and let us get out of there, especially since we are both approaching age 70. If they want to fight, that's OK, but please don't use us as pawns.[6]

We asked Mark DiGiovanni for the Turnpike tower's side of the story. He said the Beebers, like many other patrons, did not realize the Turnpike has its own way of doing things. Like most other Turnpike regulations the justification offered is safety. DiGiovanni explained:

The Turnpike likes to have their own people out there because the towers know what to do. They've got the experience to get the cars off the highway fast. They have to, because anything stopped on the shoulder of that road is a target. That's why nothing can stay on the shoulder. If they allowed cars to stop on the side of the Turnpike and the people said, "I'll be back next week for it," before two days went by, the whole Turnpike would look like a salvage yard.

They don't allow road services like AAA on the Turnpike because, if they did, they would have such an influx of equipment coming on and off the Turnpike— all those mechanics and trucks trying to fix cars—there would be no control over what was going on. AAA doesn't like it, but the main thing we say to patrons when they're AAA members is "Relax, I know you want AAA. But once we tow you, and you get an authorized Turnpike receipt and send that to AAA, they reimburse you."

But AAA customers get annoyed. They like to use that little card, you know. They don't want to hear of anything else. Once the AAA patron is that wound up and excited because they can't use that card, things get sticky. So you keep repeating, "We're here to help you."

But sometimes a [tow truck] driver has had a bad day. He's tired. Especially in a snow situation where you're constantly on the go, and you're dealing with the same problem every twenty minutes. You get to that fifteenth car and the guy starts arguing about AAA and you don't feel like explaining it again and then you've got an argument.[7]

A few days after we talked with Mark DiGiovanni, the Turnpike Authority issued an official rejoinder to Mrs. Beeber in a letter also sent to the *New Brunswick Home News.* The letter, which went out over the signature of Joseph "Bo" Sullivan, chairman of the New Jersey Turnpike Authority, presented a curious mixture of commonsense rebuttal and self-serving rhetorical overkill:

> In reference to Mrs. Charles Beeber's letter, the N.J. Turnpike has 31 garages under contract. The contract is rigid, encompassing insurance coverage ($1 million umbrella) and type of equipment. The towing equipment must be capable of handling the smallest vehicle to the largest tractor-trailer, overturns, car fires, or vehicles trapped down an embankment. The tow truck must have ample and secure storage yards.
>
> The AAA is just what the initials stand for, an automobile association. It contracts with various gas stations which, for the most part, have small equipment.
>
> Mrs. Beeber states the trooper said he would fine the tow truck operator $1,000. This is not the case. The trooper could have issued a summons for illegal U-turn, illegal tow and attempted evasion of tolls, but he did not. If he did, a judge would decide the amount of the fine. The trooper's statement is being investigated by the commanding officer of the state police on the Turnpike.
>
> I assume the services of King High Garage of Perth Amboy were satisfactory. Their records indicate Mr. Beeber's bill was $26.50, which AAA will reimburse.
>
> According to our traffic operations center, P&R Towing from Port Reading has attempted illegal tows previously and is aware of our regulations. It will be notified by the state police and our operations director that summonses will be issued for any repetition of activity.[8]

Sullivan's letter certainly starts out in a reasonable manner. But what about the trooper saying he would fine the tow truck operator $1,000? Sullivan says, "This is not the case." Perhaps what Sullivan means to say is that the trooper has no authority to fine anyone. That is true. Judges levy fines. But if a state trooper tells you, "I'm going to fine you $1,000," you listen.

The Turnpike Authority could do a better job of reducing patron anxiety about breakdowns through better communication. Other toll roads make more of an effort in this regard. In the rest areas of the Garden State Parkway, for example, are posters prominently displayed that spell out tow truck procedures. The posters explain the rates for towing charges in detail, breaking down separate charges for hook-up and mileage fees. The posters, kindly in tone, also indicate that the towing companies accept major credit cards in payment. To be sure, there is no guarantee people will read them. But those who do will undoubtedly be calmed and reassured.[9]

The Garden State Parkway at least tries to communicate its policies to its patrons. The biggest anxiety in breakdown situations comes from not knowing what to do. We said earlier that the Turnpike is "not user friendly." Alas, in the matter of communicating its towing policies, this statement is all too true.

And communication is essential on the Turnpike because, once motorists get on it, they enter a closed world. They cannot just get off anywhere; they must get off at designated exits, after paying their tolls. They are blocked from the outside world by physical barriers—tall fences and barbed wire. All along the roadway are signs advising them that no stopping is allowed. They cannot stop to take pictures. They cannot stop to picnic. They cannot stop to discipline their children. Stopping is not permitted. One can understand, then, why they might have a great deal of anxiety about breaking down on the Turnpike.

On breaking down, motorists become subject to a special set of New Jersey Turnpike Authority regulations. They may not leave their vehicle to make a call. If they want to fix their car themselves, the state police will (reluctantly) allow them two hours. Given the complexity of today's cars, very few motorists are actually able to fix their own cars. Even professional mechanics with tools in their trunk may be stymied by a lack of spare parts. Most of the rest of us simply raise the hood and poke around so as not to lose face.

After the allotted two hours, motorists have lost their freedom of action. Even if they know how to complete their repairs, their time is up. They *must* be towed away. If the turnpike were a river, these cars would be declared a hazard to navigation. Motorists may not decide who will tow them. That decision is made for them.

Some patrons find this loss of control humiliating. They do not go quietly. But a motorist who refuses to cooperate enters a will-breaking contest, especially after the tow truck operator summons the police to the scene by radio.

The worst-case scenario occurs when the patron has no money to pay for the tow. This aggravates an already delicate situation in which the towing company has performed a needed but, perhaps, unwanted service. The lack of funds exacerbates a confrontational situation. The towing company will simply impound the car, refusing to release it until all charges—including an ever-mounting daily storage fee—are paid. Most people dispossessed of their vehicle feel vulnerable, if not violated. The tow truck operator may not relish separating motorists from their vehicles, but this is an indignity motorists without funds will suffer.

Mark DiGiovanni related one such story to us. He was sitting at the dispatcher's console in Guaranteed's office in Somerset, New Jersey, when a call came in from one of his tow operators at 10:30 P.M. A young woman, about twenty-one years old, had been driving north on the Turnpike and had run out of gas near New Brunswick. She had no money and no identification. She was unable to buy gas. She had to be towed. Now her car was on a flatbed tow truck parked in front of the New Brunswick train station. She wanted the driver to take her and the car to her home in Maplewood. Since she had no money to pay for the service, the driver refused. The best he could do was to drop her off at the train station. Meanwhile, he could take her car to Guaranteed's storage yard, where it would be held for her until she could pay the tow charges.

The young woman was upset and irate; she refused to get out of the tow truck. The driver radioed Mark DiGiovanni to come down to the train station to straighten things out. DiGiovanni told the story this way:

> I went down there and explained everything just like the driver said it. She sat there crying and wouldn't get out of the wrecker. She said, "I'm not getting out of the truck," as if she was chaining herself to the truck, and that way, he couldn't drive off with her car.
> I said to her, "Get out. This is our vehicle. You're not allowed in here. You're trespassing."
> She wouldn't answer me. I said, "Ma'am, do you want me to call the police?"
> She still wouldn't answer me. So I picked up my walkie-talkie and was going to call the police, when I saw two New Brunswick police officers driving by in a car. I yelled and flagged them down. I asked them if they were on a call or something. I said, "I have a situation here which I need you guys to intervene on."
> The police explained, "Look, lady, it's state law. This guy is protected. He is towing your car. You can't pay him? The law says you don't get your car back. Simple. Okay? Since you have nothing to go with, why don't we take you down to police headquarters? You can wait there until you can show us some identification or have someone pick you up."
> "I don't want to!"
> "Look, don't start throwing a tantrum. You're going with us. Come on. Have a seat in the police car."

She finally went with them. I talked with the officers later on that evening because I was curious to find out what happened to her. It was her boyfriend's car. She had gone to visit a friend he didn't want her to see in the first place. . . .

The next day the boyfriend and her brother came down and paid the bill. They never said one word to us about it. I would have expected some sort of nastiness. All they did was walk in and say, "Hi! How ya doing?"

They paid their bill. We pushed the car out to the pump. They put gas in it, and they drove away.[10]

For tow truck operators, dealing with troubled patrons goes with the territory. So do long hours. In the case of Guaranteed Motor Towing Service, round-the-clock dispatcher service is provided by family members. On a typical day, Mark DiGiovanni spends eight to ten hours at a small desk in company headquarters on Route 27 in Franklin Township. The desk has a telephone, a scanner, and a two-way radio. At home in his bedroom, the entire setup is duplicated. What if he wants to go out for the evening? No problem. His father, Pete DiGiovanni, has a complete dispatching station in *his* home. What if both father and son want to step out? Still no problem. Uncle Mark has yet another station in *his* home. By informal arrangement, through give-and-take, somebody is always ready to take a call.

Their business is not so much a job as a way of life. Tow truck operators are like volunteer firefighters, always on duty. The difference is that the volunteer firefighter may be motivated by altruism or glory. For the tow truck operator, there is no glory; but the towing business is a profitable, recession-proof business.

Still, the life-style does take a toll. While hanging out in Guaranteed's office, we picked up a back issue of *Tow Times* ("The International Communications Medium for the Towing and Recovery Industry"). There was a letter to the editor from one Tina Harris, complaining in a good-natured way about the life of a towman's wife. The letter was written ostensibly in the form of a heart-to-heart talk with a woman contemplating marriage with a towman:

The first thing you will need to acquire as a towman's mate is an independent spirit. You will have to adjust to having some meals alone (or at midnight, whichever you prefer). A microwave oven is a great blessing. That is because your telephone will invariably ring just as he sits down to a meal, and there is a great deal of warming over to be done.

Also, your towman will almost never come "straight home" from work. He has to go by the parts store, the local law enforcement agency, or gas station. And when he calls and tells you not to worry about preparing much for supper, the translation is "You can put the roast back in the freezer because he stopped by the coffee shop with the highway patrolman after that last wreck and couldn't resist the hamburger and french fries." . . .

You will know the honeymoon is over when he stops turning the volume down on the scanner by your bed during those intimate moments. And if you wake up at three in the morning to the sound of a blaring television, noisy burglars have not invaded your home. No towman returns from a late night call without having a snack and watching a little television to unwind. This means you will have to put the melting ice cream back in the freezer, turn off the television, and cover him up while he snores on the couch. If you are deter-mined to get him into the bed, you will have to resort to trickery, as there is no way you will be able to wake him up at this point. You will have to make your own telephone ring (they always hear the phone) and say "652, go to bed, 10-4." This way, he can sleepwalk to bed without realizing what you have done! . . .

If you really love that towman, you might just as well love what he has chosen as his profession, because I can tell you one thing for sure, he will never change! And his profession is very honorable—one of service to others.

So be proud of your towman and remember that for him to be a success in the eyes of the rest of the world, he has to be a success in your eyes first![11]

Tina Harris's letter provides a window into the life of the tow truck operator. We understand that he is a human being who needs respect and understanding. But there is, after all, a two-way street here. The motorist needs these things too, and the Turnpike environment places a tremendous strain on the normal give-and-take of social interaction. For the stranded motorist, any gesture of human kindness is likely to be warmly appreciated. So much so that the relationship that develops between the tow truck operator and the motorist is not unlike that of the "Stockholm syndrome," a term developed by psychologists to explain the bonding that takes place be-tween hostages and their captors.

Precisely such an experience was brought to our attention by a col-league, Tom De Haven, from Jersey City. He was driving home in the late afternoon of Tuesday, December 1, 1987. He was about ten minutes away from his house, on the Newark Bay–Hudson County Extension of the Turn-pike, when his car suddenly and inexplicably stopped. De Haven later explained:

It's dark, around ten after five. The worst nightmare has come true. I'm on this bridge, in the fast lane absolutely stalled. I imagine myself being the object of one of those helicopter reports. Everybody is beeping and honking at me. I don't know what to do. People zoomed around me, and I thought I was going to get hit for sure.

Anyway, somebody stops behind me. I got out and he says he would push me and get me off the road. He says, "You know us New Jersey drivers. We'll kill you." So I say, "Okay." We both put our directionals on and we have to go across the roadway to the shoulder. He had just a regular, small car. It was incredibly brave of him because no one was stopping, you know. He's pushing me, and I'm dead in the water. We're creeping over to the other side. I didn't think we were going to make it. I mean, people were just zooming around— trucks and everything. Finally, we were on the downgrade, and I was moving, really rolling down the hill.

I had no brakes because the whole car cut out, power brakes and all. So the only way I can stop this thing is to use the hand brake. Actually, I figured I'd let it roll because I'm rolling towards 14A (Bayonne). I'm getting closer and closer to 14A. I said, "This is all right. I'm not out in the middle of the wilderness." So anyway, I came to a stop fifty feet from the sign for 14A where you go down that ramp. The guy comes up behind me, and I got out of the car to thank him for doing this. He says, "You can walk off the Turnpike and get some help." I said, "Well, there's not going to be any problem because thousands of people are going off right here. They all see me, so I'll get help. Thanks a lot." He takes off.

I really literally thought I was going to get help in five minutes. The reason I didn't walk off the bridge was that two weeks before you guys [the authors] came to my class to talk about the Turnpike, and you asked the students "Do you know what to do if you break down on the Turnpike?"

You said, "You can't leave your car. If you leave your car, you might get a ticket. The Turnpike toll ticket says you have to stay with your car."

If you had not told me about this regulation, I would have walked off the Turnpike. I was so close to 14A. But I didn't want to get a ticket. So I just sat in the car and waited and expected a cop to come. Meanwhile, these cars were just zooming by really fast. And now people were using the shoulder as they came off the bridge to pass cars on the right. What's happening is that they are coming around over the bridge on that shoulder trying to pass. Then they suddenly see me: *stopped dead!*

I thought I was going to get killed, so I got out of the car and stood on the passenger's side of the car. But it was freezing cold, so I got back in the car. I'm saying, "Somebody's going to be here soon. Somebody's going to tell them I'm here because thousands of cars are going by to get off at 14A." Any time I ever saw anybody broken down I always noted what mile marker it was and told the people at the booth. I figured that's what people were doing.

Then I almost got creamed by a truck that was passing on the shoulder. I was getting scared. I was cold because there was no heat. Time kept going by and no one came.

It was sixty-five minutes before a cop came. The cop pulls up in front of me and I see him gesturing to approach on his passenger side. I walked up there and he said, "What's the problem?" I said, "The car just conked out." He wants to know the plate number and the make of the car and where the car is registered. So I give him all that stuff. He jots it down—a real nice state trooper. He says, "All right. You go back to your car and get in and wait. I'll have a tow truck sent." I said, "Okay. Fine." So he pulls back out into traffic.

I walk back to the car, having been there already an hour and ten minutes—literally five minutes from the Exit, all this time knowing I could have walked off. And right off the Turnpike at Exit 14A is an Exxon station. I could have walked there a long time ago, but I'm obeying the rules. What a wimp I am. I don't want to get a ticket, you know. So I wait some more in the car. I figure, "He's called. What's it going to take, another five or ten minutes?" It took another full hour. I was out there—a five-minute walk from the tollbooth—and it took two hours for this tow truck to come.

It's this old jalopy of a wrecker. It's huge and it's clanky. It looks mud-encrusted and falling apart. This young guy, real nice, jumps out and says he'll hook me up. I said, "Where are you going to take me?" I mean, at this point, after two hours out there, I want to go home. I'm freezing. He says, "I'm taking you to Newark." I said, "Oh, no! I don't want to go to Newark. I live ten minutes away from here, five to the exit, and five minutes to my house." He says, "Well, I'll take you home. You want me to take you home?" I said, "Yes. Please take me home." He said, "I gotta check. Do you have a major credit card?" I said, "Yes, I have a major credit card. Which do you want?" He says, "It doesn't matter. We take them all." So I got in his truck, and he goes about hooking up my car.

Then he hops in the truck and calls his superior on the two-way radio. He says, "I have this guy wants me to take him into Jersey City." The boss crackles back, "Where in Jersey City?" I said, "Summit and Astor Place, right off Garfield." The kid relays the message. There was this long pause. I had this vision of someone back in Newark checking out a map. Then the word comes back, "Eighty-five dollars." God, I thought. But I was desperate, so I said to the kid, "Fine. Please just get me out of here."

So the kid hangs up the radio and starts driving and he says, "I really feel bad. Eighty-five dollars. That's a lot of money, isn't it?" I said, "Yeah, it's a lot of money, but I tell you. I've been out here two hours. I just want to get off. It's worth it to me to get off." He says, "I still feel bad." I said, "Well, don't feel bad."

So we were getting off at 14B coming toward the tollbooth, and he says, "Have you got your toll ticket?" I said, "Oh, God, my ticket's back in the car." He said, "You gotta have your ticket. You gotta pay the toll." So he stopped, He said, "I'll get it for you. Don't bother yourself." I said, "It's in the visor over the driver's side." He gets out and runs back and comes back with the ticket. I give him the money and he has his own little ticket. He pulls up and pays both of them. He says, "I want a receipt for both of these."

So then we drive down Garfield Avenue. And I'm saying, "Oh man! Where are we going to put this thing?" You can't just dump it. I have this neighbor who lets me use half of his driveway. Sometimes he keeps this huge camper in the other half, so I just have this little wedge of a driveway to park in. So I say to the kid, "I have this place I can park, but it's only a piece of a driveway." He says, "No problem. I can get it in there for you." I said, "Okay. I really appreciate it. Turn here at the next corner. You see that little driveway there?" He says, "Yeah, I see it." There's cars parked right to the edge of the driveway on both sides—right to the very edge, but, luckily, the camper isn't there. He had this big wrecker and my car behind it. I said, "Do you think you can get it in?" He says, "No problem. No problem. Which side of the driveway? Which way do you want it facing?" I said, "The far side if you can get it in there, but any way you can do it's fine. I'll explain it to the guy." He said, "No problem. You want it on that side, I'll get it on that side." So he pulls up. He was in all his glory at this point. Dragging the car was just work, but this was Art! He pulls up in this old thing and he takes the wheel with such grace and spins it with a turn of the wrist and this thing just glides perfectly in, right up to the fence. So the neighbor could get his camper in just fine. It was craftsmanship. I looked over my shoulder and I said to the kid, "That is fabulous! Wonderful! What a job!" He turns to me and says, "That's what all my girls say."

He jumped out and got the car down. He took my credit card and phoned in the numbers. It was just like going to a department store. I got my receipt and gave him a five-dollar tip, and that was the last I saw of him.[12]

We can easily identify with Tom De Haven's plight, because we Americans cherish our mobility. The fast lane of the Turnpike, where De Haven had been traveling before his mishap, invites us to put the pedal to the metal, even if we know better, to bypass both urban congestion and suburban sprawl. But a breakdown stops us dead in our tracks.

A breakdown, especially on the Turnpike, is not just a mechanical mishap. It represents coming up forcefully against the *illusion* of control, self-expression, and mastery represented by the private automobile. Motorists are no longer "rugged individualists." Now they are just helplessly adrift alongside a river of traffic. Sitting in their disabled vehicles on the shoulder, motorists are involuntarily subdued and restrained. They are fearful and apprehensive. They are dependent on the help of strangers. And they are in a very dangerous place.

The system does have some consumer safeguards built in, but no regulatory scheme can completely extricate motorists from their vulnerability. The breakdown drama is acted out dozens of times every day. The present setup inevitably leads to some fierce confrontations. There are other solutions, but they would be costly. For example, the Authority could follow the example of certain bridge and tunnel authorities. They could provide a free tow to the nearest exit, and then let motorists negotiate their own deals with private towing companies. To do this the Authority would have to acquire its own fleet of tow trucks.

The present system is a curious mixture of private enterprise and Authority control. The breakdown is regarded as the *private* problem and expense of motorists, yet they must accept a service vendor chosen for them by a *public* authority. This mixture of the public and the private is a recipe for disputes, confrontations, and arguments. And for some pretty good stories as well.

Road Hazards

Chapter

6

> "Now there was blood and glass all over.
> There was nobody there but me.
> There was a rain tumbled down hard and cold
> I seen a young man lying by the side of the road,
> Crying, 'Mister, won't you help me please?'"
>   —Bruce Springsteen,
>   "Wreck on the Highway"[1]

In a video arcade about two miles from New Jersey Turnpike headquarters, a young college student in blue jeans and a T-shirt sets down his bookbag and takes out a quarter. He has decided to play an electronic game called "Jersey Gear Jammer." He needs relief from the tension of studying for final exams. The game beckons with loud rock music and an incessant flashing sign that says, "INSERT COINS." The electronic display shows a red sports car convertible, unmistakably a Ford Mustang, with a male driver and his blond female companion.

The car is poised for acceleration on a highway, but it's not just any highway. It's a hugely wide asphalt highway with dashed white lane stripes; it bears an uncanny resemblance to the New Jersey Turnpike.

The electronic trip starts out beneath a concrete viaduct. The piers of the viaduct whiz by, the driver overtaking slower cars. Sometimes the driver passes them on the right, sometimes on the left. Finally, the car, traveling at very high speed, veers off the roadway to the right, hits an obstruction, and flips over. Several more accidents and the game is over. The student shrugs his shoulders, picks up his bookbag, and heads out to the parking lot, prepared to drive the real New Jersey Turnpike home.

On the Turnpike, there are plenty of real accidents: in 1986 there were 4,489; in 1987, 5,309. Newspaper coverage of these accidents is often alarming and sensational, and sometimes inaccurate.[2] The only fair way to evaluate these numbers is to compare the accident statistics of other major toll roads. Official records show that the New Jersey Turnpike, in comparison with twelve other major toll roads, ranks fourth highest in total number of accidents.[3] Considering that the New Jersey Turnpike has the highest traffic density of all, the record is not bad.

In the Turnpike Authority's standard press kit, "A Guide for the News Media," there is a carefully worded statement on safety, which begins: "Virtually all highway traffic between the great seaports of New York and Philadelphia passes through New Jersey. Yet, in spite of the incredible volume of traffic, the New Jersey Turnpike has consistently been *one of the safest major toll roads* in the United States" (emphasis added).[4] This is a valid claim, but from time to time it gets transformed and exaggerated by the press. For example, Gordon Bishop of the *Newark Star-Ledger* writes: "The New Jersey Turnpike is both the busiest all-purpose and safest toll road in America."[5] In another instance, Paul Overberg of the *Bridgewater Courier News* called the Turnpike "the nation's safest toll road."[6]

In actual fact, driving the Turnpike, especially in the northern sections, is a scary experience. Statistically it may be relatively safe, but it still feels frightening. Nevertheless, few people blame the New Jersey Turnpike Authority for the accidents that take place there. Although the New Jersey Turnpike has attracted a great deal of aesthetic criticism, almost no one has attacked it for bad safety design.[7] Because the Turnpike was one of the first roads to provide for physical separation of opposing lanes of traffic, it has often been held up as a model of good safety design.

Right from the start, the opposing lanes of traffic were separated by steel guardrails. As this book is being written, the old steel guard rails are being systematically replaced by an even safer 52-inch-high reinforced concrete median barrier, ten inches taller than the standard concrete divider, which is known throughout the country as "the New Jersey Barrier." This new protective wall, which is cast on location, can withstand the impact from heavily loaded tractor-trailers, preventing such vehicles from crossing over into opposing lanes of traffic. By the time this book is published, much of the roadway should have the barrier in place, a project that will have cost half a million dollars per mile.[8]

The civil engineering elements in safe roads are no great mystery; most of them have been known since Roman times. Key elements are curves, hills, and intersections. Curves are dangerous for two reasons. First, there is the danger of running off the road or flipping over when taking a curve at high speed. Second, a curve often restricts the motorist's sight distance and, thus, increases the chance of collisions with other vehicles.[9] Turnpike design specifications all but eliminated curves, or made them so gradual as to be imperceptible. The minimum radius for curves was specified at 3,000 feet. In actual fact, when the Turnpike was built, with only two exceptions, no curvature of less than a 10,000-foot radius was used.[10]

Since curves when the Turnpike was built were considered dangerous, they were engineered right out of existence. Nevertheless, today, many people find the straightness of the road unsettling. It's just not normal for a road to be so straight. Today, the Turnpike's straight design seems like technological overkill.

The Turnpike, like bronzed baby shoes and portraits of Elvis on velvet, is an artifact left over from the 1950s. There is no longer a consensus that a straight road is the best road. Instead, some critics argue, the boring nature of such roads makes them dangerous. Highway historian Phil Patton writes:

> By the time the Interstate program began in earnest, . . . it was recognized that the straight line was the highway designer's greatest enemy, in terms of both safety and aesthetics. The greatest complaint about the superhighway is the tedium of driving on it. The straightest, most boring roads, like great stretches of the Kansas Turnpike, have some of the highest accident rates in the country. Those rated as aesthetically attractive, blending curves and straightaways, are also among the safest.
> Dull highways can literally put drivers to sleep at the wheel. They also reduce their sense of distance. Designers speak of "velocitation," the tendency of drivers too long on a straightaway to underestimate their speed. The results are rear-end collisions, sportscars sliding underneath tractor-trailers, and chain-reaction crashes.[11]

If there is now uncertainty among road builders about the virtue of straight roads, with some planners favoring the factoring in of curves as a positive feature, there appears to be more of a consensus with regard to hills. Hills *are* dangerous. The reasons are fairly simple. Heavy vehicles, which are underpowered or overloaded, have to slow down to a crawl to climb up a steep hill. Such slow-moving vehicles often provoke drivers of faster cars to try to overtake and pass them on hills, with predictably disastrous results. Of course, hills are also just as dangerous on the down side, where overloaded trucks may reach excessive speeds and go out of control. As we all learned in grammar school, what goes up must come down. To reduce accidents on hills, as far back as 1939 the U.S. Public Roads Administration had advocated that maximum grades should not be more than 3 percent; which is to say that there should not be a rise of more than 3 feet in 100 feet of road.[12] These were fine standards, but they were too expensive for most road builders.

Turnpike engineers, with ample funding, easily met the standards. The hills, like the curves, were engineered into oblivion. For the motorist, they no longer exist. In fact, no long grades exceed 2 percent in the 100 miles from the tollbooths at the Delaware River to Elizabeth. Of course, this southern stretch has generally favorable topography. At the time the Turnpike was built, it was mostly flat farmland. North of the Raritan River, the route goes through a heavily developed region, which presented problems. Not that there were many hills, as such. The heights that needed scaling were chiefly man-made. In spite of these difficulties, long 3-percent grades were necessary only in two places, the major crossings at the Passaic and Hackensack rivers.[13]

Intersections are the third key element in highway safety, and they are dangerous. The Turnpike minimized the danger by eliminating the intersections and by using the now-familiar principle of limited access. There are not many exits on the Turnpike. (That is how motorists refer to them— "exits"—but the Authority calls them, perhaps more accurately, "interchanges," for, after all, motorists enter there as well as exit.) Along the Turnpike's 142-mile roadway network, there are only twenty-seven interchanges. Contrast this with almost any major East Coast highway, with its virtually continual pattern of exits. There is always political pressure to create more exits, but Turnpike engineers have tried hard to resist this pressure over the years. Very few interchanges have been constructed since the original Turnpike was completed in 1952. We are so familiar by now with the "cloverleaf" principle of grade separation that it no longer seems remarkable, but this method does sort out high volumes of traffic with few collisions. A driver can still hit a barrier, but that is preferable to hitting another vehicle, especially since the new concrete barrier is designed for vehicles to slide off, rather than collide with, the barrier.

In Chapter 10 we criticize the Turnpike for its apparent disregard of aesthetic considerations. But, to be fair, the New Jersey Turnpike was designed and built to be as safe as possible according to what was known about safety at the time, regardless of aesthetic considerations. In the realm of safety, no expense was spared.

The Turnpike's traffic engineers have continued to try to make the road as safe as possible. Jerry Kraft, senior engineer, says: "We are not just civil servants waiting for retirement. This job carries with it recognition within the profession."[14] Kraft cites a long string of "firsts" for the New Jersey Turnpike. As mentioned earlier, it was the first highway to install guardrails along its entire length. In 1962, it was the first to install a radio sign-control system, by which speed limit and emergency warning messages are activated by radio to 107 locations along the Turnpike. It was the first to provide right-hand safety shoulders on major bridges.

The most remarkable innovation was the installation of a system for automatic traffic control and surveillance in January 1976. This system enhances the Authority's ability to take advantage of the so-called dual/dual Turnpike, the twelve lanes in the 36 miles of the northern stretch of the Turnpike. This part of the road provides two separate three-lane roadways in each direction, one for cars only, the other for cars, trucks, and buses.

Separation of the roadway prevents crossover traffic (vehicles crossing over into parallel, or opposing, lanes of traffic, typically causing spectacular accidents). Separation of the commercial vehicles further improves safety and driver comfort.[15]

We asked Kraft about the dual/dual arrangement. Obviously, for the passenger car driver concerned about safety, the "CARS ONLY" lane is the wise choice. Statistically, the inner roadway for cars only and the outer roadway, which is shared by cars with trucks and buses, have roughly the same number of accidents. In the "CARS ONLY" inner lane, however, if there is an accident, one only has to worry about being hit by another car. In the outer lane, one runs the risk of being crushed by a massive 40-ton truck. We asked the obvious question: why not make all the cars go in the "CARS ONLY" lane? Kraft answered that the overriding concern is one of roadway capacity. Cars represent the bulk of the traffic. If all cars were made to use the inner roadway, it would be too crowded. By allowing cars a choice, the traffic is dispersed more evenly over both inner and outer roadways. Thus the inner roadway is 100 percent cars; the outer roadway is about 85 percent cars and 15 percent trucks and buses.

The really positive aspect of the automatic traffic control system is that whenever one roadway is congested and the other is underutilized, the surveillance system reports this condition back to headquarters instantly and police are dispatched to check things out visually. The operator can then divert the flow of traffic to the underutilized lanes through automatic sign control. In other words, he can switch the entering flow of traffic on the dual/dual from the inner roadway to the outer roadway, or vice versa, all of this by remote control.

The system makes best use of available capacity. Sensing devices embedded in the pavement at half-mile intervals along the main roadway report congestion rapidly, day and night, good weather and bad. The more serious the situation, the more rapidly it is detected. A complete blockage can be detected in three minutes or less. The required sign changes can be made immediately, and traffic can be kept moving around the obstruction. With this system, detecting an accident no longer depends on how frequently the police patrol the roadway. The system also allows dispatchers to route emergency vehicles, such as ambulances, fire engines, and tow trucks, around congested areas.[16]

Understandably, Turnpike officials are proud of the automatic surveillance and control system. Visiting dignitaries to Turnpike headquarters are always shown the main control console and the 20-foot-long electronic map display. They are truly impressive. The operations center looks like the bridge of the USS *Enterprise* on "Star Trek." The map display, with its blinking lights, shows overall roadway performance and traffic levels at all detector stations. It gives a readout of what all electronic signs on the roadway currently say. In terms of symbolism, the map seems to reflect a Turnpike Authority completely in control of its terrain. The engineer on duty resembles a Coast Guard harbor master monitoring the traffic flowing up and down a mighty river.

While the automatic surveillance and control system represents a high-tech approach to safety, there are also some low-tech operations. One of these is the litter patrol. It is not just an aesthetic matter of picking up discarded food wrappers. The litter patrol is also charged with removing anything from the roadway that might cause an accident. For example, if there is a muffler or tailpipe or hubcap on the roadway, it is possible that a motorist might come along, fail to see the object, hit it, lose control, and swerve into another vehicle, possibly leading to a multiple-car crash.

The litter patrol consists of crews of men who cruise the shoulders of the Turnpike in bright orange trucks. They pick up pieces of wood and metal, dead animals, truck parts, and even bags of household trash. More than 10,000 cubic yards of litter are collected on the Turnpike each year—enough to fill 322 large garbage trucks.[17]

Despite having designed the road to be as safe as possible, despite carefully monitoring the flow of traffic, despite faithfully picking up litter, accidents do occur on the Turnpike. The worst one, really a series of accidents, took place in October 1973. Ten persons were killed and more than forty injured in a series of collisions that sent sixty-five vehicles crashing into one another in a heavy fog that enveloped a large section of the northern Turnpike. The fog was bad enough, but it was made worse by a garbage-dump fire near the scene of the accidents that gushed forth smoke into the fog, creating an almost impenetrable smog. As this black cloud descended on the roadway, the Turnpike was plunged into virtual darkness. Like a grade-B horror movie brought to real life, suddenly there was zero visibility on both the eastern spur near Secaucus and the western spur near the Hackensack Meadowlands.[18]

In a fiery series of multiple crashes that stretched for miles along the Turnpike, trailer trucks, tankers, small delivery vans, passenger cars, and a Trailways bus were damaged or destroyed. A million dollars worth of cargo, including a truckful of whiskey, was scattered everywhere. The accidents took place during the night. There was diesel oil and tar all over the road and vehicles burning everywhere.

The accidents began in the late evening of Tuesday, October 23, and continued through the wee hours of Wednesday, October 24. At 11:30 P.M. on Tuesday, the first major accident took place in the three-lane northbound side of the westerly route in Carlstadt. Several people were injured, one fatally, in a pileup of four trucks and three cars. A contemporary account in the *New York Daily News* described the aftermath:

> There was a confused parade of rescuers to the fog and smoke-darkened scene. Many of the state troopers who came from as far away as New Brunswick and Princeton had to leave their cars and stumble on foot to the aid of the dying and injured.
> Ambulances came from a dozen communities and took the casualties to hospitals in Secaucus, Kearny, Hackensack, Newark, and Jersey City. But authorities still were looking late yesterday for one truck driver who became coated with hot asphalt from another truck and was last seen running into the swamps along the highway.[19]

After the first collision in Carlstadt, there was a second fatality when two tractor-trailers hit a passenger car 5 miles to the south at 2:00 A.M. Shortly afterward, and less than half a mile to the south, the worst crash occurred. Six people were killed as five cars and more than twenty trucks became locked together in a twisted mass of wreckage. Later, at 3:00 A.M., the fourth serious crash took place on the eastern spur in Secaucus. Two cars and a tractor-trailer collided, and two more people were killed. In addition to these four major crashes, there were about forty other minor accidents.[20]

Later, Casper La Marca, a survivor of the worst crash, described the scene from his hospital bed in Kearny: "It was the heaviest fog I've ever seen in my life, a visibility of two to three inches. I remember trying to stop between two trailer trucks. I must have been thrown clear of the car and gone off like a rocket. When I came to, I found myself under a tanker and I started crawling north. I just kept crawling north. I knew they were going to plow into me from the back. It all happened so suddenly, just like that."[21]

Some two hundred Turnpike maintenance workers were called in to help with the rescue work. The next day, even more personnel had to be called up to help with the cleanup operation. Dozens of maintenance trucks hauled away tons of debris. Tow trucks, including a number from Guaranteed Motor Towing Service, were called in to remove damaged cars and trucks. Joan Cook, a *New York Times* reporter, described the scene: "Through an eye-smarting haze that clung to the ground, the area of the accidents, particularly in the westernmost leg of the road, presented a scene from the air reminiscent of a bombed and strafed military convoy in wartime."

One of the men involved that fateful night was Robert Lyttell, then twenty-eight years old. He had been a driver for the Provan Trucking Company of Newburgh, New York, for seven years. That night he was driving an oil tanker that hit another truck in a chain collision near Kearny. The next day, in the hospital, he told about his experience:

> He was a foot or two ahead of me. I saw the outline of his marker lights and could feel the impact of everything crunching. When I came to, I was on the ground.
> I heard all the crashes behind me and everybody got panicky because you couldn't see where you were. You could hear screams and crashes. A guy a couple of rigs behind me was yelling "Help!" I turned off the electricity. Thank God the oil was not flammable.
> There were trucks with propane gas about a quarter of a mile behind me that went up like a chain reaction, they all went up. They're all dead.[22]

In Lyttell's account of the situation, he told the *New York Times* reporter that he felt very bitter toward the police. He admitted that, like everyone else, he had been barreling northward at about 70 miles per hour. He saw the lighted sign just beyond Exit 15W with the words "FOG. ACCIDENT. SPEED 35 MILES PER HOUR." But in Lyttell's opinion, that was not enough. He said: "If there had been a man at that sign with flares or a flashing light telling us to go through at five miles an hour, everyone would have crept along and been all right. Just one patrol car. Maybe you'd have been a half hour late but you'd have been all right."[23]

One can understand Lyttell's frustration. His complaint about the slow initial police response to the smoke and fog may be valid. Once the accidents took place, however, the police did react and rescue people. At least one New Jersey state trooper emerged from the disaster a hero. He was Cornel Plebani, a state trooper whose heroism was described about a year later in *Reader's Digest.*

The author of the article, Peter Michelmore, carefully set the stage by explaining Plebani's war record in Vietnam, his family situation with a wife and young son, and the routine nature of police patrol work. But the night of October 23, 1973, was not routine. When Plebani arrived on the scene, he radioed Newark: "I need heavy-duty rescues. I got a tractor-trailer jack-knifed and I got a tanker with oil spilling out on the roadway with its tractor demolished. At least three other rigs are smashed. We're all engulfed in smoke here. We can't see six inches."

The article went on to describe Plebani's repeated rescue efforts. At great risk to himself, Plebani went back to the scene a number of times, trying to pull people from the flames and debris. His hair was singed and his face scorched. When firefighters from Kearny arrived on the scene, they tried to get Plebani to leave in an amulance, but he refused and stayed on the scene, continuing to render aid.[24]

After the debris was cleared away there were a number of state and federal investigations.[25] All reports agreed that an underlying cause of this terrible series of accidents was the smoldering dump fire next to the Turnpike. The fire emanated from the old sprawling dumps in the township of Lyndhurst. After the accidents, it was revealed that fires had often raged out of control for days at the site. The situation was beyond the control of the Lyndhurst Fire Department. The nearest fire hydrants were 5,000 feet away, much too far to maintain a good water supply.

A repeat of the 1973 tragedy is highly unlikely now. Landfills are more tightly regulated. Fires are controlled more effectively. And according to Jerry Kraft, traffic engineer, there have been fewer heavy fogs on the Turnpike since 1973 and few fog-related accidents.

This may just be lucky. A more likely explanation could be the extensive development along the Turnpike. Fog requires moisture—evaporation from swamps, lakes, and vegetation. As wetlands have been increasingly replaced in North Jersey by asphalt and concrete, there are fewer sources to generate fog. It would be ironic if development is the source of improved visibility on the New Jersey Turnpike.[26]

Still, accidents do occur. What kind of accident is most typical? What are the most frequent contributing factors? According to Kraft, "One of the advantages of a toll road, especially when you have the ticket system, is that you are able to keep very, very good records. Take these records. Analyze them. Then go out on the road and do something."[27]

The Turnpike keeps elaborate records on all accidents. If a pattern or a cluster of accidents appears at a given place, that locale is studied for possible improvements. For example, if there is a cluster of accidents at a given milepost at twilight, that place might need additional lighting. If there is a cluster of accidents at a given toll plaza, that place might need additional booths to accommodate the volume of business. Wherever there is a pattern of accidents, the engineers try to formulate recommendations to alleviate the situation.

Particular attention is paid to the placement of traffic signs. The Turnpike has an unusually high volume of traffic. In any dense traffic pattern, the driver of a vehicle in the left lane has difficulty seeing a ground-mounted sign to the right of the roadway, because other vehicles, especially trucks, may block the view. Thus many ground-mounted signs on the Turnpike have been replaced with easier-to-read overhead signs. For example, all of the signs warning of an approach of an interchange one mile ahead or one-quarter mile ahead are overhead signs, even in the southern section of the Turnpike, which is the least heavily traveled.

Despite all these safety efforts, as traffic increases, fewer gaps occur in the traffic stream, so over the years accidents have tended to increase. Interestingly, however, fatalities have been going down. This makes sense, because as traffic becomes more dense, reaching excessive (and deadly) speed is difficult.[28]

A friend who often uses the Turnpike to come to work told us that his biggest fear is getting involved in an accident with an overly aggressive truck driver. He told us of his annoyance recently when driving on the northern section of the Turnpike in the outer roadway, which is shared with trucks. Although he was driving 65 miles per hour, he was forced to pull over to let a large truck get by. As it passed, he read the bumper sticker on the back of the truck: It said, "HOW'S MY DRIVING? PHONE 1-800-EAT-SHIT." This widely available bumper sticker is meant as a joke, but given the behavior of that particular truck driver, it seemed to underscore a troublesome aspect of the trucking industry. Since most truck drivers are paid by the mile, they have every economic incentive to travel as fast as they can, regardless of the danger to others.

Our friend's apprehension is well founded. Though trucks (together with buses) make up only 15 percent of the traffic on the Turnpike, they are involved in more than 30 percent of the accidents. Since truck drivers are often paid by distance traveled, they have a tendency to push their speed and to stay on the road even when fatigued. One trucker from Alabama who stopped briefly at the Vince Lombardi Service Area told us, "I just drive until I get there." No mystery, then, why trucks are statistically overrepresented in accidents on the Turnpike and overly at fault in such accidents.

Of course, this is a national problem, not just a New Jersey Turnpike problem. Although truck driving no longer requires great physical strength, it does take concentration and stamina. After many hours of driving, fatigue takes its toll. Some progress was made with the passage of the Federal Truck Safety Act of 1987, which addressed the problem of trucker licensing, trucker education, and inspection of trucks; but more obviously needs to be done.

We asked Kraft about the truck-safety problem. He told us: "Many truckers are over-the-road. They drive longer distances than passenger cars. Although many of them are professionals . . . there are still many, many truckers that are not that skilled. We have seen accidents involving truck drivers who don't know what to do in the case of unusual circumstances. They don't know how to drive in the snow, for example." [29]

Like truckers, young people appear to be overrepresented in the accident statistics. Although people under twenty-one years old make up only about 3 percent of the drivers on the Turnpike, they are involved in 6.7 percent of the accidents. Engineer Kraft speculated that this disproportion is due to a combination of inexperience and aggressiveness. When these qualities are combined with unusual conditions, we have a recipe for an accident. Although such statistics are intriguing, there is little the Turnpike Authority itself can do about the problem of young people and their high accident rate. [30]

Also of interest are the statistics on out-of-state drivers. On the New Jersey Turnpike, 70 percent of the motorists are New Jerseyans, but they are involved in only 52 percent of the accidents. It is tempting to speculate that New Jersey drivers are better drivers. A more likely explanation is that they are familiar with the roadway, confident of their sense of direction, and less likely to be confused or lost. A driver preoccupied with directions and map reading, not to mention backseat drivers, is likely to be more accident-prone. Another interesting fact has to do with the age-old controversy about the relative skills of men and women drivers. Men have more accidents than women on the Turnpike by a ratio of about six to one, but the statistic may mean less than it appears since, according to Kraft, there are far more male drivers than female drivers on the Turnpike. [31]

Careful records also are kept on the time of day of accidents. During weekdays, there are more accidents on the Turnpike during commuting hours than during the rest of the day. This makes sense, but there are also more accidents during the afternoon than in the morning. People seem in less of a rush to get to work in the morning than to get home after work. This phenomenon has been compared to a horse's proverbial eagerness to return to the barn. Also, drivers are perhaps more alert early in the day than late in the day. [32]

Records are also kept correlating accidents and the days of the week. Accidents occur more on Friday than on other days because more people are on the Turnpike, leaving for the weekend. People tend to leave for the weekend in a pack on Friday, but they do not all come back on the same day. Some come back on Sunday, but others return on Monday or even later the next week. Obviously, this kind of information is useful in scheduling the work of state troopers. More of them are on duty Fridays to cope with the high traffic and accident volume.[33]

Records are also kept on alcohol-related accidents. This is a topic that gets a great deal of media attention. So, of course, does speeding. But, surprisingly, neither has much to do with accidents on the Turnpike. The main contributing factor to accidents is not dramatic: over 50 percent of all accidents on the New Jersey Turnpike are caused by inattention. It seems hard to believe, given the massive publicity in our society about drunk driving. Despite the media blitz, drunk driving is not a statistically significant cause of accidents on the Turnpike. A recent study of drivers involved in accidents there showed that out of a total of 7,038 drivers only 144 were drunk. This adds up to 2 percent, hardly a significant figure. Turnpike officials argue that this is another benefit of a toll road. When you get your ticket and when you pay your toll, you are being exposed twice to trained personnel, both of whom have two-way radios. If they suspect you are drunk, they can radio your license plate number and a description of your vehicle to the state police. Also, of course, people know the Turnpike is heavily patrolled, and thus drunk people may avoid it altogether.[34]

One more general observation: common sense would suggest that the Turnpike in South Jersey is safer than in northern New Jersey. Heading north from the Delaware Memorial Bridge, the Turnpike goes straight as an arrow through lovely, unspoiled farmland. Passing through tranquil Salem County, the Turnpike feels safe and unthreatening. The traffic is far less dense than in the north. We interviewed many patrons about their perception of safety on the Turnpike. Everybody knew that it was more dangerous in northern New Jersey.

There is only one problem with this perception: everybody is wrong! Turnpike statisticians, through patient and plodding compilation of fact, have proved the opposite. "Bo" Sullivan, chairman of the Turnpike Authority, commented: "Our accident rate, which is low, is double in South Jersey what it is in northern New Jersey. People ask, 'How can that be?' Maybe it's because you've got a very straight road with little to hold your attention. But in the north, if you're driving along the Turnpike, there is so much going on, you're pumping adrenaline just to stay on top of it. We're keeping you alert up here. Down there you're dozing."[35]

The difference between driving on the southern and northern stretches of the Turnpike may be exacerbated by the nature of today's automobiles. They are nearly silent in operation. During the day, with the air conditioning quietly humming and the windows closed, we hear no traffic noise.

With automatic transmission and power steering and cruise control, we can drive with a single finger. In the late evening, as we lean back into our plush upholstery, we may become mesmerized by the taillights up ahead, especially on the southern stretches of the Turnpike, which lack the fiery refineries, the roaring jets, and the overall drama of the northern stretches.

We now know that a dull visual scenario is narcotizing. Research has shown that prolonged vigilance is exhausting. Indeed, one of the hard-won lessons to come out of military history is that sentries on guard duty and radar operators have a tendency to fall asleep. Even in wartime, only the fear of the death penalty keeps such people awake.

We can only conclude, knowing what we now know about inattention and accidents, that if the New Jersey Turnpike were being built today, it would be different. We now know that boring stretches of road put people to sleep or hypnotize them. But that was then, and this is now. The design of the Turnpike seemed right in its time. America was the most powerful nation in the world in the 1950s, and, therefore, it believed that its values and ideas and aesthetics and even its engineering were self-evidently correct. It believed that straight roads were not only safe roads, they were American roads. Winding and picturesque roads were too European and vaguely un-American. Straight and wide roads like the New Jersey Turnpike were American (and somehow "superior") in the same way that suburban ranch houses and large cars were. It is not accidental that disillusionment with these American artifacts set in simultaneously some years later.

Over the Fence

Chapter 7

"I'm an ant; the Turnpike's an elephant"
—John Lazarczyk[1]

If, as the last chapter suggested, driving on the New Jersey Turnpike has its peculiar dangers, what of the effect of the Turnpike on those who live along-side it, its immediate neighbors? When John and Madeline Lazarczyk bought their first and only home in Milltown, New Jersey, in 1955, the Turnpike did not trouble them. Though their backyard bordered its right of way, they were hardly aware of the Turnpike, which was down below, over the hill. All they knew was that they had achieved the American dream: a house in the country. "We loved living here," the Lazarczyks say.

"Besides," says John Lazarczyk, pointing to the tree-covered hill that has always served as a buffer between his backyard and the Pike, "the Turnpike was the perfect neighbor: no obnoxious habits, no barking dogs or loud stereos. The traffic sound? You get so used to it, it's like a waterfall. Soothing." As years went by, and five children were born, the Lazarczyks added rooms to their house. "I expected to live here all my life," Lazarczyk says.

Unlike much of suburban-sprawl New Jersey, Milltown is a real town, with a real identity. Main Street is lined with neatly painted frame houses, antique stores, mom-and-pop grocery stores, and funeral parlors. As one resident puts it, Milltown is "a pocket of yesterday."[2] There are only two police cars in Milltown, car number one and car number two. Everyone in town knows that if you get past both of them, there aren't any more. Then you can go as fast as you like. Sure, the teenagers hanging out on the corner say, "There's nothing to do in Milltown," but teenagers say that everywhere.

Main Street cuts Milltown in half, with residences on either side. Half-way down Main Street is Mill Pond, where the mill that gives the town its name once stood and where kids go fishing today. Some years ago T-shirts that said "Milltown: One Square Mile of Happiness" were printed up and sold. Milltown isn't a picture book, cutesy town. It's not wealthy enough for that. But it is a town where Norman Rockwell might have felt at home. Twenty-one-year-old Jim Lukach, a friend of the Lazarczyks' daughter Nancy, writes:

> Milltown doesn't belong in the middle of one of the country's most populated areas. . . . It should be in Kansas or somewhere. It's a small town. Everybody knows everybody else's business. It's a place where you are still judged on how you once performed on the baseball field. "Oh, it's the Lukach boy. He could field but he couldn't hit worth a damn." I can even remember the names of the eighteen kids I graduated eighth grade with. . . . Milltown's a place where the Fourth of July means something. No one misses the parade, and the afternoon is ablaze with barbecues and the beer flows freely.[3]

Basically, Milltown is working-class respectable, churchgoing: the Boy Scouts, Little League, the PTA. Few of its seven thousand people think the sign at the beginning of Main Street is corny. The sign says,

WELCOME TO MILLTOWN
A FRIENDLY COMMUNITY

and the town feels friendly as you drive east along mile-long Main Street till you get to East Joffre Avenue. Though it is the last street before the Turnpike, there's no sense there could be anything menacing behind the Lazarczyks' house. East Joffre Avenue looks like any other street in a small town: trees and lawns and kids playing and adults washing cars.

In 1987, thirty-two years after they built their house, the Lazarczyks learned to their horror that the Turnpike would be widened between exits 8A and 9, bringing two trucks-only lanes 30 feet from their bedroom window. The machine was literally moving into their garden. Their home was not being condemned—although, ironically, that might have been better; in road-widening projects, those left behind, rather than those whose homes are condemned, probably endure the greater agony. "It's funny," Lazarczyk says. "The Turnpike used to send us a newsletter called *Over the Fence.* It was about what good neighbors they were—planting trees, mowing the grass. It always had a drawing of this well-dressed guy who represented the Turnpike and this pretty woman who represented your typical homeowner chatting with each other over a low, rural-looking, wooden fence. It didn't matter to me that the real fence is tall and chain link and topped with barbed wire. But it matters now that the Turnpike wants to destroy my home. What kind of neighbor is that?"

Over the Fence was a monthly, two-page Turnpike Authority newsletter sent to all property owners bordering the Pike. It was full of tips on what to do about poison ivy growing on the Turnpike fence, how to handle litter blowing off the Pike, what to do when motorists abandoned their cars and scaled the fence onto one's property. Said *Over the Fence* about such cases: "Tell the trespasser—from behind a locked door or from an inaccessible window—that the Turnpike has instructed you to tell him to go back to his vehicle and wait for aid. Also tell him you are going to call the local police to officially record his trespassing and that you are going to call the State Police." [4]

John Lazarczyk did not mention that *Over the Fence* hasn't been arriving at his house in recent years. The Turnpike suspended publication when they found it "counterproductive." Says Jean Citrino Adubato, of the Turn pike public relations office; "It backfired. We published it to reach out, to show people living alongside the Turnpike that we cared. But what the newsletter mostly did was encourage people to complain."[5]

The Lazarczyks thought long and hard about whether they could continue living on East Joffre Avenue. Their children have grown up in the house and would be brokenhearted if they moved. Many family events have taken place at the house—birthdays, christenings, and more recently, weddings. In an insecure world, 4 East Joffre Avenue is much of what the Lazarczyk family knows of roots and traditions.

But what was the alternative? Watch as the tree-covered hill between their house and the Turnpike was obliterated? Listen forever to the drill-like noise of eighteen-wheelers gunning past their house? Smell the fumes coming in through the windows? Watch as vibration cracks appeared in the foundation and then in the walls of 4 East Joffre Avenue?

When the Lazarczyks bought their house they assumed the Turnpike would never need widening. "In 1955 we'd look out our bedroom window and yell, 'There goes one,'" Lazarczyk says. "Just for fun, me and the kids would walk to the bridge [Milltown's Main Street bridge over the Turnpike, a block and a half away] and watch for a truck." But today, the Main Street bridge shakes with the unremitting stream of machinery racketing by below. Looking down from it, it's hard not to give way to fears of being swept away. And now this ambience was to become the chief feature of the Lazarczyk's backyard.

Lazarczyk is a tall, wiry man, sixty-three as this is written and on Social Security. For thirty-one years he worked two jobs: as a laboratory assistant for Dupont in Parlin, New Jersey, and as a part-time janitor at St. Peter's Catholic School in Milltown. The Lazarczyks still have three children at home, including two in school—Nancy, a student at Rutgers University, and Johnny, a student at St. Peter's.

The Turnpike is willing to compensate the Lazarczyks if they choose to move. There is a program to buy the homes of people who abut the Turnpike widening. "But they won't give me what the house is worth," Lazarczyk claims. "And they won't pay any closing costs or pay for us to move. They said they would but now they won't.[6] So the only way I can move is to buy a much smaller house." Lazarczyk feels the Turnpike is "grinding us both ways. My house is worth less because it's next to where they're going to widen the Turnpike. But it's the Turnpike I have to deal with if I want to sell my house.

"You wouldn't believe how low the appraisal came in," Lazarczyk says. He has the option not to accept the Turnpike's appraisal and get his own, with the expectation that an effort will be made to reconcile the difference between the two. But an appraisal can cost eight or nine hundred dollars. "And, besides," Lazarczyk says, "who says my appraisal will come in any higher? No matter how high, it won't be enough money to buy a house equivalent to this one.

"Everything the Turnpike tells you sounds a whole lot better than it is," Lazarczyk says. "It's all nice and legal and fine—only I don't really have any options: either I lose my house or I live alongside the Indianapolis 500. The Turnpike sweet-talks you but, when all is said and done, they're wrecking my house.

"All my life I've done the right thing, done what I was supposed to do," Lazarczyk says plaintively. "I'm no radical." Lazarczyk turns and asks, "You don't think I am, do you?" For a moment John Lazarczyk sounds like a character in John Steinbeck's *Grapes of Wrath*, a late twentieth-century Pa Joad being driven disbelievingly off his land. But then, in his characteristic way of trying to see the bright side, Lazarczyk says, "Maybe we'll stick it out. Maybe it won't be as bad as we think."

But from past experience, John Lazarczyk is not being unnecessarily alarmist when he fears that life as he has known it at 4 East Joffre Avenue has come to an end. In Edison, New Jersey, just north of Exit 9, where a similar widening took place in 1973, a meeting of citizens whose property abuts the Turnpike was called by the Township Council in 1988. "This is ridiculous," John Niemiera of Morris Avenue said at the meeting. "How would you like to get woken up every morning at 5 o'clock by the sound of trucks cranking by? When you can't go to your backyard to talk to your neighbors or have a barbecue, it's ridiculous. When I first moved into my house, you could hear birds chirping in my backyard. Now you can't hear any birds. All you hear is the roar of trucks riding by."[7]

The Edison Township Council passed a unanimous resolution calling for the New Jersey Turnpike to find the means to lower the noise produced by traffic. A noise survey conducted by the township Division of Public Health and Human Resources found decibels as high as 85, which far exceeds permissible levels. A jackhammer at 50 feet is 88 decibels. The resolution states: "The noise conditions which have been found constitute irreparable harm to the citizens of Edison Township and cannot be tolerated." At another point in the resolution, the Township Council referred to the noise as a "life threatening condition."

Township Council member George Asprocolas said the noise of traffic on the New Jersey Turnpike was the equivalent of an alarm clock ringing constantly two feet from one's ear. And, said township resident Tom Panconi,

"The backyards are 75 feet from the Turnpike," but "the sound is even deafening in front of our homes."[8] One is reminded that John Lazarczyk's bedroom window will be only 30 feet from the Turnpike when it is widened south of Exit 9.

Frank McRitchie, who lives in East Brunswick, and whose house abuts the Turnpike, says, "We never open the windows of our upstairs, which fronts on the Turnpike." In fact, the McRitchie family can no longer look out these windows. The noise was so intense, the McRitchies put panels of insulated ceiling material between the windows and the storm windows. Then they put up heavy drapes, an acoustic tile ceiling, and carpeted the floors. Before doing this "you just thought a truck was going through the bedroom," McRitchie says.[9]

John Lazarczyk is tortured by the nagging suspicion that perhaps the widening of the Turnpike isn't necessary. "Maybe they're doing it just to keep the machine going," Lazarczyk says. "You know: widen the Pike and issue bonds, widen the Pike and issue bonds. Stay in debt forever, because that's the way to keep your power. Hey, if I thought this was being done for the citizens of New Jersey, I'd accept it. But I don't believe it. I don't trust the Turnpike."

John Lazarczyk's plight is surely not unique. Whenever a family's home is threatened by eminent domain, there is a situation rife with tragedy. Of course, the Turnpike has many other neighbors besides homeowners: farmers, corporate offices, factories, refineries. And for some of these neighbors the Turnpike is not only tolerable but necessary. Newark Airport and the Meadowlands Sports Complex could barely function without the Turnpike. Thus, homeowners are a particular kind of Turnpike neighbor. For them, whether the Turnpike operates in the citizens' interests or has a life of its own has a special poignancy.

Certainly, today, the Turnpike is less free to do what it wishes than in its early years. At that time, environmental impact statements and public hearings had not yet become routine. For example, it is unlikely that, if the Turnpike were being built now, it would be allowed to bisect Elizabeth the way it does. The Turnpike Authority may not have had any alternative but to go through Elizabeth, but, today, this might mean that the Turnpike would not be built at all. Elizabeth, like most New Jersey cities, is in deep trouble, but what is unique to Elizabeth is that the Turnpike divides the city in two, making community building doubly difficult. Just as Robert Moses' pet projects in the Bronx, the Cross Bronx Expressway and the Bronx River Parkway, destroyed viable Bronx neighborhoods one by one, so the New Jersey Turnpike carved up Elizabeth into a series of zones instead of neighborhoods. As one commentator has written: "If the turnpike has cut the heart out of any town, it's Elizabeth, where some 240 homes and businesses were bought out to make room for the road, more than any other town." Other Elizabeth property owners stayed where they were:

> Some 500 homes and small stores are left standing along the border of the turnpike—box seats to the thump and hum and whizzing that wracks the nerves of all but those who live with it, those steely folks who say they can't sleep when a rare blizzard shuts the highway down and stills the night.
> The highway runs hard past Patrick Romero's three-story house on Atlantic Street, Elizabeth, which stands 20 feet from the highway and shakes like an earthquake at least three times a day.[10]

One wonders what sentiments toward the Turnpike are likely to be in Elizabeth once the new widening project is completed. Perhaps Elizabeth is too far gone for it to matter. In 1986, chairman of the Turnpike Authority, "Bo" Sullivan, and the mayor of Elizabeth, Tom Dunn, issued a joint statement indicating they were in total agreement with the Turnpike's plans to increase its size from twelve to fourteen lanes through Elizabeth.[11]

Still, the current widening project does seem to offer something to Elizabeth that was not planned when the Turnpike was first built through that city. The project calls for 11 miles of noise barriers between the Turnpike and homes in Elizabeth as well as homes all the way south to Woodbridge. And north of Elizabeth, the projected widening cannot be accomplished without cleaning up thirty-six toxic-waste dumps and eleven landfills that surround the Turnpike in the Meadowlands. Ironically, the widening may prove to be an environmental boon for the northern reaches of the Turnpike.[12]

If the Turnpike currently exhibits some sensitivity to the needs of its neighbors, this is largely due to the battle royale it engaged in with certain citizens of East Brunswick back in the early seventies. Prior to this time, the Turnpike had never experienced major opposition from homeowners whose property flanked the Turnpike. This is nowhere better illustrated than in Arthur Warren Meixner's doctoral dissertation on the early years of the Turnpike Authority, in which, even in the chapter on pressure groups, there is no mention of neighbors as a force with which the Turnpike had to contend.[13] It took the Vietnam War, Watergate, ethnic agitation, the environmental movement, and the consumers movement to awaken such activism.

One of the most concerted efforts to stop the Turnpike's efforts at expansion took place between 1971 and 1973, when the Concerned Citizens of East Brunswick (hereafter abbreviated as CCEB) endeavored to halt efforts to expand the Turnpike from six to twelve lanes along the 6-mile stretch bordering East Brunswick north of Exit 9. The Concerned Citizens of East Brunswick stopped the Turnpike only temporarily, but they forced concessions that have become the rule in Turnpike widenings ever since. William Flanagan, recently retired executive director of the Turnpike, admits that the prolonged altercation between the Turnpike and the CCEB "was the turning point. The environment became the key issue in any Turnpike expansion. We began factoring in that gaining clearances for a project would take us longer than the project itself." [14]

In 1971 the Turnpike was prepared to take from East Brunswick property owners what it thought it needed to expand, with no concern for the environment and with little or no compensation for homeowners gravely affected. The Authority planned no public hearings on the widening. Under the principle of eminent domain, the Authority saw itself as having the right to take those portions of homeowners' property it needed, compensating them only for the purported value of their land, but in no way for the extraordinary injury to the quality of their lives. Thus, half a citizen's backyard might be taken, but there would be no compensation for the fact that he or she now had only half a yard and that, in the other half, trucks were racketing by.

A national publication that fosters mass transit learned of the Turnpike's plans and was so incensed that it published a page-length cartoon showing the Authority as a monster striding over East Brunswick citizens. It was captioned, "The Totalitarian Giant Trying to Stamp Out . . . Rights." The accompanying article said:

> The N.J. Turnpike says "we must widen in East Brunswick to 12 lanes." Meanwhile, about a couple of dozen private homes must go and the Turnpike will be moved to the backyard of others. A citizens committee has been fighting (unsuccessfully) to stop the expansion. Just as the Turnpike Giant has stepped all over the bus driver and bus rider for years, it is now doing so to private citizens—backed up as usual by New Jersey's Governor. There is no real due process when dealing with the Turnpike.
>
> Of course, the answer to traffic congestion is not more and more roads and additional traffic lanes, which only attract more automobiles. The answer is to RESTRICT THE USE OF THE PRIVATE CAR and give special right of ways to mass transit vehicles. Something the Turnpike can't understand because they are 25 years behind the times we live in. [15]

The CCEB was a grass-roots organization—mothers with baby carriages, senior citizens—whose primary organizer was Emily Alman, then a professor of sociology, now an attorney. "You have to understand that our people were basically conservative," says Alman, who has been described as having "an overdeveloped sense of justice." [16]

Some of them had lived alongside the Turnpike for years and accepted it as a fact of life. They'd scream at you only a few feet away, *"The Turnpike hasn't affected my hearing!"* when it was clear they were near deaf. One man only joined us after an eighteen-wheeler rolled off the Turnpike into his backyard. Our people had watched years of students demonstrating, blacks demonstrating, antiwar activists demonstrating, and now they thought, "We've got a reason to demonstrate too." Here was an issue they cared passionately about: their homes. And it was clear to them that the Turnpike didn't give a damn about their homes. The Turnpike radicalized our people. They had been middle-class, Silent Majority types. The Turnpike turned them into environmental warriors. Pretty soon they knew all about lead in the blood; they knew all about the connection between heart attacks and noise. The Turnpike had always said, "We don't make noise; trucks make noise." Our people didn't buy that kind of talk anymore. One woman put on her dead husband's World War II army uniform and marched to our rally shouldering a rifle. Others, when the Turnpike arrived to take borings on their property—this was news to them, that the Turnpike could come onto their property and, without their permission, take borings—put up American flags around their property and signs saying "OCCUPIED TERRITORY." [17]

What made the efforts of the CCEB especially poignant was that they were carried on in the very shadow of the Turnpike Authority at Exit 9. From the windows of their headquarters Turnpike officials could scan with binoculars CCEB rallies on the other side of the Pike. Emily Alman felt the Turnpike did more than just observe the activities of the CCEB. "For some days, CCEB officers were shadowed wherever they went by a black van. Then, when our family was away overnight, a vehicle crashed into our house. The neighbors heard it, but it was too dark to see who it was. The Turnpike was clearly trying to scare us. We didn't imagine this! We're talking terrorism here."

At one point, Alman went out onto the Route 18 bridge over the Turnpike to take some photographs for an upcoming meeting with then Governor Cahill that would follow a motorcade to Trenton. Suddenly, she was

startled by a disembodied sound. "GET OFF THAT BRIDGE!" It sounded like God. I couldn't tell where it was coming from, but I knew they could see me from the headquarters building. I felt like a character in George Orwell's *1984.* Then several state police cars converged from different directions. "No pictures of the Turnpike," the cops yelled. That was before I became a lawyer and learned to read the fine print. The rules didn't say you can't take pictures *of* the Turnpike; they said you can't take pictures *on* the Turnpike—which is bad enough.

The day before the meeting with the governor, the *New Brunswick Home News* had an editorial that argued, "This is not a political issue— Democrat and Republican alike will be poorly served and adversely affected by a transportation system that—like Topsy—just grows."[18] At the meeting that took place in Governor Cahill's office on June 2, 1971, the CCEB inquired why the state refused to consider widening U.S. Route 1, which does not pass through residential areas, instead of the Turnpike. The state commissioner of transportation, who was attending the meeting, exclaimed, according to Emily Alman, "Why, we couldn't do that. It would take away revenues from the Turnpike."

But, ironically, the federal government would have helped to pay for a Route 1 widening, whereas it would not contribute to a Turnpike widening because the Turnpike is a toll road and, as such, is ineligible for Federal Highway Trust Funds. Alman wrote to Ann Klein, then a New Jersey State assemblywoman from Morris County: "Toll roads are a double tax on the citizens of this state. We all pay enormous sums into the Federal Highway Trust Funds [predominantly gasoline taxes] and have a right to expect that any road building that does take place be paid at least in part by Federal funds."[19] The CCEB also learned to its dismay at this meeting that, as a state toll road, the New Jersey Turnpike thought it was immune from federal environmental and historic preservation regulations—which could explain why the Turnpike has been so insensitive on these questions.

One of the major causes animating the Concerned Citizens of East Brunswick was saving the Lilac Hill Mill House, a historic site that had long given character to an otherwise suburban neighborhood. The Turnpike's plan was to demolish Lilac Hill by running one of its ramps right through it. "Would you believe?" Alman says today. "At meetings the Turnpike boasted that it always ran its roadbed in a straight line—as if this was a sign of character or something. And now they were saying there was no way they could build these ramps—which, after all, were going to intrude far more into our neighborhood than the roadbed—except through Lilac Hill, when Lilac Hill wasn't the most direct route. There were lots of alternatives; they just didn't want to consider them. We couldn't help believing that people in high places would have their pockets lined if the ramp came through Lilac Hill."

We asked Alman if she meant that literally.

"You must be joking," she said. "We're talking the most basic form of corruption here."[20] Alman told us that during the years of altercations between the Concerned Citizens and the Turnpike she received many letters from Turnpike employees who wrote to her anonymously. "Several of them referred to the Turnpike as 'the Ermine Road,'" Alman said. "The New Jersey Turnpike costs more per mile than any road in history and," Alman continued, "gives the people less. They're so cheap they won't spend a cent more than they have to because they have to take care of their own. The Turnpike is like a family business."

Getting nowhere with the Turnpike in its efforts to save Lilac Hill, the Concerned Citizens applied for state historical status. This was obtained just in time; demolition equipment had already arrived at the site. But CCEB's joy at stopping the annihilation of Lilac Hill was short-lived. A few weeks later there was a suspicious fire at Lilac Hill. Luckily, it sputtered out. Then, one night, Lilac Hill burned to the ground. It was the night of the Fireman's Ball—no coincidence, Alman feels.

Nevertheless, Alman says, "We slowed the bastards down." CCEB collected funds, hired attorneys, and took the Turnpike to court. Its motto: "Stop them at the Raritan." Leonard Weinglass, of Chicago Seven fame, signed on as one of their attorneys, bringing with him considerable press attention. Said Peter Berger, another of CCEB's attorneys, at a public meeting, "Rather than become a pioneer in environmental protection, as they [the Turnpike] have in road design, they will be forced to do it heel first." [21]

But court action was something the CCEB turned to only after trying to reach an accommodation with the Turnpike. CCEB asked for earthern berms, for noise barriers. They suggested alternate routes for the ramps. They asked that the trucks-only lanes be built on the inside of the Turnpike, keeping them farther from residences. The CCEB hired noise and pollution consultants—all to no avail. The attitude of the Turnpike was, according to Alman, "We will tell you what we're going to do and when we are going to do it. It isn't your affair what the Turnpike does or does not do."

This attitude predominated at the first of many confrontations between the CCEB and the Turnpike Authority. The Concerned Citizens heard that a commissioners meeting had been called at Turnpike headquarters to discuss the widening in the East Brunswick area. They decided to attend. Not knowing how to gain entrance, a group of the Concerned Citizens entered the lobby of the Authority building. They were stopped and told they could not attend the meeting. While they milled about, uncertain what to do, another group of CCEB members mistakenly entered on a lower level, took the elevator to the top floor, and suddenly found themselves just outside the meeting room.

The commission barred them from the room. "Where are your badges?" they were asked. The CCEB knew nothing of badges, of the elaborate procedures visitors to the Turnpike Authority must follow if they wish to gain entrance. As far as the Concerned Citizens knew, this was a public meeting of a public body, and any citizen could attend. They had no idea that the Turnpike Authority functions almost as a state within a state, patterning itself more after the military than civilian government. This was at a time prior to sunshine-law, open-meeting procedures. From the Turnpike Authority's point of view, the CCEB were trespassers and a security risk. The Concerned Citizens sat down in the hall and refused to move. They also sent emissaries to the lobby, gathered up the members detained there, and spirited them into the elevators and up to the meeting before the receptionists could stop them.

In this bitter confrontation, the CCEB discovered that the Turnpike Authority was unaccustomed to submitting its ideas to public scrutiny. This was the first time it had ever been challenged. Eve Shapiro, then an East Brunswick councilwoman, later said with regard to the Turnpike Authority's attitude toward the Concerned Citizens, "What right do a group of men have to sit in an air-conditioned, sound-proof building beyond effective citizen control and impose this invisible umbrella of death on us?"[22]

As it turned out, the attitude of the Turnpike Authority toward the Concerned Citizens rallied public support. "FOR WHOM THE TURNPIKE TOLLS," screamed a headline in a local paper,[23] suggesting, as does John Donne's poem, that the Turnpike "tolls" in more than one way for all of us. Said an editorial in another newspaper, the CCEB "have won something for all of us. . . . They have made Turnpike officials look up from drawing boards to see the people instead of just cars."[24] And the *New York Daily News* chorused, "Today, a new era dawned for environmentalists."[25]

Former governor Alfred Driscoll, then chairman of the Turnpike Commission, was flabbergasted by the attitude of the Concerned Citizens, enraged that anyone would challenge the Turnpike. He was extremely proud of the Turnpike, saw it as a noble project that had been built under his stewardship in record time against all obstacles. He later told Emily Alman: "Until this day, we enjoyed the reputation as the best road in America. You have ruined that."

From the Authority's point of view, road expansion was ipso facto good. Anyone who opposed it was either crazy or un-American. Driscoll was quoted in the *New Brunswick Home News* as saying that those who protested the Turnpike widening were "rendering a disservice" to the public. Driscoll saw widening the Turnpike as natural; stopping it, "as difficult an objective as stopping Detroit from manufacturing motor cars."[26] The Turnpike Authority even invoked the name of the deity to support its plans. Says Alman, "Flanagan [the executive director] was forever saying things like, 'God created New Jersey as the corridor between New York on the one hand and Philadelphia, Delaware, and the South on the other, and it is the mission of the New Jersey Turnpike to serve that God-given responsibility."

The protests of the CCEB were now getting so much press that the Turnpike Authority reluctantly agreed to participate in a public meeting in the

East Brunswick High School on May 19, 1971. Eight hundred and fifty citizens turned out for the meeting. The Turnpike Authority presented evidence that the widening was not only necessary but would be an environmental plus for the community. The Authority offered the testimony of expert witnesses who claimed that widening the Turnpike would actually lessen noise and air pollution. Emily Alman countered with a CCEB position paper that included these remarks:

> For those members of the community living near or adjacent to the Turnpike, there has not been a reduction in noise pollution—there has in fact been an ever increasing din. For those people north of the Raritan who have already experienced the "benefits" of Turnpike expansion, there has been no relief from noise and air pollution. If in fact the Turnpike experts are prepared through new technological improvements to reduce air and noise pollution, then we believe that they should immediately institute all of these reforms on the existing road. The Turnpike Authority has had approximately 23 years to demonstrate its sensitivity to the human needs of its host communities. It has had 23 years in which to plant barrier trees, search for noise deterrents, beautify and improve its highway system so as to guarantee a maximum of health and safety to its host communities. A drive north of the Raritan suggests that few, if any, trees have been planted; that the 23 year lush growth which might have protected the communities is nonexistent, and that nothing has been done to relieve the human hardships and health hazards experienced by the host community.

As a following to the May 19 meeting, Diana Grignon of the CCEB sent a letter to the *East Brunswick Spokesman* in which she wrote: "The New Jersey Turnpike . . . [says] there is no immediate need for more lanes. . . . They have stated that the reasoning behind the further expansion is to eliminate a 4 to 10 minute delay at Interchange 9. Is the saving in time worth destroying homes, promoting deafness, polluting the air, and destroying our greenery?"[27]

Eventually, the CCEB was able to exact a $5 million environmental package out of the Turnpike Authority as a compromise solution. The Authority agreed to include sound barriers, earthern berms, and a bridge providing access to the neighborhood. The CCEB wanted more, but with their forces dissipating, they settled out of court.

"That was a mistake," Alman says.

> The Turnpike is vengeful and unforgiving. Challenge them and they'll be your enemy forever. We had to put up all the sound barriers and earthern berms on our property, not theirs. And we had to hire the contractors to do it. There's a spot where our berm approaches their berm and there's an opening between

them which creates a roaring tunnel of sound. The only place to connect the berms is on their property. To this day [1988] they refuse to do it. We have $120,000 in the bank for this purpose and can't spend it.

The fact is, over the next six to eight years the Turnpike reneged on most of the deal. They whittled the agreement down, found loopholes for not doing what they had promised. They kept taking us to court, kept wearing us down. They even took us to court over some small print which said that because of our agreement we were not allowed to speak publicly about any issue concerning the Turnpike. Unbelievable. It's like those guys had never heard of the First Amendment. We put out this release to the press: "New Jersey Turnpike Try at Silencing Citizens Group Termed Fit for Totalitarian States, Not U.S.A."[28]

But over the years our people got tired. They forgot the terms of the agreement. There was nobody holding the Turnpike's feet to the fire, because we were doing this in our spare time. Any money we spent was our money. But the Turnpike has unlimited funds from their toll collections. (That really galled us: every time any of us used the Pike we were paying their legal expenses.) The Turnpike could afford to fight us forever. Some of our people moved away or died. But the Turnpike endureth forever. It's immortal. It'll just wait you out and, eventually, you give up.

That was what John Lazarczyk was thinking now, in late 1988, as he stood looking out the back window of 4 East Joffre Avenue in Milltown: that eventually you give up. Throughout 1987 Lazarczyk had led a fight of neighbors to stop the widening. But by early 1988 he discovered that for his home to remain eligible for purchase by the Turnpike, he had to sign an agreement that says in part: "As consideration for the above, the homeowner shall not institute any action at law or equity, any administrative proceeding, or any arbitration proceeding the purpose of which is to block, delay, impede or limit construction of the project, nor shall the homeowner support any other person or entity which institutes any such proceeding."[29]

So Lazarczyk had quit fighting. He couldn't risk losing his chance to sell his home to the Turnpike. He had a year, and the year wasn't up yet. He wanted to think about it some more.

But who was that out on the hillside today, just beyond the Turnpike fence? Surveyors? And what were those guys doing out there just beyond the fence with their mallets and wooden stakes and orange plastic markers? How soon before the bulldozers arrived? Could they really just obliterate the hill and turn it into traffic lanes?

"I always liked it here," Lazarczyk said wistfully. "This is my home. Guys like me reach a certain age and they start thinking about going to live in Florida. Not me. I expected to live here my whole life. I expected to die here. But now? Now I just don't know."

Rest Area Culture

Chapter

8

"I don't want a Jersey Turnpike rest area named after me."
—Calvin Trillin [1]

"Do you know who Walt Whitman was?" We were at the Walt Whitman Rest Area on the Turnpike, milepost 30.2 on the southbound side, between Exits 3 and 4, and we were talking with a waitress in the Roy Rogers.

"Who?" Chris Sanial, a seventeen-year-old high school senior asked.

"Walt Whitman."

"Who's he?"

"That's what we're asking you. Do you know who Walt Whitman was?"

"Never heard of him."

"What do you mean, you've never heard of him? Of course you've heard of him. You've been working here a year, and this is the Walt Whitman Rest Area."

"It is?"

We thought she was kidding us, but as Chris explained, "When I came to work here a year ago they told me to answer the phone 'Marriot Corporation, Highway Division, 3-S.' How would I know this is the Walt Whitman Rest Area?"

As it turns out, the only way the public knows that the rest area at milepost 30.2 on the south side of the Turnpike is the Walt Whitman Rest Area is that there are signs out on the Turnpike telling the motorists they are approaching the Walt Whitman Rest Area. Nothing in the rest area itself indicates that it is named after America's greatest poet. And since Chris doesn't travel to work via the Turnpike but, rather, drives to the back gate of the rest area, parks in the employee lot, and walks into the concession building, it is possible she *could* work a whole year in the Roy Rogers and never know that this was the Walt Whitman Rest Area.

Chris wasn't alone. We asked the manager of the Roy Rogers if he knew who Walt Whitman was and he said, "Walt Whitman? Never heard of the dude."

We wondered how the good gray poet would feel about the honor of having a rest area named after him when it turns out that the people working in the rest area not only do not know who Walt Whitman was, they never heard of him. Of course, they have other recognition problems to deal with. The manager of the Roy Rogers told us: "A man came in the other day off the Pike and said he was Jesus Christ. Okay, that was his business. Then he started calling all the waitresses 'Babylonian whores.' I phoned the state police, but by the time they got here he was back on the Pike driving."

As we shall see, patrons approaching rest areas who see the signs don't score dramatically higher on the Turnpike honoree recognition meter. A rest area is a pit stop where one eats, eliminates, fills one's gas tank, and is gone. There aren't supposed to be any surprises, any deviations. A rest area is orderly, linear, and predictable. Like a hospital or a police station, it never closes. It is a 24-hour-a-day, 365-day-of-the-year operation. If the patron cannot tell one rest area from another, if rest areas are so uniform that a sexually ambiguous nineteenth-century American poet is honored in the same way as a meat-and-potatoes, garrulous World War II admiral named William F. "Bull" Halsey (for whom the rest area at milepost 101.7 is named), so be it. The Turnpike isn't in the education business.

Still, since motorists must move at such a fast pace on the Turnpike—they cannot, as on a country road, stop under a tree or smell a flower—the rest areas offer the only opportunity for a few contemplative or philosophical moments or, at least, to be stationary. The Turnpike has no place else with any pretense to civilization or culture. For better or worse, the rest area is the descendant of the old wayside inns of stagecoach days. While doing the research for this book, we spent considerable time in the rest areas, where we often paused to think about the Turnpike and its meaning.

The uniformity of the rest areas dictates that one's experience of them depends on what one brings to them. That and the weather, the time of the year. For example, the Molly Pitcher Rest Area at about 2:00 P.M. on a lovely summer day in late July . . .

The motorist pulls up to a nicely landscaped building. Around the building are artistically arranged boulders, shrubs, and foundation plantings. There is a flower garden in a circle out front. Over to the side is a cluster of outdoor picnic tables behind the snack bar. There is a broad lawn, carefully mowed, with a number of mature shade trees. The building is handsome enough, at least today in this sunshine, to be the information center of a national park. A large Puerto Rican family picnics on the bit of lawn underneath a small shade tree. They are talking and laughing and passing around a bottle of wine. In the distance one hears the quiet puttering of a little orange tractor pulling a large lawnmower. The driver of the lawnmower, wearing a blue baseball cap, waves to a fellow employee as he passes by. In the parking lot, a French-Canadian family is having a picnic off the tailgate of their big Buick station wagon. The parking lot is very clean. At 2:05 P.M. a crew of three teenage boys dressed in white have just completed their hourly sweep of the parking lot. Each of them carries a large plastic bag.

They do a pretty good job—missing only a couple of apple cores and one Seven-Up can. But you have to look hard to spot what they have missed. The scene is peaceful and tranquil—the social order marred only by a menacing black stretch limousine with New York plates illegally parked next to the door of the restaurant, even though the curb is clearly painted yellow.

Inside the restaurant at the Molly Pitcher wood-paneled walls are covered with western prints: a portrait of a cowboy with a ten-gallon hat and a red bandanna, a portrait of another cowboy in a sheepskin coat repairing a barbed-wire fence. Maybe this is Wyoming, not New Jersey. It's such a nice day, though, that these cultural incongruities don't matter. Nor does the fact that the wood paneling turns out to be Formica. Nor that the hanging plants aren't real. Who cares? A Coke on a day like this tastes great wherever you drink it.

In January, as the same motorist approaches the Molly Pitcher, red neon signs mounted on an overhead bridge flash incessantly: "SLOW AHEAD / ICE SNOW." The signs may not be necessary; the shoulder of the Turnpike, resembling a battlefield littered with disabled machines of war, is warning enough. Over to the right a jackknifed rig is piled onto the steel footings of an overhead highway sign. To the left, a shiny black Ford Bronco with extra chrome trim sits helplessly athwart the steel guardrail, none of its four tires touching ground.

Otherwise, the scene is totally white, with no horizon, the road and sky merging somewhere. Everybody is driving slowly, nobody wanting to join the beached cripples along the shoulders. Headlights on. No tailgating. It's 9:00 A.M., and the snow is still coming down. Progress is extra slow because just ahead are a team of snowplows, yellow lights flashing, shrouded in snow and moving in a stately procession. One wishes a painter from the Ashcan School, maybe John Sloan, could capture the scene.

This kind of driving is stressful, so the motorist pulls off the Turnpike into the Molly Pitcher Rest Area. The ramp is plowed and sanded, but the parking lot hasn't been touched. Knowing where to park is difficult. The parking lines are hidden under the deeply rutted snow, and vehicles are parked every which way. Since it is 15 degrees outside, no one stops to buy a newspaper from the half dozen vending machines outside the building. The trash cans are stuffed with empty bags of take-out food wrappers; no one wants to venture outside to empty trash cans this morning. Just outside the double glass doors of the lobby is a handcart with a half-empty white paper sack that says, "CALCIUM CHLORIDE 80 LBS" and a cardboard drum of "ATOMIC ICE MELTER PELLETS." The parking lot is a mess, but the sidewalks are clear.

Inside the building the red tile floor is wet from the melting snow people track in, though there are few customers.

The Roy Rogers manager is not happy with the Turnpike's delay in plowing his lot. He explains: "In the summer we take in $140,000 a week. Now we're down to next to nothing. The Turnpike doesn't care though; they get plenty of rent from us."

Meanwhile, the help tries to look busy. With so few people on the road, there isn't much to do. It's too late for breakfast and too early for lunch. One young woman makes a show of wiping off the Formica counter of the "Fixin's Bar" even though it is already spotless. The row of artificial hanging plants swing against the glass windows as, outside, a chain of tractor-trailers drive slowly by in the snow.

The New Jersey Turnpike has thirteen rest areas (plus a trucks-only rest area about to be built), and they are all named for famous New Jerseyans or for Americans who made a contribution to history while in New Jersey. Moving south to north, the rest areas are the Clara Barton, John Fenwick, Walt Whitman, James Fenimore Cooper, Richard Stockton, Woodrow Wilson, Molly Pitcher, Joyce Kilmer, Thomas Edison, Grover Cleveland, William Halsey, Alexander Hamilton, and Vince Lombardi. Wherever possible, the rest areas are near the homes or New Jersey connections of the honorees. Thus, the Halsey rest area is near Elizabeth, where Halsey was born.

One may quibble with some of the honoree choices. For example, other than being born in Burlington, New Jersey, James Fenimore Cooper is utterly identified with places other than New Jersey, principally upstate New York. And is John Fenwick, a founder of Salem County and a member of the Assembly of West Jersey, really among the thirteen most distinguished people to be associated with New Jersey over the centuries? Still, when one considers that most turnpikes do not name their rest areas after anyone (the rest areas on the Massachusetts Turnpike, for example, are designated by the name of the nearest town or city), the New Jersey Turnpike might be thought of as being in the vanguard.[2]

But if the intentions of the Turnpike Authority in naming rest areas for famous New Jerseyans are commendable, they have been less than successful in properly honoring the thirteen. The rest areas are virtually indistinguishable from one another. Besides the Vince Lombardi rest area, where there is a small museum of Lombardi memorabilia, there are no paintings, busts, plaques, brochures, or anything else to inform the public about the honorees. And the Lombardi "museum"—two large showcases—is strange because Lombardi's only identification with New Jersey is that he once coached a New Jersey high school football team. Is it indicative of the Turnpike's values that the only great "New Jerseyan" for whom a minimuseum has been created was a football player and coach?

Other than the Vince Lombardi, the rest areas are utterly bland and identical and franchised. Some have a Roy Rogers *and* a Bob's Big Boy, others just have a Roy Rogers. Otherwise, it is virtually impossible to tell one rest area from another up and down the Turnpike. Nothing about them—the food, the decor—suggests anything regional, anything about New Jersey. For all motorists know, once inside the concession building they could be in Alaska or Texas or Maine. Some of the rest areas, until recently, had a picture of the honoree. For example, there was a picture of Grover Cleveland in the Cleveland rest area when Roy Rogers took over as concessionaire a few years ago. The painting, says the Turnpike Authority, was "not in keeping with the new decor."[3] Now patrons of the restaurant are familiar with the visage of Roy Rogers and his maxims ("Happy trails" and the like) but not with Grover Cleveland. In time, we suspect, young patrons will come to think Roy Rogers *is* Grover Cleveland.

The blandness and uniformity of the rest areas has more than once occasioned joking in the media. David Letterman, the television talk show host, often does a "top ten" listing. On his March 12, 1987, show he offered a list of the "top ten rest areas on the New Jersey Turnpike." What Letterman was implying, of course, is that Turnpike rest areas are so dull and undistinguished that making a top ten list (even a top one list) is an exercise in the absurd.

Calvin Trillin insists he wouldn't want a New Jersey Turnpike rest area named after him:

> In my constant search for an honor I might decline, I have decided that I don't want a service area on the New Jersey Turnpike named after me. I hasten to add that nobody has suggested naming a service area on the New Jersey Turnpike after me. I just think it makes things easier for all concerned to take myself out of the running early in the game. . . .
>
> Still, you never can tell. The Turnpike Authority might decide to name one service area after an ordinary driver—perhaps the driver whose children asked to stop at the most service area restrooms on a single journey between the Holland Tunnel and the Delaware Memorial Bridge. . . .
>
> Without meaning to seem ungrateful, I'd have to say that having a service area named after you does not strike me as a completely ennobling experience. For instance, I could envision friends of mine going miles out of their way to

stop at my service area so they could complain about the staleness of my hamburger buns. The only one of the present honorees who may deserve such treatment is Joyce Kilmer, and surely the punishment for bad poetry should stop short of transforming the poet into a reststop. . . .[4]

I'd like to think that a young poet named Kilmer kept turning out verse bad enough to embarrass the state, despite warnings that if he persisted, the authorities would officially give him a girl's name. (Until then, his name had been Chuck Kilmer.) Even after the name change, he insisted on publishing the poem that began "I think that I shall never see a poem lovely as a tree." A week later, he received a letter from the Turnpike Authority that said, in its entirety, "Your place will be forever hence the place they stop to use the gents." If I'd been him, I would have declined.[5]

Philip Roth has written in a similar vein in *The Counterlife:*

"If you're from New Jersey," Nathan had said, "and you write thirty books, and you win the Nobel Prize, and you live to be white-haired and ninety-five, it's highly unlikely but not impossible that after your death they'll decide to name a rest stop for you on the Jersey Turnpike. And so, long after you're gone, you may indeed be remembered but mostly by small children, in the backs of cars, when they lean forward and tell their parents, 'Stop, please, stop at Zuckerman—I have to make a pee.' For a New Jersey novelist that's as much immortality as it's realistic to hope for."[6]

Typically, rest areas on the Turnpike are a broad expanse of blacktop filled with cars, a concession building with rest rooms, a grassy area behind or to the side of the concession building, an automotive area where gas is sold and minor repairs can be accomplished—and that's about it. The automotive and food concessions charge a premium price to the patron. Thus, at the time this was written, a large roast beef sandwich and an 8-ounce milk container consumed in a Roy Rogers on the Turnpike cost $3.50, whereas off the Turnpike they cost $3.05. A 32-ounce soda costs 99 cents at the Roy Rogers in Newark, $1.49 at any of the Roy Rogers on the Turnpike.[7]

Similarly, whereas regular unleaded gas at this writing costs, on average, 87.9 cents a gallon off the Turnpike, on the Turnpike it costs 99.9. We asked why and found, to our surprise, that the Turnpike Authority not only charges rent to its concessions, but also receives a percentage of the take. By doing so, of course, it passes along extra costs to Turnpike patrons, who have no choice but to use Turnpike services while on the Turnpike, and if they decide to exit to seek these services, will have to pay a premium on their toll tickets. So patrons are, in a sense, captives of the Turnpike.

The Turnpike has the authority to control pricing in the concession areas, as well as to control the kind and quality of food and merchandise offered. Thus, it would be perfectly possible for the Turnpike Authority to insist that gift shops offer New Jersey's finest products instead of the Hong Kong–manufactured, world-class kitsch one finds there. New Jersey's infant wine industry could receive support in gift shops, as could the state's famed fine china industry. The state's craftspeople might have an outlet for their wares, bringing financial support to them and honor to the state. Garden State vegetables might be sold, as produce is at the farmers' markets found at some New York State Thruway rest areas and, even, on New Jersey's own Atlantic City Expressway. Nourishing food, including typical New Jersey cuisine, could also be offered in the restaurants instead of, or in addition to, the fast food that nutritionists increasingly tell us is less than healthy.

It is interesting what the Turnpike provides the patron and what it does not. Rest areas commonly have video game rooms (despite the signs posted everywhere saying "NO LOITERING"), but no mailboxes. Indeed, it is impossible to mail a letter the entire length of the Turnpike, though stamps are sold (at a premium, of course) just outside the rest area gift shops, where postcards are also sold. Thus, one can, if one wishes, play games such as Kung Fu Master, Ms. Pac Man, Spy Hunter, and Contra (with its pictures of Rambo-like figures in Central American jungles), but one cannot find out anything about the history or geography of the region through which one is passing.

Sporadically, the Turnpike makes an effort to acquaint the motorist with New Jersey's heritage. Prodded by Governor Brendan Byrne in the late 1970s to promote the "positive benefits" of New Jersey, the Turnpike published a brochure listing places of interest within easy access of the Turnpike.[8] And recently "New Jersey and You" stands were placed in all rest areas, full of brochures and maps and general tourist literature of high quality. For some reason, however, these stands are always kept in the garage offices, where virtually no one goes, instead of in the lobbies, through which pass almost all of those stopping at rest areas.

Every rest area has a "Bio-Rhythm" machine in its lobby. You would probably never waste your time or money on a Bio-Rhythm machine in a shopping mall or a supermarket; there are too many other, more interesting diversions. But driving along the Turnpike is an exercise in sensory deprivation. By the time you pull off the roadway into a rest area, you are desperate for a little action. Anything is better than immediately getting back into your car and staring at the white lines again. So the Bio-Rhythm machine is as welcome to the Turnpike traveler as a canteen of fresh water to a traveler in the desert. Here at last is something that not only holds a promise of being interesting; it is a small but significant opportunity to reassert your individuality.

You put a quarter into the Bio-Rhythm machine and punch in your date of birth and the "desired graph date" (no indication as to what that is). The machine then promises to give you information on "Luck, Romance, Creativity, Health, Sex, Drive, Endurance, Finance, Friendship, and Leisure Plans," based on what, it does not state—perhaps your stars. Contrary to the implications of the machine's name, your blood pressure, pulse, and breathing rate are not taken. You might conclude from the ubiquitous presence of the Bio-Rhythm machine in the lobby of each rest area (in the Vince Lombardi there are two machines, one on either side of the memorabilia cases) that the New Jersey Turnpike Authority is high on the merits of astrology.

One of us tried the Bio-Rhythm machine and absolutely nothing happened—which was none too good for the ego. Trying it in another rest area, the quarter went in and the machine began to make its little whirring noises and squeaks. Eventually, a card came out giving high marks in the categories of "Creativity" and "Finance" but, alas, low marks in "Romance" and "Sex."

The presence of the Bio-Rhythm machines and video arcades contrasts markedly with the signs on the door at the entrance to the concession buildings at each rest area. These are unwelcoming to say the least. The doors feature a long list of the things you are not to do. You are not to "solicit." You are not to "loiter." You are not to try to "sell" anything. You may not enter "without shoes and shirt." One appreciates the Turnpike's concern for propriety but, still, wonders just what its definition of the term *loitering* is. Playing Kung Fu Master or the Bio-Rhythm machine is not loitering, but lying on the grass outside, reading a newspaper, or just loafing is? Also, we find it curious that one is required to be shod when entering the concession building, when people are invariably more careful what they step in when barefoot or in their stocking feet than when they have shoes on, something the Japanese have known for centuries. But, of course, the Turnpike is not alone among American institutions in insisting that its patrons wear shoes.

The rest areas also have Traveler's Valet cases at the entrance to the men's rooms, which vend a variety of useless objects—disguises, self-winding go-go mice, friends-and-lovers key chain sets, and tiny telescopes—though they also offer nail clippers and Alka Seltzer. An identical case is found at the entrance to the women's rooms, except that it is called "The Maid" instead of "Traveler's Valet."

Some of the rest areas also have machines that vend decals and little placards that say such things as "Happiness Can't Buy Money," "Teenager's Room—Keep Out," "I Don't Get Mad, I Get Even," and "What Did I Do?"

There is nothing wrong with these amusements if indeed they amuse. And one could celebrate the world-class kitsch available in the rest areas if one were of such a mind. The Turnpike, however, almost seems to have striven for mediocrity in the rest area experience offered. With all travel and tourist literature safely hidden, and with nothing whatsoever in evidence about the person the rest area purports to honor, the Turnpike evidently does not consider education one of its responsibilities.

"Couldn't they at least give everyone a copy of 'Trees'?" asks one motorist. "It's short." [9] He has a point. One wonders why the Joyce Kilmer Rest Area might not have Kilmer's famous poem "Trees" available on a little takeaway card for all patrons to read and enjoy. "Trees" is so short it could even be engraved in the lobby or posted in some prominent place. Once again we asked an employee if she knew anything about the person the rest area honors. The cashier in the gift shop said, "I don't know who she was." This cashier had been working in the gift shop several years, and not only did she not know who Joyce Kilmer was, she thought Kilmer was a woman.

Rest areas could not only provide Turnpike patrons with succor for their physical needs but also give them something to think about on resuming their trips. We posted ourselves in front of the Joyce Kilmer Rest Area and asked seventy-six entering patrons who Joyce Kilmer was and not one knew. Then we went inside and spoke to the manager of the Roy Rogers restaurant.

"She was a poet," he said.

Not bad, we thought, batting 500. But we still felt constrained to say, "Joyce Kilmer was a man."

"No shit," the manager said.

Our faith, not in the Turnpike but in the American educational system, was revived when, just before leaving the Joyce Kilmer, we thought, what the heck, and decided to ask one more group of people about to enter the concession building if they knew who Joyce Kilmer was.

A woman of about forty turned to her teenage daughter, smiled, and said, "Hit it, Jeanie," whereupon Jeanie broke into song:

> "I think that I shall never see
> A poem lovely as a tree."

"They did Joyce Kilmer in English class this year," Jeanie's proud mother explained.

We should have quit while we were ahead. The next people we asked, a couple wearing his-and-her plaid shorts, shrugged at each other, then at us. Finally, the woman said, "Wasn't she a movie star from Bayonne?"

At the Molly Pitcher Rest Area we had equally bad luck getting anyone to identify Molly Pitcher, the name pinned on the woman who brought water to Washington's troops at the Battle of Monmouth and then helped fire the cannons. One woman thought Molly Pitcher was a nurse in the Civil War. She had Clara Barton in mind, of course. A man told us he had seen a plaque telling of Molly Pitcher's exploits mounted at the rest area some years ago, but the plaque is no longer there and no one seemed to know where it is. It too seemed to have become a casualty of Roy Rogers.

Actually, it's more complicated. There *are* plaques at various rest areas—though they honor people other than those for whom the rest area is named. So, for example, at the Joyce Kilmer Rest Area, there is a plaque celebrating the Basilone Memorial Bridge, which spans the Raritan a little to the north.[10] The plaque honors John A. Basilone of Raritan, New Jersey, who was a marine killed in the Battle of Iwo Jima in 1945. The Turnpike Authority informed us that the plaque used to be on the bridge, but, of course, no one could read it at 65 miles per hour so they moved it to the nearest rest area. Without meaning to take anything away from Basilone, it does seem confusing at best that the rest area named after Joyce Kilmer has a plaque outside honoring John A. Basilone and a picture inside of Roy Rogers (not to mention the bitter truth that the Marriott Corporation, not Roy Rogers, now owns Roy Rogers).

One should, perhaps, applaud the catholicity of the Turnpike's taste: a war hero, a poet with a woman's name, and Roy Rogers. Something for everyone. But, of course, a very mixed message at best.

The message is even more mixed at the Grover Cleveland and Alexander Hamilton rest areas. Each sports four plaques that once were on the bridges immediately to the north of the Cleveland and to the south of the Hamilton. The giftshop manager in the Alexander Hamilton told us that a picture of Hamilton once hung "right here" (she gestured to a place in the air right over her head), "but when we built the shop we had to take down the picture."

Meanwhile, immediately outside the concession buildings at both the Hamilton and Cleveland rest areas are large plaques honoring Luke A. Lovely, Harry Laderman, Reverend John P. Washington, and the three Lewandowski brothers—Alexander, Walter, and William. Luke Lovely was the first New Jersey soldier killed in World War I. Harry Laderman was a toll collector "killed in the line of duty" in 1967. The Reverend Washington was one of the famous four chaplains of World War II, who gave up their life jackets and lives on a sinking ship to save four servicemen. And the Lewandowski brothers of Lyndhurst, New Jersey, were all killed in World War II. Obviously, these are all men worthy of memory, and the Turnpike is to be congratulated for naming its bridges after them. Our complaint is that placing these plaques in rest areas, where there is not one word about the person the rest area purports to honor, only makes whatever message the public might receive even muddier.

Obviously, as we mentioned earlier, in one rest area the message comes through loud and clear: the Vince Lombardi Rest Area, or "the Vince" as some call it. This may be because the Vince Lombardi is the most recent rest area built—and is actually owned and was built by the Marriot Corporation rather than the Turnpike itself. The rest area, built of brick and in Federal-style architecture, is much more attractive than the ordinary-looking glass and aluminum of the other rest areas. It even has a slate roof, chimneys, and a cupola with a gold weather vane. But what makes this area especially different from the others is the museum in its ample lobby.

In the Vince Lombardi showcases is a host of Lombardi memorabilia, including such books as *Lombardi: Winning Is the Only Thing,* edited by Jerry Kramer, and *Run to Daylight,* by Vince Lombardi with W. C. Heinz. In one case is a framed item called "The Lombardi Creed," which includes these words: "The many (physical) hurts seem a small price to pay for having won, and there's no reason at all that is adequate for having lost!" This may not be the most humane attitude, considering that, in any game, there must *always* be a loser; and, if there is "no reason at all that is adequate for having lost," half the people who engage in contests would have to think of themselves as utter failures—worse, bad or immoral persons.

In the cases are also photos of the Super Bowl trophy, named, as the reader is no doubt aware, "the Vince Lombardi Trophy" (Lombardi's Green Bay Packers won the first Super Bowl in 1967 and repeated in 1968). There are cups, bowls, plates, and other trophies, including the trophy from the Vince Lombardi Memorial Game in Giant's Stadium on August 17, 1979, between the Pittsburgh Steelers and the New York Jets. There are many photographs of Lombardi and his players. In short, the motorist who may never have heard of Vince Lombardi will come away with an appreciation of who Lombardi was and why he was important. Indeed, in the Vince Lombardi Rest Area crowds of motorists often mill in front of the display cases, as if hungry for food of a different sort than that which Roy Rogers and Bob's Big Boy are serving a few feet away.

Vince Lombardi, a contemporary figure, obviously has more of a constituency than the historical figures celebrated in the other rest areas. Indeed, a Vince Lombardi Committee, organized in 1978 "to perpetuate the name of Vince Lombardi and the high standards and values exhibited by him throughout his lifetime," seems to have been responsible for gathering the memorabilia found in the cases. The Lombardi family has taken a special interest in the rest area over the years. Lombardi's sons are on the committee, and his widow, Marie, has often stopped by for coffee.

The minimuseum in the Vince Lombardi Rest Area is a fine thing. It does, however, seem strange, if not wrong, that not one scrap of anything can be found in the other rest areas honoring the figures for whom they are named. This is another example of the exclusively business-engineering orientation of the Turnpike, its failure to provide amenities to its patrons. This is too bad, for with a little imagination, rest areas could be oases of good taste, humane values, education, and pleasure.

Others besides ourselves have criticized the Turnpike for ignoring its broader responsibilities. One writer, commenting on the Turnpike's blandness, suggests, not entirely tongue-in-cheek, that the Turnpike be made more of an "educational experience" by placing signs reminiscent of the old Burma Shave ones along the highway alerting the motorist to the special delights at upcoming exits. For example, this wag suggests, at the approach to Exit 5 in the southbound lanes could appear four successive signs that say:

BACK ROADS TO THE OCEAN'S SHELF
VEGGIES YOU CAN PICK YOURSELF
FIELDS OF GREEN SO VAST AND GREAT
(THAT'S WHY IT'S CALLED THE GARDEN STATE)
Exit 5—1 Mile
Mt. Holly
Burlington

Similarly, he feels the approach to Exit 4 in the southbound lanes might be heralded by:

TOWNS AND SUBURBS, OLD AND NEW
GROWING WHERE THERE ONCE WERE FEW
WHERE LIBERTY'S BELL WAS FIRST HEARD RINGING
AND WHITMAN HEARD AMERICA SINGING
Exit 4—1 Mile
Camden
Philadelphia

This writer also thinks toll tickets should be decorated with paintings of New Jersey historic and scenic sights, that facsimiles of these toll tickets should be sold in the rest area giftshops (and patrons encouraged to collect the whole set), and that a giant television screen near the Meadowlands should keep motorists up-to-date on the goings-on at the Sports Complex. Finally, letting a little Jersey chauvinism creep into his proposals, the writer suggests a series of signs just short of the New York, Delaware, and Pennsylvania borders that say:

> AS YOUR DEPARTURE DRAWS SO NEAR
> WE THANK YOU FOR YOUR VISIT HERE
> PLEASE COME AGAIN TO NEW JERSEY'S PLACES
> (WE LIKE YOU FOLKS FROM LESSER PLACES)[11]

To all of this we say, Well, why not? However silly, it's a start.

But if the present Turnpike is boring and banal, this has not stopped stories from growing up around certain places along the Pike, including some of the rest areas. A former student of ours, who wishes to remain anonymous, recently wrote:

> When I was waitressing at the Joyce Kilmer Howard Johnson's[12] on the Turnpike . . . the night shift (11–7) sold other items over the counter than donuts. Or in back, more accurately, themselves, to be specific. A truck stop to service your every need, so to speak. This was . . . supposedly the reason for Ho-Jo's puritanical insistence that we look like nuns behind the counter during the day—no makeup, hair in a bun (with a net), no jewelry except for a wedding band and a watch, and skirts hemmed at a mid-ankle length. (Once I almost quit over defending my right to have pierced ears.) Anyway, nothing like the platinum blond, beehived waitresses with makeup so thick Tammy Faye would have been envious who somehow managed to work the night shift during that era. Is it true? I don't know for a fact—but I certainly wouldn't doubt it. And the places they were reputed to have done it!—not only ergonomically unappealing, but challenging to the basic human anatomical structure.[13]

We reprint this letter without being able to prove whether prostitution ever flourished at the Joyce Kilmer Rest Area. If it did not, the story is still interesting because, like all folklore, it answers a need. Prostitution on the Turnpike appeals because it tends to undermine the Turnpike's image of military, inhuman efficiency. One wants to believe that somehow, amid all that concrete and steel, sin, if not love, might blossom.

There is something about the Turnpike that seems to excite sexual desire, perhaps as a means to relieve the terrible boredom and anonymity. Or perhaps the authoritarian nature of the Turnpike excites rebellious instincts—and what better way to rebel than to do something taboo—to have sex on the Turnpike, the least likely of places (reminiscent of Rita Jenrette's disclosures, some years back, that she and her congressman husband would occasionally have sex in and around the Capitol Building—in the cloakrooms and even, once, on the steps, for its danger turn-on). A newspaper story describes the Vince Lombardi Rest Area as a major homosexual cruising spot at night. "The state police make vice sweeps several times a week. This year they arrested 120 people—college professors, lawyers, and dentists among them." [14]

We placed an advertisement in the *Targum,* the Rutgers University newspaper, asking readers who had unusual anecdotes about the Turnpike to send them to us. Surprisingly, unless Rutgers University students are a particularly lustful lot, most of the anecdotes we received were about sex. One stands out:

> I am a Rutgers College senior. . . . Since I do not have a car, I depend on rides home (I live in northern N.J. about one hour from school) from friends when I go home on weekends. Sometimes I get a male friend to drive me. I've known him for about a year. I always offer him $ for gas and tolls, but he never takes it. He wants something else in payment instead.
>
> My father would drop me off at his house (if I was going back to school) and my friend and I would make small talk for a while as we drove along. The next thing I knew I'd be giving him a blowjob on the Turnpike.
>
> Sometimes, we'd go and park in the back at the Thomas Edison rest area. I don't know why Thomas Edison. Seems ridiculous, but you can say "Thomas Edison" to me to this day and I get excited. In fact, this is what my friend would say; it was our code. He'd say, "Thomas Edison?" and I'd nod, and then he'd pull into the Thomas Edison and park way in the back and I'd give him a blow job. Sometimes if it was dark on the way home on a Friday night in the winter we'd have intercourse in the back seat, but that was a lot more nervous because that way nobody could be the lookout.

The letter goes on with much graphic detail. Some of this student and her male friend's sexual exploits took place not in the rest area but on the roadway itself:

> One time we were approaching the toll-booth at Exit 9 and he didn't tell me until the last possible minute because he was about to come. Well, eventually, I realized the car was slowing and looked up to realize we were almost there. Well, I stopped and he threw his coat over his penis. Then after we pulled away I finished the "job." Also, another time, with the same guy, we were stuck in traffic on the turnpike—there'd been some kind of wreck—and I did "it" again. As a matter of fact, *every* time he's driven me from or to school, we've had sex as my way of paying him for the ride.
>
> I really sort of like it, especially in the Thomas Edison, where we could take our time. Well, relatively. It's dangerous, I know, but it's also very arousing and exciting. Sometimes I'd think: "If I ever get killed having sex on the Turnpike,

what a way to die. . . ." Do you think Thomas Edison would approve? Sometimes, after we had sex at the Thomas Edison, we'd go inside and have a coke.
We'd sit there and laugh. What would the people in the other booths have
thought if they knew what we had been doing out in the parking lot?
  I can't give you my name. I'm sure it's obvious why.[15]

There is no way we can prove the veracity of this letter. The fact, however,
that our respondent seems blissfully unaware of the moral implications of
trading sex for transportation would seem to speak for its authenticity. Of
course, her letter could have been sent to us as a joke or it may be a fantasy.
Apparently, sexual fantasies involving a New Jersey Turnpike setting are not
unusual. Nancy Friday, in her book *My Secret Garden: Women's Sexual
Fantasies,* reports a fantasy involving a woman speeding on the Turnpike
and her sexual activities with three state police officers.[16]

If the letter to us from the student is a fantasy, it is a very American one
because of the immediacy of its connection between the automobile and
sex. Whether the letter is fiction or fact, and as far as we know it *is* fact, it
would seem to suggest that, at least in the imagination of some, the Turnpike is not as antiseptic, not as sexually neutral, as it first appears.

It is also not as hermetically sealed or isolated or locked off from the rest
of civilization. Few if any patrons know that one can walk right off the Turnpike if one wishes. Although the Turnpike is fenced all along its 142-mile
length, at each rest area there is a back gate and a parking lot just beyond the gate for rest area employees. They—waitresses, mechanics, and
others—know how to reach this gate from the streets of the closest town.
Most employees, therefore, do not drive to work on the Turnpike and pay
tolls but, instead, as for example at the Grover Cleveland rest area, drive
down Calvin Street in the town of Sewarn, which dead-ends into the employees' parking lot and the back gate. They park, walk through a small
opening alongside the gate, and go in the back door of the concession
building.

The back gate itself is only used by the police or fire fighters or the Turnpike Authority in emergencies. But the pedestrian opening is there twenty-
four hours a day. At the Grover Cleveland we stood by the back gate
pondering what would happen if one just walked out. Would one be arrested? Would one find oneself irreparably separated from one's autmobile
and stranded in some strange limbo?

That day a man who lives at the foot of Calvin Street was washing his
car outside his ranch house. Just standing there 25 feet from the Turnpike
back gate washing his car as if the Turnpike didn't exist. Screwing up our

courage, we walked through the pedestrian opening in the back gate and came up to Glenn Csordos, forty-eight, whose home is at 76 Calvin Street and has lived there since 1965. Years ago, Csordos had two jobs, one of which was as a mechanic at the Grover Cleveland Rest Area. "Yeah, I'd come home from the other job, have dinner with my wife and kids, then just walk over there and do a four-hour P.M. shift. If my wife or kids needed me they could just yell to me over the fence, 'Hey, Dad.'"

We asked if there were any advantages or disadvantages living so close to the Turnpike, almost on it. "Well, one advantage," Csordos said, "is that when it snows, they plow Calvin Street immediately." The Turnpike Authority itself plows Calvin Street so rest area employees can get to work, most of them driving—though some rest areas are near bus routes and their employees take the bus to work, get off, and walk a few blocks to the back gate of the rest area.

"What about disadvantages?" we asked Csordos, thinking he would talk about the noise of the traffic or fumes. "Oh, we never notice the Turnpike," he said. "In fact, I don't think I could sleep if they ever stopped the traffic. If there's been a wreck and the traffic comes to a halt in the middle of the night, I bolt upright in bed scared stiff."

Csordos said the only time he'd experienced the Turnpike as a disadvantage was during the great New York blackout in 1965. Apparently, the Turnpike didn't want traffic to continue north into totally darkened New York City and detoured people off the Pike into local streets through the back gate of the Grover Cleveland Rest Area. "You should have seen all that traffic bumper to bumpering down Calvin Street." Csordos said the hard part was people knocking on his door asking to use his phone. "I said, 'Okay, you can use it, as long as the state policeman stands by'—which the cop did." Csordos says he had several offers from people who wanted to rent a bed from him for the night.

We asked him if, other than that, he'd ever experienced the Turnpike and the rest area as a disadvantage. What about all those trucks at night? At night, truckers will, by the hundreds, pull into a rest area like the Grover Cleveland and leave their engines idling for hours. Sometimes they'll catch a few hours sleep, then get breakfast in the Roy Rogers (which puts away the hamburgers at 2:00 A.M. and starts serving breakfast) and motor up to the markets of New York, beating the commuter traffic into the city and getting to their offloading destinations just as the markets are opening.

Csordos said, "Nah, the trucks don't bother me. I kind of like sitting on my porch and looking at them at night, their lights and smoke—all those guys just making a buck like you and me. They never bother anybody."

Were there any other advantages to living right behind the Grover Cleveland Rest Area on the New Jersey Turnpike? "Oh, yeah," said Csordos. "Like sometimes me and the wife have just come home from work and nobody feels like cooking, so I say, 'Let's go over to the Turnpike and have a hamburger.' So we just walk onto the Pike through the gate. We get a hamburger and some fries and some coffee—they make good coffee at Roy Rogers—and we sit around the rest area and look at the people, wondering where they're from, where they're going. It's like we're traveling too—without any of the drawbacks. So we sit there a while, maybe have another cup of coffee, and then, when we've had enough 'traveling,' we just go home through the gate again and watch the Cosby show. Having the Pike right here—well, it's just a little something extra, if you know what I mean."

So Bad, It's Good

Chapter

9

"I got the N.J. T'Pike Blues
I got the N.J. T'Pike Blues
With the front wheel a thumping
And the wipers a pumping
The brights lines a shining
The fog is a blinding
The cotton-picking, ever loving N.J. T'Pike Blues."

    —Dan Fogarty, chorus from "N.J. T'Pike Blues"[1]

The average person driving down the New Jersey Turnpike might think, "What a ghastly highway" or "What is that smell?" Friends, upon hearing that we were writing this book, would say, "Why?" and then add, "Why would anyone want to devote time to something so gross?" Even our publisher suggested (to be fair, after more than one glass of wine and half in jest) that we insert a scratch-and-sniff page in the book where readers unfamiliar with the Turnpike might experience "Eau de Rahway."

But if the Turnpike isn't beautiful, this does not mean that it and the arts are total strangers. The rest areas, as we have seen, are not oases of civilization and culture, but the Turnpike has long had an appeal to artists. Offbeat New Jersey art photographer Jim Coleman calls the Turnpike "minimalist heaven." According to Coleman, the Turnpike is "*the* punk highway. It's so unbelievably awful, it's wonderful. They should put the whole thing in the Smithsonian."[2]

Although for the motorist the Turnpike may be something to get to the end of as quickly as the law will allow, for artists its grittiness has a reverse chic. Artists have a love-hate relationship with the Turnpike, reflecting their love-hate feelings about New Jersey in general—the same feelings that are the basis of the many Jersey jokes. The Turnpike is so bad, it's good. One finds this true in popular songs, in fiction, in poetry, in painting, in sculpture, and in film.

Joseph Cosgriff's 1981 novelty song "I Like Jersey Best,"[3] distributed locally, illustrates the duality of feelings toward not only the New Jersey Turnpike but New Jersey in general. The song begins:

Travelin' down the turnpike
Headin' for the shore
A thought just then occurred to me
I'd never thought before

I've been a lot of places
Seen pictures of the rest
But of all the places I can think of
I like Jersey best.

So far the song seems an unequivocal celebration of New Jersey, possibly written by someone in the State Office of Tourism.[4] But as the song progresses, its author does not fail to note, with wry humor, New Jersey's pretensions and drawbacks:

> Lots of dineries, oil refineries
> Our highways make you cough

goes one pair of lines, and

> Drinking spots and used car lots
> Make the place just grand

goes another. We are further told that "forty-seven shoe stores / line Route 22," and that "our Giants could go all the way / if they could just win one." "I Like Jersey Best" is, thus, a song that likes New Jersey. At the same time, what it likes are some of the state's most negative aspects. So bad, it's good.

Such complex feelings about New Jersey and the Turnpike have not always been expressed in popular songs. As we saw earlier, in the 1950s the Turnpike was celebrated for its efficiency; in the 1960s and early 1970s it was seen as the despoiler of the environment. It was only in the late 1970s and in the 1980s that the dualistic nature of feelings about the Turnpike—it's so bad, it's good—emerged fully. We see this evolution of feelings through the songs of Chuck Berry, Paul Simon, and Bruce Springsteen.

Rhythm-and-blues artist Chuck Berry wrote "You Can't Catch Me" in 1956.[5] In it, the Turnpike is seen as a place where one may go fast and feel free, where one can escape from the commonplace and ordinary cares of life. Berry sings that he has

> bought a brand new airmobile
> Custom made, it was a flight Deville
> With a powerful motor and some hideaway wings
> Push in on the button and you will hear her sing.

The singer decides to take his "brand new airmobile" out for a spin on the New Jersey Turnpike:

> New Jersey Turnpike in the wee, wee hours
> I was rolling slowly 'cause of drizzling showers.

The singer is then challenged by another car, as if the New Jersey Turnpike is the kind of place where one can drag race freely—which was close to the truth in the road's early years. The singer leaves his challenger in his wake, only to excite the interest of the state police. He leaves them in his wake as well, such is the freedom from laws and strictures of all kinds that the Turnpike represents:

> Here comes a flattop
> He was moving up with me
> Then come waving goodbye
> In a little ole souped-up jitney
> I put my foot in my tank and I began to roll
> Moanin' siren, 'twas a state patrol
> So I let out my wings and then I blew my horn
> Bye bye New Jersey
> I've become airborne

Then follows the refrain:

> Now you can't catch me
> Baby you can't catch me
> 'Cause if you get too close
> You know I'm gone like a cool breeze.

"You Can't Catch Me" reflects the 1950s' unqualified enthusiasm for automobile culture. Americans did not yet connect the automobile with ecological and energy worries, and roads like the New Jersey Turnpike were still seen as the world of tomorrow.

In marked contrast is the classic sixties song "America," by Paul Simon.[6] This enormously popular song is about America's search for meaningful values at a time when the old shibboleths no longer mean anything. America is fighting in Vietnam, and the young people in the song represent the emerging counterculture opposing the war. The song is full of the malaise and despair of the sixties, and ultimately the New Jersey Turnpike becomes the symbol of that malaise and despair.

The song begins with the quixotic dream of finding the America of our ideals and of our dreams. The characters in the song do not find it. Or, rather, they discover that maybe there wasn't anything to find in the first place. We repeat the lyrics below in their entirety:

> Let us be lovers
> We'll marry our fortunes together
> I've got some real estate here in my bag
> So we bought a pack of cigarettes
> And Mrs. Wagner's pies
> And we walked off to look for America.

"Cathy," I said, as we boarded a Greyhound in Pittsburgh
"Michigan seems like a dream to me now
It took me four days to hitchhike from Saginaw
And I've come to look for America."

Laughing on the bus
Playing games with the faces
She said the man in the gabardine suit was a spy
I said, "Be careful. His bowtie is really a camera."

Toss me a cigarette
I think there's one in my raincoat
We smoked the last one an hour ago
So I looked at the scenery
She read her magazine
And the moon rose over an open field.

"Cathy, I'm lost," I said
Though I knew she was sleeping
"I'm empty and aching and I don't know why."
Countin' the cars on the New Jersey Turnpike
They've all come to look for America
All come to look for America.

Countin' the cars on the New Jersey Turnpike
And they've all come to look for America
All come to look for America
All come to look for America.

In "America," there is a close correlation between the fact that the narrator is "lost" and that he is "countin' the cars on the New Jersey Turnpike." He is "empty and aching" and he doesn't "know why" because the Turnpike represents the American dream—an automobile for everyone, a highway big as the sky. This should be automotive heaven, but it isn't. It's a kind of hell of loneliness and despair.

We had a Turnpike experience some years ago that underscores the loneliness theme of the song. Back then, many more cars in America were big—but the story would have almost as much validity now. Picking up a foreign visitor to the United States at New York's Kennedy Airport, and coming out to New Jersey and onto the Turnpike, we became aware of our foreign friend's silence. He stared out of the window, didn't say a word. Finally, we asked him what was the matter. "Everyone looks so lonely," he said. "This giant road and all these little heads in these big machines. In Europe you have four or five people in each car, everyone talking. Brrr," he shivered.

"It's just the Turnpike," we joked.

"Yes," he said, noncommittally. "But these people look like prisoners. If I drove regularly on this road, I would commit murder."

During the weeks of his visit, the Turnpike kept coming up in our foreign colleague's lectures. One day we played him Paul Simon's song "America." He listened to it over and over.

"That's it," he said.

"What?"

"America. This song is what America is all about."

He was fascinated by the passage in which the narrator and Cathy are "playing games with the faces" on the Greyhound bus. He repeated it over and over: "She said the man in the gabardine suit was a spy / I said 'Be careful. His bowtie is really a camera.'"

"That's the way the Turnpike is," he said.

"But that passage isn't taking place on the Turnpike," we pointed out. "The Turnpike hasn't come into the song yet."

This detail didn't bother our foreign friend. Nor did he think Cathy and the narrator were joking about spies on buses. As he put it, "That's what the Turnpike does to you. It makes you paranoid."

All this happened before we began writing this book. We recalled it only as we took a fresh look at the song and realized "America" was not just another syrupy Simon and Garfunkel song. It has a powerful message about anomie. We *are* empty and aching and don't know why, and the New Jersey Turnpike—or what it stands for in the song—might just be the reason.

If Chuck Berry's "You Can't Catch Me" illustrates 1950s feelings about the Turnpike, and Paul Simon's "America" illustrates late 1960s and early 1970s feelings, the internationally popular rock music of Bruce Springsteen best exemplifies late 1970s and contemporary ambivalence toward the Turnpike and New Jersey in general—the so bad, it's good feeling. How is one to feel about songs like "Born to Run," in which Springsteen says that New Jersey is "a death trap, it's a suicide rap?"[7] Springsteen's New Jersey is a place from which to run if one is to survive, yet there was for several years a strong movement in the state to get "Born to Run" declared the state song, a strong indication, once again, that one can love the very things one abhors.

In Springsteen's "Jungleland," a nightmarish vision of life in New Jersey and the Greater Metropolitan area, there is a line, "Man, there's an opera out on the Turnpike."[8] "Opera" connotes culture, and, indeed, the next line is, "There's a ballet being fought out in the alley." These lines, however, are surrounded by images of police, guitars like switchblades, rats, and the general sense that life is a jungle. The "opera" indicates that the Turnpike is a powerful place. But it can also be a malevolent one.

Springsteen's "State Trooper" is set entirely on the New Jersey Turnpike:

> New Jersey Turnpike
> Ridin' on a wet night
> Neath the refinery's glow
> Out where the great black rivers flow.
>
> License, registration
> I aint got none
> But I got a clear conscience
> Bout the things that I done
>
> Mr. State Trooper
> Please don't stop me
> Please don't stop me
> Please don't stop me.
>
> Maybe you got a kid
> Maybe you got a pretty wife
> The only thing I got's
> Been botherin' me my whole life.
>
> Mr. State Trooper
> Please don't stop me . . .
>
> In the wee wee hours
> Your mind gets hazy
> Radio relay towers
> Lead me to my baby.
>
> Radio's jammed up
> With talk show stations
> Just talk, talk, talk
> Till you lose your patience.
>
> Mr. State Trooper
> Please don't stop me . . .
>
> Hey somebody out there
> Listen to my lost prayer
> Hi ho silver-o
> Deliver me from nowhere.[9]

"State Trooper" is sung in a mournful monotone, its guitar accompaniment evocative of endlessly turning wheels, of boredom, and of despair. The road troubador singing it sounds more than a little depressed.

Why, then, do so many people like the song? They like it because it tells the truth about the reality many people live along the Turnpike, and there is beauty in that truth. Who hasn't at some point in his or her life felt utterly alienated and afraid of being stopped by a pitiless state trooper, perhaps while riding with no license and registration on a megahighway like the New Jersey Turnpike?

What a bleak landscape this song describes! If "ridin' on a wet night" were not enough, one is "neath the refinery's glow / Out where the great black rivers flow." This is a hellish place. The only light comes from the Hades-like gas flares of the refineries. The rivers (the Hackensack and Passaic are probably intended), which might under other circumstances be highways to freedom, here are so polluted, so degraded, as to be black, poisonous, probably lethal.

But there is more. There is a disparity between the condition of the singer and what he imagines is that of the state trooper. The state trooper has a kid, a pretty wife, but "the only thing I got's / Been botherin' me my whole life." Life, Springsteen seems to be saying, is miserable enough for me out on this wet night, on this horror road, in this killer landscape, but I also have this terrible problem. Isn't that enough? Do you have to finish me off by stopping my car and hassling me?

The singer knows he can turn to no one for help. Talk radio won't help him. He hopes that in some mysterious way the radio relay towers will "lead me to my baby." Perhaps the singer's problem, the thing that's been "botherin' me my whole life," is his inability to connect with anyone, his total alienation. In the plaintive last verse of the song, Springsteen fairly shrieks his anguish, hoping against hope that someone will "listen to my lost prayer / . . . Deliver me from nowhere."

"Nowhere" is, of course, the singer's condition, his mental and moral state; but it is also the Turnpike, that utterly dehumanized environment. The Turnpike is the objective correlative of the singer's experience of life. It is the embodiment of his despair.

And yet? And yet there is something wonderful about it. If the Turnpike can evoke such strong feelings, if it can personify everything that is wrong with this young man's life, then it has considerable power. One may not like it, may even hate it, but one cannot take it lightly. The Turnpike has gotten into the singer's pores, has gotten down deep into his soul; and as we listen to the song, we realize that it has gotten into ours as well.

Bruce Springsteen sings another song in which the New Jersey Turnpike is featured: "Open All Night." It is also part of the *Nebraska* album, which was recorded when Springsteen's fortunes as an artist were at their lowest ebb. As with "State Trooper," Springsteen accompanies himself alone on the guitar.

The scene in "Open All Night" is once again the New Jersey Turnpike, with a lone rider contending with state troopers who wait ominously beneath overpasses. Radios are "jammed up with gospel stations / Lost souls callin' long distance salvation," and the singer hopes the "deejay" will hear "my lost prayer / . . . Deliver me from nowhere." Once again, the sense that the Turnpike is physically nowhere, but also the embodiment of a spiritual nowhere, comes through.

One of the verses in "Open All Night," which evokes the work of painter Edward Hopper (and particularly makes one think of his painting *Nighthawks*), goes:

> Early north Jersey industrial skyline
> I'm a all set cobra jet creepin' through the nighttime
> Gotta find a gas station, gotta find a pay phone
> This turnpike sure is spooky at night when you're all alone
> Gotta hit the gas cause I'm runnin' late
> This New Jersey in the mornin' like a lunar landscape.[10]

The key images for the Turnpike are "spooky" and "like a lunar landscape." The singer is utterly alone in an unfriendly technological landscape. And yet "lunar landscape" has its positive features. There is something clean about it, albeit uninhabited. The Turnpike is a kind of desert, with nothing to distract you from your car, the road, and the sheer nothingness out there. Clearly, what is open all night is the Turnpike itself, a lonely but enthralling landscape to which you are attracted almost despite yourself; a landscape so ugly it's splendid; a landscape you hate so much, you love it; a landscape that is so bad, it's good.

If the Turnpike has excited the imagination of songwriters, it has also been important to novelists. The best-selling novelist Fletcher Knebel is a prime example. In *Dark Horse,* Eddie Quinn, a commissioner of the New Jersey Turnpike Authority, becomes a surprise candidate for president when the Republican party's nominee dies twenty-two days before the election.

Quinn is a onetime truck driver and Teamster Union functionary. In a smoke-filled room the politicians desperately try to come up with a fresh face, a candidate who, though little known, is unlikely to offend anyone. In the late-night discussion Eddie Quinn's selection seems to make sense. The party insiders figure he will appeal to America's love for the automobile.

One of Quinn's supporters reveals that Eddie Quinn is something of a prophet of the open road; he wrote a book, *A Miracle of Wheels: A Study of Metropolitan Expressways in the United States.* He also has quite a reputation in New Jersey: "'Eddie made a big hit in our state a couple of years ago,' said Pete, 'when a bunch of radical kids tried to tie up the Turn-pike. Eddie went down personally and directed operations. He got traffic flowing again inside a half hour. He also got off a line that's still being quoted, "There is no right of anybody, anywhere, any time to block a public highway." ' " [11]

Eddie Quinn, it is revealed, has highways in his blood. As a onetime roommate of his at Seton Hall University in New Jersey says, "He's queer for asphalt." Specifically, it is the New Jersey Turnpike in Quinn's blood. He was born in the backseat of a Model-A Ford while his father was driving his mother to a hospital in New Brunswick, New Jersey. Quinn's friend Pete Stackpole informs the assembled politician-kingmakers, "Eddie Quinn was born at the spot that some years later became the tollgate . . . at Exit Nine . . . of the New Jersey Turnpike." [12]

The action of the novel returns to this very spot toward the story's conclusion. Eddie Quinn, now the Republican presidential candidate, has been making a speech in Philadelphia and is due in New York City. "Hell with the plane, Pete," he says. "Nice straight haul up the Turnpike out of Camden."

"More wear and tear, Eddie. Your throat sounds like a rusty gate already."

"No. Riding relaxes me. Especially the Turnpike." [13]

The decision to drive is a tragic mistake. Near Exit 9, the New Brunswick interchange, Eddie is involved in an automobile accident that nearly takes his life. There is a fatality in the car that caused the crash, and though he is blameless, Eddie Quinn loses the presidential election because of the negative publicity. The *New York Times* dwells on the irony of "a son of the highways, born at Exit Nine, who became a political casualty of the expressways." [14]

Tom De Haven, whose breakdown on the Turnpike was discussed in Chapter 5, is a talented novelist from Jersey City. Among his books is *Jersey Luck,* another novel in which the New Jersey Turnpike receives consider-able attention. Its central figure, Jacky Peek, falls in love with a high-strung, punky young mother named Neetsie, who is married to a very jealous, highly volatile New Jersey Turnpike toll collector whose name is Anthony but is called "Ant."

Neetsie tells Jacky about Ant's work: " 'It's all right, but the job rots the brain. Ant was better off pumping gas. At least he moved around. This booth work has made him a very edgy person.' She laughed. 'He's always saying he's gonna quit. He wants to be a jail guard.' " [15]

One day, Jacky and Neetsie go to the Jersey Shore. They get on the Turn-pike and Jacky takes the "CARS ONLY" lanes, whereupon Neetsie comments, "Ant always takes the truck side, even at rush hour. He says only nervous drivers take the Cars Only side and nervous drivers are the ones that kill you." On the way back from the shore, Jacky and Neetsie

> get on the Turnpike north, and who hands me the toll ticket? Anthony. I didn't recognize him and Neetsie was lighting a cigarette, not paying any attention. But Anthony was a girl-watcher and my van was built high. He looked straight past me as he leaned out of his booth. And he spotted her. He yanked the ticket back. And clutched at my shirtsleeve.
>
> "*Ant?*" Neetsie said. "Hi, Ant. What're you doing here—somebody get sick?"
>
> I looked at her and she was blushing but that's all. She didn't seem stricken or panicked or guilty. Then she stretched out her neck and gave a Lucille Ball sort of gulp, being deliberately comic. Ant said her name sharply. The car behind me beeped. I snatched the toll ticket and stepped on the gas.
>
> Neetsie fell back against the passenger door and slung out her arms like some crime boss drilled at lunch. Her cigarette dropped. She stared at me in horror. . . .

> "You are marked for slow death," read the note I found stuck in my door when I got home. "I know where you live, prick. I can get you any time I want."
>
> It wasn't signed, but it was printed, in fiber tip, on the back of a computer-punched New Jersey Turnpike toll ticket.[16]

Richard Ford, a young novelist who has come to prominence in the 1980s, sets *The Sportswriter* largely in New Jersey. The novel is about a man who has lost his wife, his child, and his ability to write. Because of these misfortunes, he seeks anonymity, "and New Jersey," Frank Bascombe says, "has plenty to spare." Bascombe feels New Jersey "is the perfect landscape for . . . loneliness." Other states might offer some, but "New Jersey's is the purest loneliness of all."[17] Emblematic of New Jersey's anonymity and its loneliness for Bascombe is the New Jersey Turnpike. There are a number of striking and effective descriptions of life along the Turnpike and of the Turnpike landscape.

In one of his trips up the Turnpike, Frank Bascombe is traveling with his girlfriend, Vicki Arcenault, who looks out at the landscape one sees from the Turnpike and says, "Looks like someplace the world died out there, doesn't it?"

"I like it out there," Bascombe replies. "Sometimes you can imagine you're in Egypt."[18]

Vicki Arcenault is the daughter of a Turnpike toll collector:

> She smiles up at me sweetly and puts her hand inside my thigh in a way she hasn't done before, and I have to keep from swerving and causing a big pile-up. We are just now passing Exit 9, New Brunswick, and I take a secret look over along the line of glass booths, only two of which are lighted OPEN and have cars

pulling through. Indistinct, gray figures lean out and lean back, give directions, make change, point towards surface roads for weary travelers. What could be more fortuitous or enticing than to pass the toll booth where the toll-taker's only daughter is with you and creeping up on your big-boy with tender, skillful fingers?[19]

Vicki Arcenault's father, Wade, is a toll collector at Exit 9, the same exit where Eddie Quinn of *Dark Horse* was born and nearly died. Wade Arcenault, who like most other New Jerseyans in *The Sportswriter,* comes from somewhere else, is a Texan who is described as "a cheery, round-eyed, crewcut fellow with a plainsman's square face and hearty laugh. I instantly recognize him from Exit 9, where he has taken my money hundreds of times but doesn't recognize me now."[20]

Wade Arcenault tells Bascombe a story about a fellow toll collector that underscores the importance of the New Jersey Turnpike as a place where one cannot only lose oneself but also get a fresh start:

> "There's a fellow works for us up at Exit 9. I won't say his name. Except in 1959, he was living out west near Yellowstone. Had a wife and three children, a house and a mortgage. A job, a life. One night he'd been to a bar and was on his way home. And just after he left, a whole side of a mountain collapsed on the bar. He stopped in the middle of the highway, he told me, and he could see back in the moonlight to where a lot of lights had been that were all gone because this huge landslide had taken place. Killed everybody but him. And do you know what he did?" Wade raises his eyebrows and squints, both at the same time.
>
> "I've got a pretty good idea." Who in the modern world wouldn't?
>
> "Well, and you'd be right. He got in his car and drove east. He said he felt like somebody'd just said, 'Here, Nick, here's your whole life being handed to you again. See if you can't do better this time.' And he's reported dead right now out in Idaho or Wyoming, or one of those states. Insurance paid. Who knows where his family is? His kids? And he works right beside me on the Turnpike happy as a man can be."[21]

Ford's New Jersey Turnpike is a supremely rootless place, a place where a man may escape from his former identity in the anonymity the Turnpike offers. Wade Arcenault's fellow toll collector once had all the trappings of civilization: "A wife and three children, a house and a mortgage. A job, a life." And then he found the perfect opportunity to run away from all that.

A peculiarly American story, a peculiarly American fate. America, the land where one may start over, reinvent oneself, the great American opportunity and the great American tragedy, working itself out on the New Jersey Turnpike.

And what a switch from the standard American myth—that it is in the

West where one may be anonymous, where one may truly get lost. Wade Arcenault and his colleague are from the West. And they have come East to disappear, to experience that special brand of American aloneness. The characters in this novel remind one of those in Sam Shepherd's plays— *True West,* for example—or movies such as Wim Wender's *Paris, Texas* (the script of which was written by Sam Shepherd). Only they haven't escaped West but, instead, found employment on the New Jersey Turnpike, as if the Turnpike is somehow misplaced geographically, as if it represents a new, a different, kind of West.

The poems of Allen Ginsberg, arguably America's greatest living poet, evoke a similar vision of New Jersey and of the Turnpike. Ginsberg, Newark-born, Paterson-reared, once the disciple of William Carlos Williams, has a kind of fatal attraction to the Turnpike and its environs. In his poem "Don't Grow Old," about the death of his father, Ginsberg writes,

> Near the Scrap Yard my Father'll be Buried
> Near Newark Airport my father'll be
> Under a Winston Cigarette sign buried
> On Exit 14 Turnpike NJ South
> Through the tollgate Service Road 1 my father buried
> Past Merchants Refrigerating concrete on the cattailed marshes
> past the Budweiser Anheuser-Busch brick brewery
> in the B'Nai Israel Cemetery behind a green painted iron fence
> where there used to be a paint factory and farms
> where Pennick makes chemicals now
> under the Penn Central power Station
> transformer wires, at the borderline
> between Elizabeth and Newark, next to Aunt Rose
> Gaidemack, near Uncle Harry Meltzer
> one grave over from Abe's wife Anna my father'll be buried.[22]

In "Don't Grow Old" Ginsberg describes the ultimate industrial landscape, of which the Turnpike is the central or linking ingredient. Here even a cemetery must be squeezed between chemical plants, breweries, billboards, power stations. It is perhaps the only green for miles around (and, at that, a dingy green), this home of the dead.

In another poem, "Bayonne Entering NYC," the Turnpike and its landscape are again evoked:

> Megalopolis with burning factories—
> Bayonne refineries behind Newark Hell-light
> truck trains passing trans-continental gas-lines,
> blinking safety signs KEEP AWAKE

Giant giant giant transformer,
electricity Stacks' glowing smoke—
More Chimney fires than all Kansas in a mile,
Sulphur chemical Humble gigantic viaducts
networked by road side
What smell burning rubber, oil
"freshens your mouth"
Railroad rust, deep marsh garbage-fume
Nostril horns—
city Announcer jabbering at City Motel,
flat winking space ships descending overhead
GORNEY GORNEY MORTUARY [23]

The poem goes on in this vein for some pages. The "KEEP AWAKE" signs are, of course, a Turnpike trademark. The Gorney mortuary's sign, with an illustrated clock framed on both sides by "GORNEY," is a familiar landmark in Elizabeth at the edge of the Turnpike.

For Allen Ginsberg the New Jersey Turnpike might be likened to the Moloch that animates his greatest poem, "Howl." In "Howl," Ginsberg asks, "What sphinx of cement and aluminum bashed open their skulls and ate up their brains and imagination?" And he answers that it is "Moloch whose mind is pure machinery! Moloch whose smokestacks and antennae crown the cities! Moloch whose love is endless oil and stone!" [24] For Allen Ginsberg, the New Jersey Turnpike is not just a road; it is the quintessence of roads, the road reaching nightmare proportions.

The vision of the Turnpike as a hellish place is not just typical of great and established poets but of beginners as well. Gale Abrahamsen of Northvale, New Jersey, a student at Rutgers University, wrote a poem in 1988 called "N.J. Turnpike," which she shared with us. The poem is full of horrible imagery:

Iron skeletons, space-age dinosaurs, devouring
the sky and tearing at the clouds, causing
blood to ooze from the flaming black smokestacks
which scream in rage—rage because man still
walks the Earth as master.
They vomit black smoke and poison the sky.

At the end of the poem Abrahamsen writes: "TURNPIKE ENDS HERE—PLEASE PAY TOLL." [25]

As discussed in Chapter 4, there is very little graphic art with the Turnpike as subject matter. Photographers are simply not allowed to pursue their trade there. This is, of course, true of painters as well, at least of painters who work directly from life. One painter, however, Marguerite Doernbach, a Trenton resident in her early seventies who has lived and painted all over the world and been the subject of a recent retrospective show,[26] has a number of works with the Turnpike as subject. One of these, the phantasmagorical *Turnpike at Newark* (1964), graces the cover of this book. Its swoops and curves seem perfectly to capture the perpetual mobility of the Turnpike, its place in American life as the ultimate industrial landscape. Says Doernbach, "I think the Turnpike is beautiful. It's horrible too, but it has its own aesthetics. I have this love-hate thing about the Turnpike. It's awful—but is there a more dramatic place on this earth?"

Among Doernbach's Turnpike pictures are woodcuts, oils, and goaches. A large oil called *Under the Turnpike Bridge* (1965) is a painting of the understructure of the bridge that connects the New Jersey and Pennsylvania turnpikes. Says Doernbach, "Lots of people would think it was ugly, but, for me, it's like a cathedral—in fact it reminded me specifically of Gloucester Cathedral in England. The huge pillars—they're chunky, romanesque."

Another oil, *Cracking Towers at Elizabeth* (1963–1965), is a night scene of the refineries, the flaming gas towers, the tank farms appearing incandescent in the darkness, the total industrial landscape. It seems to be a picture of Hades. "It is," says Doernbach. "But isn't it beautiful?"[27]

The Turnpike has also inspired sculptors. Although he did not produce any works that can be considered specifically "about" the Turnpike, the world-renowned abstract sculptor Tony Smith calls the Turnpike a major influence on his art. In an interview, Smith said:

> When I was teaching at Cooper Union in the first year or two of the fifties, someone told me how I could get on to the unfinished New Jersey Turnpike. I took three students and drove from somewhere in the Meadows to New Brunswick. It was a dark night and there were no lights or shoulder markings, lines, railings, or anything at all except the dark pavement moving through the landscape of the flats, rimmed by hills in the distance, but punctuated by stacks, towers, fumes, and colored lights. This drive was a revealing experience. The road and much of the landscape was artificial, and yet it couldn't be called a work of art. On the other hand, it did something that art had never done. . . . Artificial landscape without cultural precedent began to dawn on me.

Tony Smith's drive on the unfinished Turnpike that night was significant because it led him to see art in an entirely new way. It was not the kind of art that could be put in a frame or displayed in a museum. It was the American-built environment, what Smith called "created worlds without tradition." Such worlds, Smith tells us, eventually began to have a profound effect on his sculpture.[28]

In addition to its influence on Tony Smith's sculpture, the Turnpike is itself part of an enormous environmental sculpture being created in the Meadowlands by the artist Nancy Holt. Holt, with support from the National Endowment for the Arts, is working on the site of a mile-long, 57-acre, 10-million-cubic-yard landfill known as "Mount Trashmore." The garbage mountain towers above the Turnpike's eastern spur at mile 108, near Exit 15E. Holt's "Sky Mound" is "expected to create spectacular visual effects, from the mound itself, from the Turnpike, from a railroad car, from an airplane. . . . At sunrise and sunset, light will reflect to the center of the mound and radiate down the side of the hill in eight distinct rays."[29] "Sky Mound," which has been described as a "modern-day Stonehenge,"[30] will also serve as a naked-eye observatory, park, and as a gas well. The vast quantities of methane gas being generated by the garbage that, over decades, became the mesalike mountain one finds there today, will be extracted and sold to a utility company. When it is completed, "Sky Mound" will be seen by countless millions of people each year—those who visit the site, those who fly over it on the approach to Newark Airport, and, especially, Turnpike patrons.

American cinema is also taken with the New Jersey Turnpike, sometimes as just a road but other times as a road representing all roads. Car culture is a large part of the New Jersey experience, since it is virtually impossible to get to and from most points in New Jersey without an automobile. New Jersey, which has long led the nation in the number of road miles per capita, bears a close resemblance, both in size and life-style, to the city of Los Angeles, which we normally think of as preeminent in automobile culture. A number of films about car culture take place in New Jersey. *Eddie and the Cruisers,* for example, is an otherwise forgettable film in which the automobile, the road, rock 'n' roll music, and the Jersey shore are inexorably linked.

Numerous films and television dramas have used the New Jersey Turnpike as a location, as many as six in 1985 alone. One genre, the coast-to-coast auto race movie, inevitably has footage on the Turnpike or, as in the case of *Cannonball Run,* pretends to, actually using another location, no doubt near Hollywood. In *Gumball Rally* (Warner Brothers, 1976, directed by Chuck Bail), the racers tear out of a garage in Manhattan at dawn in an effort to reach Long Beach, California, in less than thirty-four hours, their previous record. Passing through the Lincoln Tunnel, the lead car drivers say, "Here's the Jersey Turnpike—6 minutes 58 seconds. We're ahead of last year." There follow a number of scenes involving tollbooths, state police officers, and typical Turnpike footage of all kinds. Indeed, the New Jersey Turnpike is the only road in the film identified as such.

Still, in *Gumball Rally* and others of its lowbrow ilk, the Turnpike is presented simply as a major road. It has no symbolic importance. Among the films in which the Turnpike enjoys a larger meaning is John Schlesinger's important 1969 film *Midnight Cowboy,* which won several Oscars, including one for Best Picture of the Year. Joe Buck, played by Jon Voight, approaches New York City on his long odyssey away from his West Texas roots. Boarding a bus, the gum-chewing, would-be professional stud, heads northeast through the hardscrabble Bible Belt to find his fortune. Toward the end of the trip he awakens seated next to a nun and surrounded by drunken American Legionaires. Turnpike overpasses go by, power pylons, the familiar scenery along the northern stretches of the New Jersey Turnpike—tank farms, marshes, chemical plants, and stacks of toxic-waste drums. A plane roars off the ground from Newark Airport. And then Joe Buck's portable radio, to which he has been listening constantly as he passes through the country, intones the familiar "Seventy-seven, WABC." It is Ron Lundy, the ABC disc jockey. Turning to the nun beside him, Joe Buck exclaims joyously, "That's New York talking there, ma'am." All through the voyage north the tension has been building, the noise increasing, the crowds getting larger. Now, on the New Jersey Turnpike, Joe Buck prepares to meet his fate in New York. Thus Schlesinger uses the familiar notion of the Turnpike as gateway as a symbol of Buck's entry into a larger world.

The Turnpike again appears at the end of the film when Buck and Ratso Rizzo, played by Dustin Hoffman, embark on a journey to Miami seeking a new life. Again a bus is boarded, it passes through the Lincoln Tunnel, and soon it has embarked on a journey beginning on the Turnpike. *Midnight Cowboy* is a film that is many things, but chief among them is a classic American road movie. And the Turnpike brackets both ends of the movie as a kind of framing device, providing an entrance and exit to the story.

Another interesting film in which the Turnpike is featured is Jonathan Demme's 1986 *Something Wild.* It begins in Manhattan, when a wild young woman, played by Melanie Griffith, all but kidnaps an uptight, pompous young accountant, played by Jeff Daniels. She takes him through the Holland Tunnel and onto the New Jersey Turnpike, en route to a New Jersey motel. There she handcuffs him to the bed and turns him into her love slave. In this road film the Turnpike and New Jersey are seen as places where one may be "wild," may do unexpected things, may be totally unconventional. In *Something Wild* the Turnpike is the route to an America alternative to New York, the beginning of trans-Hudson America, the beginning of the American West. It is the route you take to liberate yourself from the dubious blessings of civilization.[31]

We have looked at popular songs, novels, poetry, paintings, sculpture, and Hollywood films in which the Turnpike embodies key American ideas and values. Although these artifacts are of uneven merit, highbrow and lowbrow, they share an interest in the Turnpike that often goes beyond the simple fact of its existence. They acknowledge the symbolic importance of the Turnpike.

Marguerite Doernbach writes poetry about the Turnpike in addition to painting it. In a poem titled "Observations," she says that we must

> Break the speed of this
> turnpike life
> before the grand exit.[32]

For Doernbach and many of the other artists discussed in this chapter, the Turnpike is more than a road. It is an emblem of American life as we live it late in the twentieth century.

Characteristically, the attraction of these artists to the New Jersey Turnpike is of an ambivalent nature. They are horrified by it, but it fascinates them. They are repelled by it, but they also find it dazzling. They deplore it, but they declare through their works that it is inimitable. They find the Turnpike representative of all that is worst in American civilization—its materialism, its short-sighted utilitarianism, its love of bigness for its own sake, its ruinous attitude toward nature, its almost totalitarian uniformity—and yet they find themselves irresistibly drawn to it. For artists, almost despite themselves, the Turnpike is so bad, it's good.

Tunnel Vision

Chapter

10

"Terrible plans are afoot for the New Jersey Turnpike. They want to make it pretty."

—James Ahearn[1]

Imagine the Calkins family of Lynchburg, Virginia, eagerly anticipating their first visit to New York City. They're on the New Jersey Turnpike, the flaming refineries of Linden just behind them. Now, as Jim Bob Calkins fights to hold onto the wheel in denser traffic than he has ever imagined, much less driven in, he steals a look at the giant cranes of Port Elizabeth, the massive Conrail switching yards, the endless concrete expanse of Newark Airport. United Airlines Flight 846 out of San Francisco roars in over his head and he instinctively ducks.

"Careful," his wife, Thelma Lee, snaps.

Jim Bob is nervous. What do they do with the car when they get to New York City? And, meanwhile, can they survive this infernal New Jersey Turnpike? One false move, they're dead.

"Dad?" It's little Jim Bob, Jr., from the back seat.

"Whatya want?"

"Dad?"

"Yeah, what is it? You gotta pee? What?"

"Dad, why's it so ugly?"

"What? What's so ugly?"

"This road. Why's it so ugly?"

Not an atypical conversation among riders on the New Jersey Turnpike. Some love the way it looks; many hate it. But we've never met anyone who didn't have strong feelings about the aesthetics of the New Jersey Turnpike. When we told a colleague we were including a chapter in this book on aesthetics, she said, "Now I *know* you guys are nuts."

"*What* aesthetics?" she added. At the time, we had no ready answer. Later, we wish we'd answered that even pure aesthetes probably spend more time looking at public works like the New Jersey Turnpike than reading poetry or contemplating paintings or listening to music.[2] The Turnpike-inspired art discussed in Chapter 9 may, on balance, be less significant than the aesthetics of the Turnpike itself. As Frank Lloyd Wright once wrote, "I forsee that roads will soon be architecture too . . . great architecture."[3]

To ignore, or to simply dismiss, the aesthetics of public works is to insure the insularity of both the fine arts and public works. The Turnpike, with its stripped-down, no-frills look, does not exist outside recent aesthetic history but is an embodiment of it. The Turnpike informs Italian futurism on the one hand and the Bauhaus international style on the other. It is also representative of traditional American ideas and values, especially the American penchant for a spare and minimalist aesthetic that emerged from our Puritan and frontier past.

American design has always stressed the functional over the decorative, the vernacular over the genteel. As a result, museum curators and art historians often point to such artifacts as clipper ships and farm tools as the embodiment of American beauty in design. The clipper ship was built to sail rapidly in order to make money, and its celebrated beauty was an unintended by-product. The iron plow was designed to cultivate the earth using as little energy as possible, but in time the iron plow came to have meaning and aesthetic value far beyond its function: three of them appear on the New Jersey State Seal and State Flag. After a while the idea of functional beauty became a truism of American aesthetics. Don't worry about beauty: just worry about function. If it is really functional, it will be beautiful.

By the 1930s, aestheticians began to compile lists of typically American artifacts. Perhaps it started as a parlor game, but gradually it took on an aura of high seriousness. Could you make a list of artifacts—things or objects—that might be considered uniquely American?

One key player in this game was a professor at Barnard College in New York, John Kouwenhoven. In 1954, Kouwenhoven wrote an essay titled "What's American about America?" In this essay, Kouwenhoven argues that certain artifacts are quintessentially American. "I am aware of the risks of generalizing," Kouwenhoven writes, "and yet it would be silly . . . to assert that there are not certain things which are more American than others."[4]

Kouwenhoven went on to present a list of twelve items he considered typically American: the Manhattan skyline; the gridiron town plan; the skyscraper; the Model-T Ford; the Constitution; Mark Twain's writing, especially *Huckleberry Finn;* Whitman's *Leaves of Grass;* comic strips; soap operas; assembly-line production; chewing gum; and jazz. These things, Kouwenhoven argues, are process- rather than product-oriented. They all involve movement and change. They have an open-ended, unfinished, loosely structured, improvised quality and may be added to infinitely. They are distinctly nonclassic, non-European, nontraditional. And, finally, they are vernacular, virtually unconcerned with form. They put form after function (or substance or meaning) in importance and embody the notion that form should be derived from, should follow, function.

Other items might be added to Kouwenhoven's list. The American (as opposed to European) film—or shall we say the *movie*—is one. Modern dance, the action paintings of Jackson Pollock, patchwork quilts, the mobile sculptures of Alexander Calder, strip architecture, and mobile homes are others.

What of the New Jersey Turnpike, America's mightiest road? Like the other artifacts mentioned, the New Jersey Turnpike was created unselfconsciously, with thought only to whether it would work, not how it would look. From the start it had no pretensions to beauty or to art. Is there something characteristically American about the New Jersey Turnpike? Would it belong on an updated Kouwenhoven list? We wrote John Kouwenhoven in rural Vermont, where he now lives in retirement, and asked what he thought. Kouwenhoven responded: "I know nothing about the New Jersey Turnpike except what an infrequent user of it learns from first hand experience. It would not have occurred to me to contemplate it as a successful, or admirable, or characteristic example of the vernacular mode. . . . I see it as an example of the interaction of the vernacular tradition with an especially arrogant form of Baron Haussmannism." [5]

We also believe the Turnpike is aesthetically neither successful nor admirable, but we think it *is* characteristic of American vernacular. Kouwenhoven may not accept it as typical of the vernacular because he does not like it. But the vernacular can just as easily give us McDonald's arches as Shaker chairs. And it can just as easily give us the New Jersey Turnpike as New York's beautiful Taconic State Parkway.

The Turnpike was built the way public works have traditionally been erected in this country. For much of its history, America has been a frontier culture where the arts have had to take a backseat. Survival was what was required, and there was little time or money for embellishments. Add to this Puritan biases against the arts as the devil's handmaiden, as distracting, if not seducing, otherwise dedicated folk from the Lord's work, and one sees, in America's earliest days, a heady brew mitigating against the artistic temperament. No wonder American artists long felt this country did not nourish their spirits; that to be an American artist necessitated leaving one's native land.

The notion that there is something virtuous about form following function begins with the Puritans and continues on the frontier, but it is very much alive in our culture today. Americans still find the merely beautiful troubling, if not sinful. One can trace a straight line from the Puritans and the frontier right down to today and included will be some of America's most revered thinkers and builders, all believing that function must supersede form, that form is frivolous—something for long-haired artists and decadent Europeans.

Emerson, for example, tells us, "All beauty must be organic; . . . outside embellishment is deformity." [6] The Shakers, who created many plain things now considered beautiful, state that to attempt the beautiful is not only sinful but "absurd and abnormal." [7] Frank Lloyd Wright declares that true American houses "get rid of the attic and . . . the dormer . . . get rid of the . . . basement" and "lower the windows and doors." [8] In short, irrespective of Wright's considerable achievements as an architect, the "true" American house sacrifices all charm for utility. Given these values, it is easy to understand why Americans would quite naturally travel, borrowing the title of a Tom Wolfe book, *From Bauhaus to Our House.* [9] Le Corbusier's international-style concept of architecture as "machines for living" was transplanted to very fertile ground indeed in America.

This American penchant for celebrating utility at the expense of aesthetics is the constant theme of European commentators on the United States. Tocqueville wrote in a chapter in *Democracy in America* called "In What Spirit the Americans Cultivate the Arts" that Americans "habitually prefer the useful to the beautiful." [10] Dickens wrote in *American Notes* that "it would be well if there were [in America] . . . a wider cultivation of what is beautiful, without being eminently and directly useful." [11] Modern American architecture and engineering have produced their marvels, and the clean, stripped-down look can be beautiful if what one is seeking is a noble shape. But when this look is employed without respect for its surroundings, or as a money-saving device only—building the most for the cheapest, the biggest bang for the buck—aesthetic horrors ensue.

The New Jersey Turnpike was built in this spirit. It is the perfect embodiment of the late 1940s, early 1950s idea of making things practical and inexpensive but, in the end, dull, if not ugly. The Turnpike is the Levittown of American roads. Riding it, one begins to question whether form need always follow function. On the Turnpike, one even entertains thoughts as perverse as maybe it should be the other way around.

Lewis Mumford could have been speaking about the Turnpike when he complained about the "brutal assaults" of engineers who "aim solely at speed and volume of traffic, and bulldoze their way across country to shorten their route by a few miles without making the total journey any less depressing." [12] In response Turnpike admirers would maintain that it is safer and more efficient than such roads as the Merritt Parkway in Connecticut, with its lovely landscaping and graceful curves. From Turnpike proponents' perspective, aesthetics are not only unnecessary but are also dangerous distractions.

As we have seen, however, curves and highway vistas may be positive safety factors. Also, safety and efficiency aren't everything. One realizes on the New Jersey Turnpike that streamlining alone may be bankrupt, brutalizing, perhaps even totalitarian. With no ornamention to delight the eye, with no grass divider and scarcely a tree on the northern stretches, one rides the Turnpike hunched over, looking neither to left nor right, in a kind of tunnel. Yet as bad as the Turnpike is as an aesthetic experience, some celebrate it precisely for what is wrong with it, as if in a burst of democratic enthusiasm, like Candide, one decides that whatever is is good. James Ahearn, his tongue only partly in his cheek, complains:

> Terrible plans are afoot for the New Jersey Turnpike. They want to make it pretty.
> They want to take our big shouldered, exhilaratingly scented, six-lane, dual-dual freeway and turn it into Wimp Street. They want to, if you please, make another Garden State Parkway out of it.
> Now, I have nothing against the parkway. It is a nice place to go for a Sunday drive with your Aunt Agatha. . . . But New Jersey it ain't.

Ahearn was remarking on the plan to plant thousands of trees along the upper reaches of the Turnpike, shielding some of New Jersey's most unusual, if not bizarre, sights. After cataloging some of the choicest vistas from the Turnpike, Ahearn writes:

> And here—the ultimate treat for the turnpike connoisseur—is the *pièce de résistance* of the turnpike, the Bayway Refinery. . . . Big fat steel retorts. High-rise cracking towers. Miles and miles of piping. And the flares! Pipes sticking up halfway to the clouds, venting off waste gases in orange flame, day and night. To coin a phrase, what does Earth have to show more fair?
> But all this isn't enough for the Governor. No, sir, he wants to pretty up the turnpike. He wants trees and bushes planted. He wants flowers, for God's sake.
> What? Ivy growing on the Pulaski Skyway? Arbor vitae screening off those marvelous steel barrels? Little sissy plants struggling to hide the scars on the guardrails where some semi from Harrisburg flipped week before last? No, no, it won't do.
> Pass the word. "Save the Turnpike." It's New Jersey. It's us.

For Ahearn, the plan to landscape the Turnpike is an insult to New Jersey toughness. New Jerseyans, he suggests, take pride in "toughing it out." They are a distinct species of human that thrives on toxic wastes and horrific sights.[13] As if supporting Ahearn's vision, at Newark Airport, just off the New Jersey Turnpike, one may purchase T-shirts that say, "NEW JERSEY: ONLY THE TOUGH SURVIVE."

There is, thus, a macho aspect of the Turnpike with which men, in particular, identify. Tennessee trucker Jerry Jonas thinks the Turnpike is the ultimate "hairy highway." One newspaper celebrates the Turnpike as "the greaser highway."[14]

David Aaron Clark writes in a similar vein about his love affair with the New Jersey Turnpike:

> I've traveled other roads, believe me. None of them measures up. . . . If you want a simple world, one you can believe in, a linear world, the turnpike awaits. There's gas, food, newspapers, bathrooms, the backseat of your car to sleep in. . . . The New Jersey Turnpike is truth unvarnished. It speaks of crooked politicians now one with the asphalt, of anonymous tankers trucking in more toxic waste, of an endless string of donkeys driving cars with seats stuffed with and wheelwells full of coke and pot.

To "do" the New Jersey Turnpike, Clark says, you need a "real" car. No BMW's or Hondas need apply.

> I drive a 1967 Chrysler 300 with a 400 cubic inch engine. . . . The thing goes from 0 to 60 in about eight seconds. . . . I'll admit the left rear taillight's been out for a while. I'll fix it soon, really. The front fenders are slightly battered from parking in tight places, but mostly intact.
>
> Adding to this ambience is the glove compartment, which springs open whenever the car hits a bump. On the dashboard, among various anonymous food and drink stains, is one of those unspillable coffee cups with a glued-down holder. . . . Mine says, "I love New Jersey Turnpike Coffee." My car is that kind of car, and the turnpike is that kind of road.[15]

Paul Overberg, like James Ahearn, feels it would be a mistake to plant trees along the Turnpike. They might eventually obscure the unparalleled industrial landscape of the northern Pike. "Children," he writes, "are especially attentive along this stretch, especially when night transforms it into a fantasy world of looming, lighted bulk and flame and sometimes thunder." Overberg wonders whether "green is really better."[16]

Russell Roemmele, editor of *New Jersey Motor Truck Bulletin,* has similar views. "Frankly," he writes, "I have never understood the embarrassment of New Jersey residents about the roadside along the New Jersey Turnpike. Should we be ashamed of our industrial might? . . . Many times each week I travel the Turnpike north. . . . I am not looking for trees. I am content to pass the big tank farms in Carteret and their complicated piping, an art form as satisfying to me as any modern art. . . . Why should we put trees there? Rather, we should be bragging about this reality that is only a dream in most other nations.[17]

This kind of sensibility is reminiscent of *Learning from Las Vegas.*[18] In that landmark book, architect Robert Venturi and several associates argue that we can rage against Las Vegas as being tacky, but there are good reasons it looks the way it does. If one can overcome European-oriented cultural biases, much can be learned from Las Vegas. We quite agree. One can learn from Las Vegas just as one can learn from the New Jersey Turnpike. But like Turnpike enthusiasts, Venturi and his colleagues often slip over the line between learning and celebrating. They oppose trees in Las Vegas for the same reason Turnpike aficionados oppose trees. Trees in Las Vegas would block the several-story-high neon signs of which Venturi is enamored. Trees would be a lie, a coverup.

We asked Steven Izenour, one of the authors of *Learning from Las Vegas,* whether his book helps us understand the New Jersey Turnpike. "What we were trying to do in *Learning from Las Vegas,*" Izenour replied,

> was to show that, amongst all the chaos in Las Vegas, there is order. We were trying to get people to see what they don't want to—or won't—see: that in all that jumble of roadside there is reason and order not unlike that which one finds in European cities, only of a different sort.
>
> The Turnpike *is* order. The landscape you see from the Turnpike is exciting— the refineries, the garbage mountains—but the Turnpike itself has attempted to rub out any vestige of individuality. The Turnpike isn't strip architecture—which is what Las Vegas is. The strip is personalized, localized, individualized (though it was more so before the franchises). So the strip—Las Vegas—has folk art aspects.
>
> The Turnpike was designed all at once. It doesn't feed off its surroundings. It *is* its surroundings. So the trip isn't important on the Turnpike the way it is on the strip. On the Turnpike you just wait to get to the end.

Nevertheless, Izenour expressed enthusiasm for the Turnpike. "I like it best," he said,

> in the wee hours—around 3:00 A.M. There's hardly any cars then, just trucks lining up, motors revving in the rest stops, getting ready to make the last haul into New York City. It's like Carl Sandburg. Powerful. And then I like it again at the end of the day when the trucks are heading back out of the city and beginning their trek across the country from where they came.
>
> The Turnpike is tidal. It goes up and down. The pace quickens and it slackens. It's as if the Turnpike is part of nature. It's alive.[19]

If Izenour is enthusiastic about the Turnpike, others have their doubts. Peter Blake, author of *God's Own Junkyard* and a critic of *Learning from Las Vegas,* says in an article called "Vulgarian Chic" that many of those who celebrate what he considers the detritus and banalities of American civilization "wouldn't be caught dead living next door to a McDonald's." Says Blake, the argument advanced by people like Izenour and Venturi is that,

> in an egalitarian democracy, the common man and woman are, by definition, King and Queen. Their taste—and not that of some elite—should and does

shape the physical environment in which such a democracy flourishes. Their
concerns tend to be with relatively simple and straightforward things: with in-
stant communication; . . . with things that work well in areas that affect
people—which, by and large, in a country of enormous distances, mean things
relating to fast, individualized transportation—superhighways, and their innu-
merable appurtenances and excrescences.[20]

Blake believes that aesthetics cannot thrive when efficiency and simplicity
and cheapness and the lowest common denominator are the exclusive
values of builders; or, to put it another way, when form remains entirely
subservient to function. The New Jersey Turnpike is an example of how the
exclusive reliance on form following function can produce an unwhole-
some aesthetics that does little to gladden the mind or heart.

The Turnpike is an artifact left over from the 1950s. In the future, America can do better. In recent years, America has developed an excellent cuisine, created a sophisticated wine industry, become the center of the art
world, expanded its understanding of the sexes and their roles, and begun
to develop an aesthetic in which the feminine view of reality is increasingly
an equal partner. In such an environment, the blight, and lack of imagination, and, yes, unrelievedly masculine aspects of the New Jersey Turnpike
appear ever more glaring and out of touch with intelligent, contemporary
ways of solving transportation needs.

Pop art enthusiasts and apologists for all forms of vernacular construction
are drawn to the New Jersey Turnpike because of what they consider its
"honesty." But the Turnpike is one of the largest public works projects in
history, and its negative aspects, like those of Las Vegas, are too pernicious
to be ignored.

In *The Highway and the City,* Lewis Mumford argues that our highways
"are not merely masterpieces of engineering but can be consummate works
of art; a few of them, like the Taconic State Parkway in New York, stand on
a par with our highest creations in other fields." This is because, Mumford
argues, from the inception of these projects aesthetics was not thought of as
something extra, as frivolous, but as an integral part of the total project. The
difficulty with such projects as the New Jersey Turnpike, Mumford feels, is
that "the engineer regards his own work as more important than . . . other
human functions . . . [and] does not hesitate to lay waste to woods, streams,
parks, and human neighborhoods in order to carry his roads straight to their
supposed destination." Highway engineers often lack "historic insight and
social memory." There are other considerations in building roads, Mumford
feels, than "aiming at high speed or continuous flow alone."[21]

The New Jersey Turnpike could have been built with both beauty and
efficiency; but beauty was never part of the plan. The Turnpike never envi-

sioned itself as a parkway, that is, as a linear park. It did not see one of its functions as delighting the eye or providing enjoyment to the motorist. It saw itself as a superhighway and its role as simply that of getting motor vehicles from one point to another with minimum cost and maximum efficiency.

But as Phil Patton, in his book *Open Road,* argues, "A superhighway could also be a superparkway." As early as 1943, the Highway Research Board insisted that beauty be a major component in "the design of every road, whether it be local, country, interregional or international." The best superhighways, says Patton, "occupy an area between engineering and landscape design," and there is no reason why all highways might not be "gardens for machines."[22]

Early highway builders, Patton argues, "were landscape architects before they were highway engineers. They laid out their roads by walking the line, physically traversing the terrain, as Olmsted [Frederick Law Olmsted, creator of New York City's Central Park] had in laying out his parks." But roads such as the New Jersey Turnpike were designed from maps and aerial photographs, not from the ground. In a chapter titled "The Triumph of the Engineer," Patton writes that the engineers were hardworking, well-meaning men. But they saw their "historical purpose in the accomplishment of the mundane raised to a huge scale." They were dedicated to the "highway system sometimes to the point of peripheral blindness." They suffered, in short, from tunnel vision.[23]

In 1979, Governor Brendan Byrne asked the New Jersey Turnpike Authority to improve landscaping on the road as part of the state's new emphasis on tourism. Said Byrne: "The Turnpike has been widely described as giving a distorted picture to the millions of motorists whose only knowledge of our state comes from their view of the Turnpike corridor. The successful development of creative landscaping approaches in the heavily industrialized sections of the corridor would be an accomplishment of national significance."[24]

The Turnpike Authority did, in response to the governor's request, plant seventy thousand trees, but many of them, because of their tender age, quickly died of pollution or entanglement in the tall, tough grasses that grow beside the Turnpike. It was a question of too little, too late. The Authority deserves credit for beginning to address an extremely difficult problem, but the Turnpike, for the most part, appears the same.

The New Jersey Turnpike is what it is—an industrial product of the late 1940s and early 1950s. It is an artifact, realized in steel and asphalt, that is an emblem of its time. It is the realization of its designers' concepts. They did not worry at all about how the Turnpike would look; they worried only about whether people would use it. It is said that during the first three months of operation, on many afternoons, Paul Troast would look out the window of the new administrative building at Exit 9 and actually count the cars as they went by—like an impresario checking the house from backstage. After the first full year, it was clear that the Turnpike would be a financial success: the bonds would be retired ahead of time.

Had the designers of the Turnpike known this in advance, they might have provided amenities found on many other roads—attractive trees and wildflowers, a grassy median on the northern stretches, materials of a more organic-looking, less industrial nature. They *might* have done this; it is not certain. For the Turnpike was built at a time when America had just passed through its greatest economic crisis and its greatest war. This history, coupled with the traditional American penchant for favoring utility at the expense of beauty, might have mitigated, in the early 1950s, against the creation of a road on which beauty was considered anything but superfluous regardless of what monies were thought to be available.

Governor Driscoll and his engineers wanted a road that would work and pay off the bond issue. They were willing to spend whatever it took to push the project through, but not a penny more. Everything for efficiency; nothing for beauty. New Jersey got what it deserved back in 1952—no more, no less.

The New Jersey Turnpike moves more vehicles more miles than any other roadway in the world. Its immense scale is an embodiment of the American love of bigness. Its twelve lanes—twenty if one counts the paved shoulders on both sides of each dual/dual—make it the widest road in the world. It could very well appear on lists of the Ten Wonders of the Modern World. But it offers little for the soul.

One thing the Turnpike dramatically does do is teach Americans some lessons in aesthetics. First, that beauty is not an extra; it is a necessity. And second, that if form follows function, beauty does not inevitably result. The Turnpike is dramatic evidence of the limits to the vernacular idea. The vernacular may have made sense in the early years of the nation's history, when conquering a continent did not allow for European niceties. But now, in the waning years of the twentieth century, America can no longer afford to define itself aesthetically in such a limited manner. The Turnpike tells us where we have been and where we need to go in the development of an American aesthetic of which we may be proud.

But, meanwhile, Jim Bob Calkins is a few miles down the road from where Junior had asked him "Why is it so ugly?" and Jim Bob is still thinking about the question. The roadway is rising up under the Pulaski Skyway now. The swamps are spread out in every direction. But these aren't swamps like any Jim Bob has known before. The chrome-colored water looks lethal. Rusting factories, surrounded by mud and reeds, stand around on blasted islands of high ground.

Still, Jim Bob is impressed. This is a powerful place. Ugly? Well, yes and no. It's too powerful-looking to be ugly. So what is it? Overwhelming? Unbelievable? Gross? Incredible? Magnificent? Ugly? All those things?

"Well," Jim Bob finally says to Junior, "I don't know if it's ugly exactly."

"Well, then, what is it?" Junior persists. "Smell it, Dad. It stinks. Smells like a fart."

"It's . . . well, it's . . ." Jim Bob struggles to come up with an answer for his son. To hell with it, he finally decides. This is too tough to explain to an eight-year-old. Besides, if he doesn't attend to the driving they're going to all get killed on this thing. An eighteen-wheeler is bearing down on their tail, like the sombitch plans to move into the backseat. Jim Bob can see the trucker glowering down at him. Jim Bob would like to get out of the car and hit the guy. Reluctantly, he swerves right, into the slow lane.

"You're right, Junior," he says, resigned. "You're right."

"No, Daddy," pipes up Sally Mae from the back seat. She hasn't said a word since they crossed the Delaware Memorial Bridge into New Jersey. Jim Bob thought his daughter was asleep. Sally Mae is a sophomore in high school. Everyone says she's "the sensitive one."

"You're wrong, Daddy," Sally Mae says. "It isn't ugly; it's incredible. I can't wait to tell the kids back home that I did the whole New Jersey Turnpike, the whole thing. This is the most righteous, awesome road in the world. It's obscenely great. Look at that out there: garbage mountains, toxic-waste city. Lordy, I love it.

"This is the rockers' highway. This is Bruce Springsteen's road. This is it. This is where it's happening. 'New Jersey Turnpike,'" she sings,

Ridin' on a wet night
Neath the refinery's glow
Out where the great black rivers flow.

"Bruce!" she yells out the window. "Bruuuuuuuuuce!"

The Future
of the Turnpike

Chapter  11

Futurist Alvin Toffler has a favorite story. Imagine a tribal group of Indians living in a remote jungle somewhere in South America. They have no knowledge of advanced civilization. They pass their days in their peaceful village beside a large river from which they draw their livelihood. The men teach their sons how to make fish traps. The women teach their daughters how to prepare food and weave baskets from the riverside reeds. There are no wars and no epidemics.

The fondest dream of the adults in this society is that their children's lives will resemble their own. Traditional songs and stories about the river are passed from generation to generation. This way of life is all they have known, and they have every reason to expect it to continue. Meanwhile, they are unaware that 300 miles upstream a giant dam is being built for a hydroelectric project. Their way of life is about to change abruptly, since their branch of the majestic river is soon to be reduced to a trickle, but they have no warning of the impending change. The moral of the story is obvious: we ignore the future at our peril.[2]

Toffler's story was very much on our minds when we asked William J. Flanagan, the recently retired executive director of the New Jersey Turnpike, about the long-term future of the roadway. It was a hot July afternoon at the Jersey shore in Allenhurst. We were sitting around on the porch of Flanagan's gracious seaside villa, strewn with white wicker furniture on the vast wraparound veranda, the yellow-and-white awnings shutting out the oppressive heat.

Flanagan, his white hair framing his red Irish face, thought a moment. He said that automobiles may be further downsized and may have to become more fuel-efficient. He also speculated about ways to utilize more fully the existing capacity of the roadway, such as instituting flexible hours for business and industry. However, he continued, "the Turnpike will be there forever. The bonds go beyond the year 2,000, so investors will make certain it stays open. There'll always be a Turnpike, because the automobile will continue to be a primary form of transportation."[3]

Certainly the short-term future for the Turnpike seems bright. The road is popular and heavily traveled. Toll revenues are plentiful enough to repay the bond holders and to maintain the roadway. The Turnpike has had no major embarrassments like the Mianus bridge collapse on the Connecticut Turnpike or the Schoharie Creek bridge collapse on the New York State

Thruway. Assuming the public accepts presently anticipated toll increases, sufficient revenue will accrue for expansion projects and improvements along the existing route.

Flanagan feels that the New Jersey Turnpike, rather than being an anachronism, is a model for the future in other states. He may be correct. In 1987 the U.S. Congress passed a highway act, one of whose provisions has enormous implications for the future of automotive travel in America. It calls for the construction of seven "pilot project" toll roads.[4] Basically these new toll roads are to be set up with the federal government providing 35 percent of the total construction cost as seed money. The remaining 65 percent may be raised through the sale of bonds.

The seven states slated to participate in the projects are said to be very enthusiastic about the plan, since they will be putting up no tax monies themselves. The Congress is pleased because it has to put up only a fraction of the total cost. The bond houses are pleased because, with federal backing, the projects carry very little risk and considerable potential profit. The highway construction industry is understandably delighted because the interstate program, with only 3 percent of its mileage awaiting completion, is officially slated to wind down in 1990.[5]

If new toll roads like the New Jersey Turnpike are to be built, this suggests the Turnpike could be very much a part of America's future. Projecting the future is always difficult, however, especially in the long term. We ourselves are uncertain about the long-term future of the Turnpike.

Therefore, we present three scenarios, or possible futures, for the reader to contemplate: (1) continued, if not endless, expansion, based on the availability of current fuels and minerals; (2) the "greening" of the Turnpike—that is, its gradual abandonment as it proves wasteful and out of sync with a newly emerging, less mobile culture; and (3) a high-tech future based on the development of new energy sources and alternative means of travel.[6]

Let us begin with the "expansion" scenario. In the 1980s, motorists began to complain that the New Jersey Turnpike was becoming horribly jammed just south of New Brunswick. Every weekday afternoon at 4:00 P.M. southbound traffic would start to back up at this spot. The reason? It was there that the Turnpike narrowed from twelve lanes to six. As a result, the Turnpike has embarked on a massive $2 billion widening program. Experts have called this the most ambitious expansion program ever undertaken by a toll road.[7]

Some futurists had hoped the computer revolution would make it possible for more office workers to stay at home. Marshall McLuhan, the Canadian scholar of mass media, predicted a world shrunk by modern advances in communications, where everyone was linked in a vast network of electronic systems. Nevertheless, road mileage in the United States has been increasing in recent years at a rate faster than that of the population, and this is especially true in New Jersey. In fact, New Jersey has more miles of paved road per capita than any other state in the nation. New Jersey is not only the most densely populated state but also the most densely "roaded."

Thus, of all Americans, New Jerseyans may most feel they have an inalienable right to adequate highway space. In 1988, traffic levels on the Turnpike increased 4 percent over the 1987 level.[8] Imagine such an increase, year after year.

The logical consequence is preditable: why restrict the Turnpike to its present twelve-lane configuration? (Indeed, as part of the current widening program, the highway *will* be expanded to fourteen lanes in the Elizabeth area.) In the future, the Turnpike may continue to expand indefinitely. In a few years, we could go from twelve lanes to eighteen. Then from eighteen to twenty-four. From twenty-four to thirty, from thirty to thirty-six . . . Perhaps William J. Flanagan was correct: there will always be a Turnpike. It will just get wider and wider. There are no logical limits to the growth process, because the Turnpike is the corridor of choice for anyone moving north or south along the eastern seaboard—especially for trucking companies because, for them, time saved is money earned. As long as the Turnpike is able to move the traffic quickly, truckers will pay high tolls without complaint in order to avoid congestion.

What would a thirty-six-lane Turnpike be like? If we calculate that each pavement lane will be twelve feet wide and that every cluster of three such lanes will require an inner shoulder of five feet and an outer shoulder of ten feet, we are talking about a roadway more than 600 feet wide. For purposes of comparison, such a roadway will be wider than the length of two football fields.

Because of its giant scale and magnitude, a thirty-six-lane Turnpike will take its place, alongside the Mississippi River, as one of the great wonders of America. The Big Asphalt will have the same imaginative power as the Big Muddy. Tourists from the Midwest will book narrated "motorcoach cruises" months in advance and take slides of their trips to show their friends back home.[9] The New Jersey Turnpike will bulk even larger in the American mind than it does today—featured in story, song, and film.

What would it be like to live alongside and travel on a thirty-six-lane Turnpike? Imagine a latter-day homeowner in Milltown, New Jersey, where

John Lazarczyk once lived, with his property abutting this giant Turnpike. It is springtime, and he has the day off from work. He pours himself a mug of coffee, exits through the thick, soundproofed back door, and strolls out to his backyard. He peers over his back fence. It is morning rush hour. The noise is thunderous. He sees myriad cars, vans, buses, and trucks rushing past. It is like having a grandstand seat at the Indianapolis 500. A few particles of carbon exhaust waft into his coffee mug. He flicks them out with his finger and they land near his wilted forsythia. Our homeowner's pulse quickens. He looks out toward the horizon, but there isn't any: just vehicles and more vehicles, taking up the entire landscape. And then he sees a bit of the unnaturally red sun rising feebly over the black exhaust clouds that dominate this vast automotive scene.

The Milltown homeowner has set aside the day to visit his father, a retired Turnpike toll collector, in St. Elizabeth's Hospital up in Elizabeth. His father had been complaining of shortness of breath and had gone into the hospital for some tests. He gets into his car. It is small, made of lightweight materials such as aluminum and plastics. Since it's a diesel, it takes a couple of minutes to start and warm up. But, then, a diesel gives him more mileage than his gasoline engine gave him years ago. Of course, diesels tend to be dirtier and noisier, but they're the only cars you can buy now that the Supreme Court has overturned the Clean Air Act as an unreasonable restraint on interstate commerce.

He drives up to Interchange 9 at New Brunswick to get on the Turnpike. He decides to take one of the twelve northbound lanes for cars, buses, and trucks. Driving in the six "CARS ONLY" lanes doesn't suit his style. As he enters the roadway, he tries to increase his speed to that of the passing traffic. It's tricky. His downsized car is not very powerful, and the trucks are big and closely spaced. He inches forward. The cigar-smoking driver of a huge Peterbilt swears, brakes a bit, letting him in. He's made it. He sighs with relief, chokes on the exhaust fumes surrounding him, and settles in for the long drive north.

For the "expansion" scenario to work, there will have to be continued political acceptance of the Turnpike *as a toll road.* But the future collection of tolls cannot be taken for granted. To be sure, after nearly forty years of unquestioned rule of its own domain, the Turnpike Authority has developed some sensitivity to citizen complaints and more public-relations savvy. But old habits die hard. Even in the late 1980s, the Authority still manages, despite the best efforts of its press officers, to come across as arrogant and out of touch with the ordinary citizen.

Occasionally, the Turnpike *has* been creative about softening its public image, as when it began, some years ago, offering free coffee, tea, or milk at its rest areas from 9:00 P.M. on New Year's Eve to 7:00 A.M. on New Year's Day. The Authority also instituted, in 1988, a new program of providing a modest amount of gasoline to motorists whose cars have run out of gas.[10]

These good efforts, however, were offset by such public-relations fiascos as the anger generated by William Flanagan's pension bonus and the suspicions triggered by the current widening program. In the future, if enough such episodes occur, there may be political pressure to abolish the Turnpike as an independent authority. If the Turnpike were to be taken over by the state Department of Transportation, it would have to compete, along with all other state highways, for scarce revenues, since it would no longer collect tolls.

In 1988, nearby Connecticut abandoned tolls on all highways and bridges in response to citizen complaints.[11] This could happen in New Jersey someday as well.[12] But it is more likely that the demise of the Turnpike as we now know it would come about otherwise: through a radically diminished supply of fuel. Two events in the 1970s gave us an idea of what may lie ahead. In 1973 the Arab oil embargo brought long lines at the gas station. Then in 1979, with the fall of the Shah of Iran, there were again disruptions in the gasoline supply.

The long-term future of the New Jersey Turnpike is closely linked to the future of the internal-combustion engine. Different modes of transportation have come and gone in the corridor, so what is to preclude new changes? In the nineteenth century, the Delaware and Raritan Canal was a thriving commercial waterway. Today, it is a linear state park, used by hikers, boaters, and anglers. The once-busy towpath is overgrown with trees. Who in the 1850s, when the canal was in its heyday, could have foreseen such a change? Until recently, there was no reason to doubt that the role of the automobile in American life would continue to expand. But this is no longer a certainty.

In the future, if the price of gasoline increased, people would begin to restrict their driving. Even if the Turnpike Authority maintained its independent status, there would still be a fundamental problem: as the volume of traffic fell, so would Turnpike revenues. As revenues fell, the Turnpike would be forced to increase tolls. During the gasoline shortage of 1979, the

Oklahoma Turnpike Authority raised its rates in an effort to compensate for traffic losses.[13] But increased tolls usually depress traffic volume, jeopardizing a toll road's ability to pay interest on its tax-exempt bonds. In turn, bond-rating services would lower the rating of roads like the Turnpike, making it more expensive to borrow new money.

The argument can be advanced that some people, in the face of a gasoline shortage, will pay any price for the available supply. This "inelasticity of demand" may well be true for Americans who love their dream automobiles. But experience shows that the federal government may step in and reorder people's priorities. In past oil shortages, the government allocated fuel supplies on a priority basis for agriculture and home heating. Agriculture has a strong claim on oil because of food production, and home heating oil can be a life-or-death matter in the Snow Belt.[14]

We learned in the 1970s that automobile gasoline consumption can also be restricted through "nuisance" rationing. One device is to allow only so many gallons for each gas station visit. Another is to restrict purchases to odd or even days of the calendar, depending on the last digit of the motorist's license plate number. When the supply is acutely short, gas stations simply lock their doors and send their attendants home.[15]

In New Jersey during the 1970s, a system of colored flags for gas stations was devised—a green flag indicated a full supply, a yellow flag indicated that only limited quantities would be dispensed, and a red flag meant that no gasoline was available. Under "yellow flag" conditions, motorists lined up for scarce gasoline. Sometimes, the lines stretched for blocks. In at least one widely reported incident, a motorist who allegedly tried to cut in line was shot.

It doesn't take much of an imagination to conjure up a future reminiscent of that in the 1982 film *The Road Warrior,* starring Mel Gibson as Max. In it, gasoline is the most precious commodity in the world. People kill without compunction for a few gallons of gasoline. Film critic Roger Ebert describes Max's role: "He happens upon a small band of people who are trying to protect their supplies of gasoline from the attacks of warriors who have them surrounded. Max volunteers to drive a tanker full of gasoline through the surrounding warriors and take it a few hundred miles to the coast, where they all hope to find safety. . . . The pursuers and defenders have various kinds of cars and trucks to chase or defend the main truck, and the whole chase proceeds at breakneck speed as quasi-gladiators leap through the air from one racing truck to another, more often than not being crushed beneath the wheels." [16] The film suggests that gasoline shortages may accompany the collapse of Western civilization.

In 1979, the relationship between gasoline and the Turnpike's survival became clear. In July, during the height of the summer vacation travel season, William Flanagan said publicly that the fear of gasoline not being available for long trips had cut deeply into Turnpike revenues. [17] If it happened before, it can happen again. This problem is a genuine cloud on the horizon for the Turnpike and other toll roads.

At present private automobiles make up 85 percent of traffic volume on the New Jersey Turnpike; trucks and buses account for only 15 percent. In the future, as gasoline supplies dwindle, a dramatic change in these numbers may take place. We do not begrudge motorists the comfort and convenience of the private motor car. It is pleasant to be able to go where you want, when you want, with your AM-FM casette – compact disc console playing the music of your choice. Compared with public transportation, the automobile offers more privacy, independence, and, for some, a greater sense of security. It is no wonder that urban planners have had difficulty persuading people to leave their cars at home and take the bus to work. In a future with scarce resources, private car usage may no longer be voluntary. Even if it is impossible to prohibit cars on rural roads, they will probably be banned from major highways or certainly those, like the Turnpike, where access is controlled.

Already in the 1980s, there are strong hints of this kind of change in our future. According to New Jersey Transportation commissioner Hazel Gluck, "We're in a big transition. We want to be moving people instead of cars. The State Department of Transportation is no longer just a highway department. When we look in an area, we no longer look just for road solutions, we're looking for transit solutions." [18]

State officials in the Department of Transportation believe public transit will have to be the centerpiece of future plans for the New Jersey Turnpike. Perhaps the first step will be voluntary car pooling with favored lanes. The next step will be mandatory car pooling for all lanes. At this stage, desperate motorists may hire passengers to come along for the ride just to fill their vehicles. Others may resort to trickery, like using inflatable dummies (as has already been reported in Washington, D.C.) to achieve the necessary number of passengers.

The next phase may see more vans and minibuses, which combine some of the convenience of the automobile with the fuel economy of the bus.

And, of course, there will be more buses, because buses have vast passenger capacity and efficient diesel engines.[19]

Whatever the vehicle mix, there would likely be a restructuring of the toll system on the Turnpike. The Authority's voracious appetite for tolls is presently fed by millions of single-occupancy vehicles, each of which pays a toll. In the future, as the system switches to larger vehicles, each with a number of passengers, the toll revenues may collapse. It will be unlikely that buses will generate tolls to equal those lost from private cars. At that point, the Department of Transportation, however unwillingly, will have to step in and take over a bankrupt Authority.

In our own time, traffic congestion is a terrible problem. But in this version of the future, it will be the absence of traffic that is typical. First fuel shortages will start to choke off economic prosperity. People will not be able to get to work. Goods will not get to market. The escalating cost of moving goods will affect every business and household. There will be no food on the supermarket shelves. The economy will spin into a severe recession and then a depression.

Pushing our time frame into the twenty-first century requires more imagination than speculation. Eventually, after much suffering and dislocation, the world would, one hopes, develop a viable new civilization. But by then the automobile will have become as obsolete as the stagecoach, and the Turnpike will be covered with weeds. Schoolchildren studying transportation will be taken by their teachers on walking tours of the overgrown roadway, much as tour guides explain the old Roman roads to tourists in Europe today. Teachers will explain to their classes about automobiles and roads and how it all used to be. Poets will haunt the melancholy route and imagine the ghosts of old truckers passing quietly through the night.

In this scenario, the Smithsonian Institution in Washington will have an exhibit featuring one of the last surviving tollbooths, salvaged from a junkyard in Elizabeth, a relic of days gone by. Collectors of Turnpike artifacts will gather at annual conventions to buy and sell scarce Turnpike ephemera such as decorated coffee mugs, Roy Rogers place mats, early issues of the Turnpike newsletter, and old toll tickets, which will cost perhaps a hundred times more than the toll would have been. The conventioneers will gather in a hotel lobby near one of the abandoned toll plazas and swap stories about the good old days. And they will remember—sometimes accurately and sometimes not—what the New Jersey Turnpike once was.

There is a third scenario we might offer: a high-tech one, based on the development of alternate fuels and means of travel. This has already moved beyond mere speculation. Solar automobiles are close to a reality, as are automobiles powered by plentiful hydrogen. Such vehicles will not pollute.

Autmobile expert Richard P. Brennan has written in detail of how the rapidly evolving technology of microelectronics and sensors might work in cars of the future. Radar warning systems and radar-assisted brakes, designed to perceive an approaching collision and apply the brakes faster than a human driver could, would be developed. The system would not necessarily eliminate collisions, but it would reduce the impact. Says Brennan, "It is possible that drivers of the future will have microprocessors monitoring their engine speed, temperature, workload, and acceleration; radar systems warning them of obstacles and applying the brakes when needed; and the roadway controlling traffic."[20]

Thus the Turnpike of the future would have greatly enhanced non-automotive uses. Already there has been speculation about its real estate and development potential, especially the air rights above the Turnpike. If we could build a sports arena over a railroad station in Manhattan, why not build enormous malls over the Turnpike in New Jersey?

As New Jersey becomes more densely populated, the state may closely resemble today's Japan. If we take the Japanese transportation example as instructive, we can predict greater use of magnetic levitation systems. Perhaps, in time, the inner roadway of the Turnpike in the dual/dual system will be given over to rail traffic and the outer roadway to bus and truck traffic. Still other lanes might be for Buck Rogers hovercraft, which skim over the surface of the Turnpike.

There are many futuristic innovations that are not speculative and remote. Based on presently known technology, we can readily envision a Turnpike of the future where patrons' vehicles are marked with bar codes on the left rear window that can be read quickly by optical scanners mounted at on-and-off ramps. Rates would vary not just based on distance, but also on time of day. By then, tolls would be very expensive, but substantial discounts would be offered to off-peak motorists. Patrons would simply receive a bill, based on their individual usage, at the end of each month. Imagine vehicles of the future equipped with an on-board navigational system that would allow motorists to turn driving duties over to their automated vehicles. The equipment would be programmed to avoid obstacles while following a system of lights embedded in the roadway. Such devices, mounted on all cars, would allow closer spacing of vehicles and greater roadway capacity.

Some of the most intriguing ideas about the future of transportation come from the world of science fiction. For example, viewers of the popular television series "Star Trek," which appeared from 1966 to 1969, will remember the transporter, which was capable of taking apart the molecules of the cargo (whether human beings, animals, or packages) and sending these molecules to predetermined coordinates in a remote place, where they were then reassembled. In a typical episode of "Star Trek," a crew member who had completed his mission might radio to Montgomery Scott, chief engineer of the Starship *Enterprise,* the now famous line, "Beam me up, Scotty!" Perhaps someday there will be a Turnpike where vehicles and their occupants are "beamed" from one end to the other.

Isaac Asimov, the celebrated science fiction writer, has speculated about the future of the New Jersey Turnpike. Asimov, educated as a biochemist, envisions a future with abundant solar and nuclear energy. With his gift for vivid imagery, Asimov writes:

> Since there will be no automobile exhaust to foul the air, the New Jersey Turnpike will be enclosed with glass on top to allow sunshine on pleasant days, and to ward off snow and rain in inclement weather. The glass will be fitted with artificial lights to be turned on at night.
>
> After dark, particularly, the New Jersey Turnpike will be a softly luminous strip weaving across New Jersey with people visible inside: sitting down, reading their papers and books, playing bridge on collapsible tables they've set up, eating dinner, or otherwise passing the time until the digital mile-indicators tell them it's time to be getting off.[21]

This auspicious prediction evokes an earlier America, when it was possible to imagine the industrial reality of a New Jersey Turnpike as congruent with our pastoral ideals. Asimov's futuristic Turnpike fits comfortably into the landscape. One can imagine a tableau where strawberries and asparagus and tomatoes and peaches grow alongside this environmentally gentle Turnpike, and where the machine coexists peacefully with the garden. Our spirits are lifted by Asimov's gentle prophecy. He foresees everything—except for one detail—before you exit, you will still have to pay your toll.

Notes

Preface

1 The Authority building is actually in East Brunswick Township, just outside the city limits of New Brunswick. The Authority, however, uses a New Brunswick mailing address and always refers to itself as being in New Brunswick. We do the same.

2 Joseph Sullian, interview of July 8, 1988. As this book was going to press, in very late 1988, Sullivan resigned as Turnpike Authority chairman to again seek the Republican nomination for governor of the state. He had sought it once before, in 1980. See P. L. Wycoff, "Sullivan Resigns as Turnpike Chief to Study Run for Governor in '89," *Newark Star-Ledger,* November 15, 1988, p. 25, and David Wald, "Sullivan to Test Water in the Governor's Race," *Newark Star-Ledger,* December 21, 1988, p. 3.

3 Fletcher Knebel, *Dark Horse* (New York, 1972).

4 New Jersey Turnpike Authority, "Annual Report, 1987" (Trenton, N.J.), chart facing p. 12.

5 Jerry Kraft, Operations Department, New Jersey Turnpike Authority, New Brunswick, N.J., interview of May 20, 1988.

6 Karen Levey, "Artist Shows Tough Love for Garden State on T-shirts," *New Brunswick Home News,* May 6, 1988, p. C-10.

7 Jill Ross quotation based on telephone interview with Peter Parisi on October 20, 1987. Both were formerly editors at *New Brunswick Home News.*

8 Jo Astrid Glading, "Turnpike Moves Cars and Offers Ringside View of the Worst of N.J.," *New Brunswick Home News,* June 12, 1988.

9 William Haywood, "The Garden (State) of Eden," in "Time Off" section of the *Princeton Packet,* May 11, 1988, p. 17.

10 Irvin Molotsky, "A Party for the Pike? Too Little, Too Soon," *New York Times,* October 21, 1979, p. NJ-14.

11 American Icons Symposium, March 4, 1987.

12 James P. Johnson, in *New Jersey: A History of Ingenuity and Industry* (Northridge, Calif., 1987), p. 385. We should note that within Johnson's statement is a quotation from Angus K. Gillespie, one of the authors of this book, though Gillespie's comment was made many years before we began to write *Looking for America on the New Jersey Turnpike,* and, in any case, it is Johnson's attention to Gillespie's comment, and seeming agreement with it, that is important.

13 Linda Keller Brown, "American Studies at Douglass College: One Vision of Interdisciplinarity," *American Quarterly* 27, no. 3 (August 1975): 342.

14 Paul Bradley quoted in Johnson, *New Jersey,* p. 385.

15 The reference is to *The Education of Henry Adams,* esp. chap. 25, "The Dynamo and the Virgin" (New York, 1931), pp. 379–390.

16 James Almoney, Public Information Department, New Jersey Turnpike Authority, New Brunswick, N.J., interview of November 1, 1979.

17 Letter from Horace A. Tani, Public Information Department, New Jersey Turnpike Authority, New Brunswick, N.J., October 29, 1979.

18   Arthur Warren Meixner, "The New Jersey Turnpike Authority: A Study of a Public Authority as a Technique of Government, 1949–1965" (Ph.D. diss., New York University, 1978).
19   Leo Marx, *The Machine in the Garden* (New York, 1967); Alan Trachtenberg, *Brooklyn Bridge: Fact and Symbol* (New York, 1965); John A. Kouwenhoven, *Made in America* (New York, 1949).
20   Robert A. Caro, *The Power Broker: Robert Moses and the Fall of New York* (New York, 1974).
21   Annmarie Hauch Walsh, *The Public's Business: The Politics and Practice of Government Corporations* (Cambridge, Mass., 1980).

Chapter 1
The Machine in the Garden State

1   Bob Curso, quoted in "A Day in the Life of the Turnpike," *Bergen Record,* December 6, 1987, sec. A, p. 1.
2   John Fasselly, telephone interview of January 25, 1987.
3   Marx, *Machine in the Garden,* p. 354.
4   Michael Aaron Rockland quoted in Dan Collins, "New Jersey Gets a Bit of Respect," *U.S. News and World Report* 102, no. 18 (May 11, 1987): 24. To be fair, there have been periodic attempts to think of New Jersey in more realistic terms. Governor Thomas Kean temporarily named New Jersey "the Invention State." Said Kean, "Scientists have long found that there is something in the air, water or whatever it is here in New Jersey that makes it a very fertile laboratory for their inventions" (David P. Willis, "Kean Renames Fertile Garden State," *Daily Targum* 118, no. 122 [April 8, 1987]: 1). Kean's statement, however, was greeted by laughter from many New Jerseyans who did not need to be reminded that there *is* something in the state's air and water.
        New Jersey's reputation as toxic headquarters of America is underscored in the film *Toxic Avenger,* advertised as "New Jersey's First Superhero," produced by Lloyd Kaufman and Michael Herz (Lightning Video, 1986).
6   Truck drivers as they enter New Jersey routinely say on their CBs, "Entering the Garbage State, ten-four."
7   Supporting this "western" idea is the existence in New Jersey of two permanent and well-attended rodeos.
8   From *The Life Story of Daniel Boone,* author anonymous but probably Boone himself (Dayton, Ohio, 1856), pp. 26, 27.
9   *Report by the New Jersey Conservation Foundation,* discussed in "Jersey Discovers Pains and Perils in Office Growth," *New York Times,* July 5, 1987, sec. 8, p. 10.
10   John Cunningham, *New Jersey: A Mirror on America* (Florham Park, N.J., 1978), p. 9.
11   Rebecca Felsen, "Carlin Sends Frenzied Audience into Fits of Laughter," *Daily Targum* 119, no. 130 (April 25, 1988): 1.
12   David Aaron Clark, "Turnpike Is a Road for Life," *Bergen Record,* September 10, 1985, p. 5. For further reading on the Jersey joke, see Michael Aaron Rockland, "What's So Funny about New Jersey?" *New Jersey Monthly* 3, no. 6 (April 1979): 49,

and "Jersey Culture and the Jersey Joke," *Journal of Regional Cultures* 4, no. 2 (Fall–Winter 1984) and no. 1 (Spring–Summer 1985): 1–13.

13 "A Day in the Life of the Turnpike," p. 1.
14 Patricia Ard, Morristown, N.J., interview of May 14, 1987.
15 Quoted in Tony Hiss, "Reflections: Experiencing Places—I," *New Yorker,* June 22, 1987, p. 63.
16 Alexis de Tocqueville, *Democracy in America,* 2 vols. (New York, 1954).
17 Philip Slater, *The Pursuit of Loneliness* (Boston, 1970), p. vii.
18 William Wallen, "Telling Drivers Where to Get Off," *New York Times,* October 26, 1980, N.J. sec., p. 32.
19 "A Day in the Life of the Turnpike," p. 1.
20 Rosemary Lyon, Washington, D.C., interview of December 12, 1987.
21 Barbara Sigmund, Princeton, N.J., interview of March 17, 1987.
22 Herbert Kells, New Brunswick, N.J., interview of April 6, 1988.
23 Wallen, "Telling Drivers," p. 32.
24 Ibid.
25 Pat Fitzgerald, Summit, N.J., interview of December 8, 1986.
26 David Cohen, telephone interview of January 12, 1987.
27 Barbara Sigmund, interview of March 17, 1987.
28 We attended one such talk at Douglass College on April 25, 1987, where Dan Patterson spoke.
29 Bishop, *Gems of New Jersey,* p. 290.
30 John McPhee quoted in "A Day in the Life of the Turnpike," p. 1.
31 Paul Overberg, "'Romance' Spans the Turnpike," *Bridgewater Courier News,* October 22, 1979, sec. A, p. 8.
32 Meixner, "New Jersey Turnpike Authority," p. 66.
33 Lynn De Filippo, New Brunswick, N.J., interview of June 3, 1986.
34 Ayn Rand, *Atlas Shrugged* (New York, 1967), p. 260.
35 Patrick Sarver, "Off the Beaten Track," *New Jersey Monthly* 13, no. 9 (July 1988): 70.
36 Judy Muller, "They Only Come Out at Night," *New York Times Magazine,* April 3, 1988, p. 34.

Chapter 2
Building the Pike

1 Franklin Gregory, "Al Driscoll's Leadership Put the New in Jersey!" *Newark Sunday Star-Ledger,* January 16, 1972, p. 37.
2 Cunningham, *New Jersey,* pp. 21–24.
3 Peter O. Wacker, *Land and People: A Cultural Geography of Preindustrial New Jersey: Origins and Settlement Patterns* (New Brunswick, N.J., 1975), pp. 1–55.
4 S. S. Moore and T. W. Jones, *The Traveller's Director; or a Pocket Companion,* 2d ed. (Philadelphia, 1804), pp. 17–18.
5 Joseph C. Goulden, *The Best Years: 1945–1950* (New York, 1976), pp. 3–6.
6 Kenneth T. Jackson, *The Crabgrass Frontier: The Suburbanization of the United States* (New York, 1985), pp. 232–233.

7 Alvin S. Felzenberg, "The Constitution of 1947," in *The Governors of New Jersey 1664–1974: Biographical Essays,* ed. Paul A. Stellhorn and Michael J. Birkner (Trenton, N.J., 1982), pp. 214–215.

8 Lillian M. Schwartz, telephone interview of July 13, 1988.

9 Russell Mullen, New Jersey Department of Transportation, Trenton, interview of December 21, 1979.

10 Alan Trachtenberg, *Brooklyn Bridge: Fact and Symbol* (New York, 1965).

11 David McCullough, *The Path between the Seas: The Creation of the Panama Canal, 1870–1914* (New York, 1977).

12 Lillian M. Schwartz, telephone interview of July 12, 1988.

13 Meixner, "New Jersey Turnpike Authority," p. 282.

14 New Jersey Turnpike Authority, "Annual Report, 1949," p. 22.

15 William H. Whyte, Jr., *The Organization Man* (New York, 1956); David Riesman, *The Lonely Crowd* (New Haven, 1953).

16 Sloan Wilson, *The Man in the Gray Flannel Suit* (New York, 1955).

17 Nathan Miller, *The U.S. Navy* (New York, 1977), p. 326.

18 The selections and assignments, beginning at the southern terminus, were as follows: J. E. Greiner and Company, Section 1, from Deepwater to Woodbury, highway and structures; Gannet, Fleming, Corddry, and Carpenter, Inc., Section 2, from Woodbury to state Route 38, highway and structures; Parsons, Brinckerhoff, Hall, and Macdonald, Section 3, from Route 38 to South of Hightstown, highway and structures; DeLeuw, Cather, and Company, Section 4, from Hightstown to the south bank of the Raritan River, highway and structures; Fay, Spofford, and Thorndike, Section 5, from south abutment of Raritan River bridge to south abutment of Morse's Creek bridge, highway and structures; Edwards and Kelcey, Frederic R. Harris, Inc., O. J. Porter and Company, Associated, Sections 6 and 7, from south abutment of Morse's Creek bridge to northern terminus of Turnpike at Route 6, highway; Ammann and Whitney, Section 6, from south abutment of Morse's Creek bridge to Belleville Turnpike; structures; and Howard, Needles, Tammen, and Bergendoff, structures from south abutment of Belleville Turnpike to northern terminus of Turnpike at Route 6, and also general consultant to the Authority for the entire project. From New Jersey Turnpike Authority "Annual Report, 1950," January 24, 1951, p. 24.

19 William L. O'Neill, *American High: The Years of Confidence, 1945–1960* (New York, 1986), p. 7.

20 Editors, *Civil Engineering,* January 1952, p. 25.

21 George W. Burpee, "Studies Plus Judgment Establish Economic Feasibility," *Civil Engineering,* January 1952, pp. 35–36.

22 New Jersey Turnpike Authority, "Annual Report, 1950," pp. 77–81.

23 Walsh, *The Public's Business.*

24 Paul L. Troast, "Limited-Access Turnpike Relieves Congestion," *Civil Engineering,* January 1952, p. 27.

25 Meixner, "New Jersey Turnpike Authority," p. 623.

26 Russell Mullen, interview of December 21, 1979.

27 Enoch R. Needles, "Revenue Bonds Build 118-Mile Expressway," *Civil Engineering,* January 1952, p. 34.

28 Ibid., p. 35.

29 Burpee, "Studies Plus Judgment," pp. 37–38.

30 Letter from Richard P. McCormick, July 13, 1988.
31 Charles M. Noble, "Standardized Design and Careful Scheduling Speed Construction," *Civil Engineering*, January 1952, pp. 40–50.
32 Ibid., pp. 41–42.
33 Ibid., p. 43.
34 O. J. Porter and L. C. Urquhart, "Sand Drains Expedited Stabilization of Marsh Sections," *Civil Engineering*, January 1952, pp. 51–55.
35 O. H. Ammann, "Deck Plate Girders of Record Span Adopted," *Civil Engineering*, January 1952, p. 61.
36 Ibid., p. 62.
37 Letter from James Fisher, August 10, 1988.
38 David Davidson, Bedminster, N.J., interview of November 7, 1979.
39 John R. Deitz, "Flexible-Type Pavement Selected," *Civil Engineering*, January 1952, p. 72.
40 Ibid., pp. 75–76.
41 Carl H. Peterson and Stanton C. Funk, "Mechanized Roadbuilding—the Answer to Tight Schedules and Tough Specifications," *Civil Engineering*, January 1952, p. 86.
42 Roland A. Wank, "Service Facilities Designed for Maximum Public Convenience," *Civil Engineering*, January 1952, pp. 89–93.
43 Kathleen Troast Pitney, telephone interview of July 13, 1988.
44 Kalman Seigel, "Jersey Dedicates Incomplete 'Pike,'" *New York Times*, December 1, 1951, p. 15.
45 Current policy of the New Jersey Turnpike Authority is not to permit billboards on the roadway right-of-way. Billboards on adjacent land, however, are under the control of the various adjacent municipalities. When the Authority is notified, as a neighbor, of zoning that may permit billboards to be erected, it is Authority policy to oppose such billboards at zoning hearings. Sometimes the Authority wins these cases; sometimes it does not. (Joseph A. Sullivan, chairman, New Jersey Turnpike Authority, New Brunswick, N.J., interview of July 8, 1988.)
46 Seigel, "Jersey Dedicates."
47 "Jersey Turnpike Will Help Realty," *New York Times*, January 20, 1952, sec. 7, p. 1.
48 David Popenoe, *The Surburban Environment: Sweden and the United States* (Chicago, 1977), p. 3.

Chapter 3
A River of Cash

1 Samuel B. Meli, in *Pike Interchange*, May 1988, p. 3.
2 "Report to Trustees for April and for the Twelve Months Ended April 30, 1988," New Jersey Turnpike Authority, New Brunswick, N.J.
3 "The New Jersey Turnpike: A Guide for News Media," Public Information Department, New Jersey Turnpike Authority, New Brunswick, N.J., June 1976, p. 16.
4 Meixner, "New Jersey Turnpike Authority," p. 495.
5 Ibid., p. 271.
6 Sergeant William Darough, Toll Collections, New Jersey Turnpike Authority, telephone interview of July 5, 1988.

7   Elizabeth Graffin, Personnel Department, New Jersey Turnpike Authority, telephone interview of July 5, 1988.
8   Meixner, "New Jersey Turnpike Authority," p. 348.
9   Discussion of toll collection procedures based on our attendance at Probationary Collectors Training Center at Milltown, N.J., February 11, 1987.
10   Discussion of patron without funds based on our experience at Interchange 18W, lane 16, on August 29, 1987.
11   Discussion of patron schemes to cheat toll collectors based on our interviews with Sergeant William Darough and Lieutenant Richard John Scott, February 11, 1987.
12   *Trailblazer,* July 1987, p. 2.
13   Lieutenant Richard John Scott, interview of February 11, 1987.
14   Letter to Governor Brendan Byrne, Trenton, N.J., April 10, 1975.
15   Letter from Robert E. Ramsen, director of Toll Collections, New Jersey Turnpike Authority, New Brunswick, N.J., April 16, 1975.
16   Letter from Robert E. Ramsen, November 23, 1976.
17   Michael Aaron Rockland, "Unhappy Motoring: One Turnpike Driver's Never-ending Search for the Perfect Toll Collector," *New Jersey Monthly* (August 1986): 80.
18   Letter from Sheldon W. Wernick, in *New Jersey Monthly* (October 1986): 8.
19   Letter from James Mustillo, in *New Jersey Monthly* (October 1986): 8.
20   Letter from Les Heimann, in *New Brunswick Home News,* July 3, 1988, p. H-2.
21   Marvin and Lillian Israel, Princeton, N.J., interview of November 19, 1987.
22   Senior Turnpike official who asked not to be identified, interview of May 20, 1988.
23   "Postal Pledge to Customers," U.S. Postal Service, poster dated October 1987.
24   The Turnpike's problem with customer service is part of a larger national problem. For example, see cover story, "The Hapless American Consumer: Why Is Service so Bad?" *Time,* February 2, 1987.
25   "Report to Trustees for April."
26   The river metaphor is based on the prose poem written by Pare Lorentz for his documentary film *The River.* See Benjamin A. Botkin, *A Treasury of Mississippi River Folklore* (New York, 1955), p. vi.
27   We do not mean to suggest that the money is misappropriated. Of course, the financial statements of the New Jersey Turnpike Authority are subject to periodic audits by independent certified public accountants. Other roadways, however, may have less money available for such overhead expenses as administration, data processing, risk management, professional fees, fiduciary fees, pension funds, and so on.

Chapter 4
The Authority of the Authority

1   Our informant wished to remain anonymous.
2   "The New Jersey Turnpike—In Brief: Facts about America's Busiest Toll Highway," Public Information Department, New Jersey Turnpike Authority, New Brunswick, N.J., 1976.
3   Meixner, "New Jersey Turnpike Authority," p. 280.
4   *Newark Star-Ledger,* May 10, 1988, p. 43.

5   *Bergen Record,* March 27, 1988, p. 21.
6   *Newark Star-Ledger,* May 18, 1988, p. 42.
7   *Bergen Record,* May 20, 1988, p. 17.
8   Meixner, "New Jersey Turnpike Authority," p. 277.
9   *Bergen Record,* January 10, 1988, p. 19.
10 Ibid., February 11, 1988, p. 17.
11 *New York Times,* February 14, 1988, p. 41.
12 *Trenton Times,* May 20, 1988, p. 18.
13 Letter to Michael Rockland from Kathleen Regiec, August 8, 1987.
14 Emily Alman, Highland Park, N.J., interview of March 21, 1988.
15 Joseph Sullivan, New Brunswick, N.J., interview of July 8, 1988.
16 Letter to the *Newark Star-Ledger,* April 18, 1988, sec. A, p. 15.
17 Guy Sterling, "State Spent $650,000 to Defend Two Troopers," *Newark Star-Ledger,* May 22, 1988, sec. 1, p. 35.
18 Eric Neisser, telephone interview of August 11, 1988.
19 Arthur Miller, telephone interview of May 31, 1988.
20 "A Day in the Life of the Turnpike," *Bergen Record,* December 6, 1987, p. 1.
21 Quoted in ibid.
22 Steve Giegerich, "City on Wheels," *Asbury Park Press,* July 8, 1984, sec. C, p. 1.
23 Joseph Sullivan, interview of July 8, 1988.
24 William Flanagan, Allenhurst, N.J., interview of July 11, 1988.
25 "A Day in the Life of the Turnpike," p. 53.
26 John McKeegan, "Drug Busts Bursting Out All Over on Turnpike," *New Brunswick Home News,* October 21, 1987, sec. A, p. 1.
27 Giegerich, "City on Wheels," p. 2.
28 Words and music by David Kent Little, Crazy Cajun Music, 1970.
29 Mary Hufford, interview of November 12, 1979. This interview is in the California State University, Fullerton, Oral History Program Archives.
30 John McKeegan, "More Arrests for Weapons on State Roads," *New Brunswick Home News,* May 10, 1988, p. 1.
31 Austin O'Malley, New Brunswick, N.J., interview of February 13, 1987.
32 Caesar Clay, New Brunswick, N.J., interview of February 13, 1987.
33 Giegerich, "City On Wheels," p. 2.
34 *Woodbridge News Tribune,* February 12, 1987, p. 37.
35 David Levinson, New Brunswick, N.J., interview of June 10, 1987.
36 Docket No. A-3312-86-T4, Superior Court of New Jersey, Appellate Division.
37 Ibid.
38 *Popular Photography* 94, no. 10 (October 1987): 17.
39 Robert Seidenstein, "The Turnpike and the Constitution," *New Jersey Law Journal,* March 12, 1987, p. 398.
40 As we write this, however, New Jersey state police officers have petitioned President Reagan to pardon Messerlian and Wolkowsky, with the support of state police Superintendent Colonel Clinton Pagano and State Attorney General Carey Edwards. For their part, the New Jersey Civil Liberties Union has objected to the manner in which the petition was circulated—on the job and at public expense. Eric Neisser, legal director of the NJCLU, points to "pressure" being brought on state troopers to sign the petition.

Finally, the family of Joseph Topolosky has been phoning and writing the White House to oppose any pardon for the troopers. Says Richard Freysinger, Topolosky's half brother, the state police still aren't "playing by the rules." See Guy Sterling, "ACLU Faults Troopers on Petition," *Newark Star-Ledger,* November 30, 1988, p. 30. See also Guy Sterling, "Jersey Troopers Petition for Pardons of 2 Comrades Convicted in Killing," *Newark Star-Ledger.* November 27, 1988, sec. 1, p. 18.

41   Arthur Miller, interview of May 31, 1988.

Chapter 5
Waiting for a Tow

1   Mark DiGiovanni, Somerset, N.J., interview of September 6, 1987.
2   Ibid.
3   All the interviews with Rutgers University students took place during a single session, November 5, 1987.
4   Pete DiGiovanni, Somerset, N.J., interview of September 6, 1987.
5   Mark DiGiovanni, interview of September 6, 1987.
6   Letter from Mrs. Charles Beeber, *New Brunswick Home News,* August 26, 1987, p. A-16.
7   Mark DiGiovanni, interview of September 6, 1987.
8   Letter from Joseph A. Sullivan, Chairman, New Jersey Turnpike Authority, in *New Brunswick Home News,* September 16, 1987.
9   Paul Onto, Patron Services Supervisor, Garden State Parkway, telephone interview of July 5, 1988. Posters are displayed throughout most of the year at the three major restaurants (Montvale, Monmouth, and Cheesequake) and the other six restaurants as well. The complete policy is detailed in booklets of regulations available at tollbooths.
10   Mark DiGiovanni, interview of September 6, 1987.
11   Letter from Tina Harris in *Tow Times,* December 1986, p. 8.
12   Tom DeHaven, New Brunswick, N.J., interview of December 10, 1987.

Chapter 6
Road Hazards

1   Bruce Springsteen, "Wreck on the Highway," from *The River,* CBS, QCL-S, 22203-2.
2   For example, the *Bergen Record* carried an otherwise excellent feature story on the Turnpike, "N.J.'s City on Wheels: True Grit and Imagery," on December 6, 1987. A prominent bar graph on page 52 made the statement, "In a Five-State Comparison the New Jersey Turnpike Ranked: No. 1 in Traffic Accidents." This statement was incorrect. It reported 4,489 accidents for the New Jersey Turnpike in 1986, which was correct. But it reported less than 2,000 accidents for the New York State Thruway; the actual number should have been 6,175. Thus the bar graph was misleading. The Turnpike should have been ranked second, not first. Accident statistics for 1985 compiled by International Bridge, Tunnel, and Turnpike Association show the New York State Thruway first, with 5,914 accidents; the Illinois Tollway second, with 5,450 accidents; the Garden State Parkway third, with 4,110 accidents; and the Turnpike

fourth, with 3,781 accidents. Major toll roads with fewer accidents include the Florida Turnpike, the Kansas Turnpike, the Maryland Turnpike, the Massachusetts Turnpike, the Atlantic City Expressway, the Ohio Turnpike, the Oklahoma Turnpike, the Pennsylvania Turnpike, and the Richmond-Petersburg Turnpike.

4   "The New Jersey Turnpike: A Guide for News Media," April 30, 1987, p. 13.
5   Gordon Bishop, "Gems of New Jersey: Roads," *Newark Star-Ledger,* September 2, 1984, sec. 2, p. 1.
6   Overberg, "'Romance' Spans the Turnpike," p. 8.
7   Unpublished data provided by the Operations Department of the New Jersey Turnpike Authority show 178,838,750 vehicles traveled the 144 miles of the roadway during 1986 for an average annual density (vehicles per mile) of 1,241,936. In 1986 there were 4,489 accidents, yielding an accident rate of 0.36 percent, lower than the corresponding figures for the New York State Thruway, the Ohio Turnpike, the Pennsylvania Turnpike, and the Florida Turnpike. Briefly, accident rate is calculated as follows: if we take the number of vehicles and the roadway length, we can compute the average density. If we then divide the number of accidents by the average density, we arrive at the accident rate.
8   "The New Jersey Turnpike: A Guide for News Media," pp. 13, 13-A.
9   Harry R. DeSilva, *Why We Have Automobile Accidents* (New York, 1942), pp. 270–271.
10 Noble, "Standardized Design," p. 40.
11 Phil Patton, *Open Road: A Celebration of the American Highway* (New York, 1986), pp. 132–133.
12 DeSilva, *Automobile Accidents,* p. 272.
13 Noble, "Standardized Design," pp. 40–41.
14 Jerry Kraft, Operations Department, New Jersey Turnpike Authority, New Brunswick, N.J., interview of November 12, 1979.
15 "The New Jersey Turnpike: A Guide for News Media," p. 9.
16 "Automatic Surveillance and Control on the New Jersey Turnpike," undated and unpaginated booklet, Sperry Systems Management, Great Neck, N.Y.
17 *Bergen Record,* December 6, 1987, p. 52.
18 *New York Times,* October 25, 1973, p. 1.
19 *New York Daily News,* October 25, 1973, p. 1.
20 Ibid.
21 *New York Times,* October 25, 1973, p. 1.
22 Ibid.
23 Ibid.
24 *Reader's Digest,* November 1974, p. 112.
25 The most complete report is the National Transportation Safety Board's *Highway Accident Report, 1973* (USTD 1.117; 75-2), "Series of Motor Vehicle Collisions and Fire under Limited Visibility Conditions."
26 Jerry Kraft, interview of May 20, 1988.
27 Ibid.
28 Unpublished tables provided by the Operations Department of the New Jersey Turnpike Authority show, for example, that in 1952 the fatality rate was 6.11; in 1962 it was 2.17; in 1972 it was 1.93; and in 1982 it was 0.96.
29 Jerry Kraft, interview of May 20, 1988.

30   Ibid.
31   Ibid.
32   Ibid.
33   Ibid.
34   Ibid.
35   Joseph "Bo" Sullivan, chairman, New Jersey Turnpike Authority, New Brunswick, N.J., interview of July 8, 1988.

Chapter 7
Over the Fence

1   The material in this chapter concerning John Lazarczyk and his family is taken from interviews conducted on June 12, 1987, and February 15, 1988.
2   Shirley Yannich, "Milltown, New Jersey," unpublished 1983 paper, p. 3.
3   Jim Lukach, "Milltown: Snow on the Angel's Wings," unpublished 1987 paper, p. 1.
4   *Over the Fence,* March 1981, p. 2.
5   Jean Citrino Adubato, New Brunswick, N.J., interview of March 12, 1987.
6   Sal Maggio, a neighbor of John Lazarczyk, confirmed that the Turnpike had promised to compensate for these expenses and then reneged. "In the beginning they were telling us they would pay closing fees, moving costs, etc. It winds up that they decided not to give anybody anything." See Elizabeth Mitchell, "Milltown's Residents by Pike's Path Doubt Agency Buyout Pledge," *New Brunswick Home News,* January 20, 1988, p. A-13.
7   Jon McKeegan, "Costly Road to 'Pike Sound Barrier," *New Brunswick Home News,* May 9, 1988, p. 1.
8   Ibid.
9   Ibid.
10   "A Day in the Life of the Turnpike," *Bergen Record,* December 6, 1987, p. 53.
11   New Jersey Turnpike Authority press release no. 15, May 15, 1986.
12   See John McKeegan, "Turnpike Widening Will Mean Landfill Closures, Waste Cleanup," *New Brunswick Home News,* October 21, 1987, p. B-2.
13   Meixner, "New Jersey Turnpike Authority."
14   William Flanagan, Allenhurst, N.J., interview of July 11, 1988.
15   *Over the Road* 3, no. 4 (September–October 1971): 2–3.
16   Louise Saul, "Overdeveloped Sense of Justice Explains Emily Alman's Leadership," *East Brunswick Sentinel,* July 21, 1971, p. 12.
17   Material in this chapter concerning Emily Alman is taken from extensive interviews with her in Highland Park, N.J., on October 23, 1979, and March 21, 1988. The authors wish to thank her for making all of the files of the Concerned Citizens of East Brunswick available to them.
18   "What Road Will the Governor Take?" *New Brunswick Home News,* June 12, 1971, p. 22.
19   Letter from Emily Alman to Ann Klein, March 29, 1972.
20   We have no evidence connecting the Turnpike and organized crime, although we did hear this charge more than once in the course of our research. Whether there is any

truth to the charge or not, some New Jerseyans obviously believe it, perhaps, in part, because of New Jersey's long history of corruption.

Some of our readers may think we should have followed up on this subject. At an early stage of our research, however, we determined that we could not write both a broadly cultural work, which endeavors to explain the significance of the Turnpike, and at the same time pursue in-depth investigative reporting.

21   *East Brunswick Sentinel,* July 19, 1972, p. 3.
22   "Quote of the Week," *East Brunswick Spokesman,* May 15, 1971, p. 1.
23   Louise Saul, "For Whom the Turnpike Tolls," *East Brunswick Spokesman,* May 5, 1971, p. 1.
24   "Turnpike Fight a Courageous One," *East Brunswick Sentinel,* May 12, 1971, p. 18.
25   Marsha Gates, "Citizens Ecology Group Wins Turnpike Suit," February 6, 1972, sec. CJ, p. 1.
26   "Turnpike Authority Chairman Raps Opponents of Widening," *New Brunswick Home News,* September 29, 1971, p. 1.
27   *East Brunswick Spokesman,* May 26, 1971, p. 22.
28   Press release of September 13, 1972.
29   Agreement between the Authority and the Homeowner, sec. 4, Covenant Not to Sue and Release and Limitation on Consultants.

Chapter 8
Rest Area Culture

1   Calvin Trillin, "The Road Not Taken: I Don't Want a Jersey Turnpike Rest Area Named After Me," *Newark Star-Ledger,* April 6, 1987, p. 15.
2   The Turnpike Authority informs us that the thirteen names were chosen from among seventy-four submitted by Turnpike staff members. (Letter from Jean Citrino Adubato, public relations specialist, to Michael Aaron Rockland, August 11, 1987.)
3   Ibid.
4   Recently, the second annual Joyce Kilmer Bad Poetry Contest was held at Columbia University in New York. The evening opened with a reading of "Trees," each line of which was loudly greeted with snickers. Various parodies of Kilmer's "Trees" were introduced, including Ogden Nash's famous

I think that I shall never see
A billboard lovely as a tree
Indeed, unless the billboards fall
I'll never see a tree at all.

One student offered: "I think that I shall never see / An M.B.A. so D.O.A. as you." Jeff Rake, a sophomore at Columbia, won second prize in the contest, a crown fashioned from twigs from a holly bush at the Joyce Kilmer Rest Area on the New Jersey Turnpike. See Gregory Jaynes, "No, Not a Curse but a Jersey Prize for Worst Verse," *New York Times,* December 5, 1987, p. 29.
5   Trillin, "The Road Not Taken."
6   Philip Roth, *The Counterlife* (New York, 1986), p. 237.

7   For more information on Turnpike concession pricing, see P. L. Wyckoff, "Toll Road Burgers on a Roll," *Newark Star-Ledger,* November 20, 1988, sec. 1, p. 18.

8   Paul B. Brown, "Pike 'Guides' Motorists to Jersey Sights," *Newark Star-Ledger,* July 31, 1979, p. 7.

9   James Fisher, who taught in the American Studies Department at Rutgers in the 1986–1987 academic year and now teaches at Yale.

10   Or, rather, the writers of this book know it spans the Raritan, but Turnpike bridges are designed in such a bland and featureless way that motorists are usually not aware of crossing them. This makes for smooth traffic flow but total obliteration of major landscape features.

11   Wallen, "Telling Drivers," p. 32.

12   Every ten years the Turnpike Authority puts concessions in the rest areas out to bid. Howard Johnson's was the first concessonaire of Turnpike food. Since the fifties, Ho-Jo's has been followed in quick succession by the Gladieaux Corporation, Marriot Hot Shoppes, and the combination of Roy Rogers and Bob's Big Boy, both of which are actually owned by Marriot.

13   Undated letter to Michael Aaron Rockland, received June 4, 1987.

14   "A Day in the Life of the Turnpike," *Bergen Record,* December 6, 1987, p. 52.

15   Undated letter to Michael Aaron Rockland, received April 12, 1987.

16   The fantasy reported in Friday's book is as follows: "I am speeding on the New Jersey Turnpike. Two policemen stop me. I tell them I will 'do *anything* not to get a ticket.' They make me get in the back seat and spread my legs wide (one of them is in the front seat, the other in the back seat). While one of them drives, the other one has me. They take turns. And then they meet a friend and he gets in on it too" (*My Secret Garden: Women's Sexual Fantasies* [New York, 1973], p. 114).

Chapter 9
So Bad, It's Good

1   Dan Fogarty, "N.J. T'pike Blues," an unpublished song, used with the permission of the artist. The rest of the lyrics are worth repeating:

It's 39 lanes going both ways
39 lanes you see
39 lanes my friend for you
And 39 more for me.

(Chorus)

14 miles from Exit 12
There's a sign that I have read
About a man that died right there
With a gas mask on his head.

(Chorus)

The Admiral Halsey stop ahead
It doesn't have a bar
But I'll get gasoline for me
And some coffee for my car.

(Chorus)

2 Jim Coleman, Princeton, N.J., interview of September 18, 1987.

3 Words by Joseph Cosgriff, performed by the Phil Bernardi band, copyright © 1981.

4 So much so that four state assemblymen introduced a bill (Assembly No. 3012, January 11, 1983): "An Act designating a State jingle: Be it enacted by the Senate and General Assembly of the State of New Jersey: (1) The State jingle shall be the words and music of the song entitled 'I Like Jersey Best,' composed by Joseph Cosgriff." One fears the assemblymen did not listen as carefully to the song as they might have.

5 "You Can't Catch Me," words and music by Chuck Berry, Big 7 Music Corporation (BMI), 1956.

6 "America," words and music by Paul Simon, Charing Cross Music, Inc. (BMI), 1968.

7 Bruce Springsteen, "Born to Run," *Born to Run* album, Columbia Records, 1975.

8 Springsteen, "Jungleland," *Born to Run.*

9 Springsteen, "State Trooper," *Nebraska* album, Columbia Records, 1982.

10 Springsteen, "Open All Night," *Nebraska.*

11 Fletcher Knebel, *Dark Horse,* p. 11.

12 Ibid., pp. 32, 13.

13 Ibid., p. 280.

14 Ibid., p. 327.

15 Tom De Haven, *Jersey Luck* (New York, 1980), p. 66.

16 Ibid., pp. 67, 71–73.

17 Richard Ford, *The Sportswriter* (New York, 1986), pp. 81, 97, 98.

18 Ibid., p. 60.

19 Ibid., p. 59. It is noteworthy that in both De Haven's and Ford's novels the central figures are excited by the idea of flaunting sexuality in the face of authoritarian toll collectors. We discussed this issue—the Turnpike as sexual turnon—in Chapter 8, "Rest Area Culture."

20 Ibid., p. 26.

21 Ibid., p. 270.

22 Allen Ginsberg, "Don't Grow Old," in *Mind Breaths, Poems 1972–1977* (San Francisco, 1977), pp. 79–87.

23 Ginsberg, "Bayonne Entering NYC," in *The Fall of America, Poems 1965–1971* (San Francisco, 1972), pp. 35–39.

24 Ginsberg, "Howl," in *Howl and Other Poems* (San Francisco, 1959), pp. 9–22.

25 Gale Abrahamsen, "N.J. Turnpike," unpublished poem. Used with permission.

26 See *New York Times,* January 10, 1988, NJ sec., p. 22.

27 Marguerite Doernbach, Trenton, N.J., interview of February 3, 1988.

28 Samuel Wagstaff, Jr., "Talking with Tony Smith," *Artforum* 5, no. 4 (December 1966): 17.

29 Barbara Westergaard, *New Jersey: A Guide to the State* (New Brunswick, N.J., 1987), p. 395.

30 Lila Locksley, "A Flowery Mountain by the Pike," *Bergen Record,* August 16, 1988, sec. A, p. 31.

31 In addition to those mentioned, the following are films with segments filmed on the Turnpike: *The Heartbreak Kid* (Warner Brothers, 1970); *Ginger* (Ginger Productions, 1970); *Bogart Slept Here* (Warner Brothers, 1975); *Heroes* (FRP Productions, 1977); *Century III Series* (U.S. Information Agency, 1977); *Fast Break* (Columbia Pictures, 1978); *The Wanderers* (Aspen Productions, 1978); *The Paul Simon Movie* (Paul Simon Productions, 1980); *Honky Tonk Freeway* (Kendon Films, 1980); *Body Heat*

(The Ladd Company, 1980); *I Ought to Be in Pictures* (Twentieth Century-Fox, 1981); *The Muppets Take Manhattan* (Henson Associates, 1983); and *Wise Guy* (MGM/UA, 1985). In addition, the Turnpike has been used extensively for made-for-television films and weekly television shows. A complete list is available from the New Jersey Turnpike Authority, New Brunswick, N.J. 08903.

32   Marguerite Doernbach, "Observations." Used with permission.

Chapter 10
Tunnel Vision

1   James Ahearn, "Beauty Is More than Asphalt Deep," *Bergen Record,* January 10, 1985, sec. C, p. 1.
2   Our colleague's attitude is by no means atypical. An assumption virtually universal among intellectuals is that aesthetics is synonymous with the fine arts. Thus, in a recent special issue of *American Quarterly* devoted to "Modernist Culture in America" (39, no. 1 [Spring 1987]), public works were not even mentioned. Ten articles dealt with poetry and painting and fiction and criticism, as if these were the only fields in which modernism has expressed itself.
3   Wright quoted in Patton, *Open Road,* p. 127.
4   John Kouwenhoven, "What's American about America," in *Beer Can by the Highway* (Baltimore, 1988), p. 41.
5   Letter from John A. Kouwenhoven to Michael Aaron Rockland, April 14, 1987. We wrote back suggesting "Robert Mosesism" instead of "Baron Haussmanism." Letter from Michael Aaron Rockland to John A. Kouwenhoven, May 15, 1987.
6   From the essay "Beauty," in *The Literature of Architecture,* ed. Don Gifford (New York, 1966), p. 116.
7   Elder Frederick Evans of the Shaker settlement at New Lebanon, speaking to Charles Nordorf. Quoted in John Kouwenhoven, *The Arts in Modern American Civilization* [a more recent, and less fortunate, title of Kouwenhoven's classic *Made in America*] (New York, 1967), p. 93.
8   Frank Lloyd Wright, "Building the New House," in *An Autobiography* (New York, 1977).
9   Tom Wolfe, *From Bauhaus to Our House* (New York, 1981).
10   Tocqueville, *Democracy in America,* 2:50.
11   Charles Dickens, "It Would Be Well if They Loved the Real Less and the Ideal More," in *America in Perspective,* ed. Henry Steele Commager (New York, 1947), p. 104.
12   Lewis Mumford, *The Highway and the City* (New York, 1953), p. 247.
13   Ahearn, "Beauty," p. 1.
14   "A Day in the Life of the Turnpike," *Bergen Record,* December 6, 1987, p. 1.
15   David Aaron Clark, "Living between Exits on the New Jersey Turnpike," *Targum Sun,* July 31, 1985, p. 9.
16   Overberg, "'Romance' Spans the Turnpike," p. 8.
17   Russell Roemmele, quoted in Clark, "Living between Exits," p. 9.
18   Robert Venturi, Denise Scott Brown, and Steven Izenour, *Learning from Las Vegas* (Cambridge, Mass., 1977).
19   Steven Izenour, telephone interview of January 5, 1988.

20 Peter Blake, "Vulgarian Chic," *Interior Design* (September 1986): 262.
21 Mumford, *Highway,* p. 247.
22 Patton, *Open Road,* pp. 71, 72, 128.
23 Ibid., pp. 141, 143–151.
24 Letter from Brendan Byrne to Turnpike Authority chairman Francis G. Fitzpatrick; quoted in Paul B. Brown, "Turnpike Facelift Asked," *Newark Star-Ledger,* March 21, 1979, p. 23.

Chapter 11
The Future of the Turnpike

1 William J. Flanagan, Allenhurst, N.J., interview of July 11, 1988.
2 Alvin Toffler, *Learning for Tomorrow: The Role of the Future in Education* (New York, 1974), pp. 3–4.
3 William Flanagan, interview of July 11, 1988.
4 The original seven pilot projects were slated for California, Texas, Pennsylvania, South Carolina, Georgia, Florida, and Colorado. Since then two states have been added— West Virginia and Delaware. As this book is being written, only the Pennsylvania project has been started. It is the Mon Valley Project, running from the Pittsburgh area south to the West Virginia line.
5 John J. Hassett, International Bridge, Tunnel, and Turnpike Association, Washington, D.C., telephone interview of January 12, 1989.
6 For more on futures methodology, see Theodore J. Gordon, "The Current Methods of Futures Research," in *The Futurists,* ed. Alvin Toffler (New York, 1972), pp. 164– 189. "Greening" refers to *The Greening of America* by Charles Reich (New York, 1970), a book that predicted the abandonment of technology and the embracing of new, more humane values.
7 *Newark Star-Ledger,* January 2, 1989, p. 18.
8 Ibid.
9 A self-guided tour is already available on audio cassette tape. See "Ride with Me: New Jersey-Delaware I-95 South" (1987) by RWM Association, P.O. Box 1324, Bethesda, Maryland 20817.
10 Jean Citrino Adubato, telephone interview of January 11, 1989.
11 The major impetus was a tragic accident. In December 1983 a truck driver accidentally rammed a line of cars waiting to pay their tolls at Stratford, Connecticut. Seven people were killed. The public was outraged. If the cars had not stopped to pay their tolls, there would have been no accident. Political pressure to abolish the toll stations mounted. The toll stations on the Connecticut Turnpike were closed forever at 11:00 P.M. on October 9, 1985. By 1988, all tolls throughout Connecticut, including bridge tolls, were eliminated. To pay for it, Governor William O'Neill proposed an increase in the gasoline tax of nine cents per gallon to be phased in over a ten-year period. Expensive as it is, the governor was able to persuade the legislature that his plan was a more broad-based way to collect revenue. (Source of information was a telephone interview with William Keish, Connecticut Department of Transportation, Hartford, on June 30, 1988.)
12 Is it possible to duplicate the Connecticut experience in New Jersey? Some public

policy critics have argued that if tolls were eliminated, the state of New Jersey would become eligible for more federal money. We asked a senior official, Russell Mullen, at the New Jersey Department of Transportation about this idea. He told us that New Jersey would get more federal money if tolls were eliminated, but not enough to be helpful. Mullen said, "There is no way for New Jersey to shift its tax burden elsewhere. Elimination of tolls is not a panacea."

He went on to explain that New Jersey now gets about $35 million per year from the federal government for restoration, rehabilitation, and resurfacing interstate highways. To this sum New Jersey adds another $10 million, yielding about $45 million per year to maintain the current interstate highways in the state, which Mullen says is about half of what is actually needed.

"What if the New Jersey Turnpike were added to the interstate mileage?" we asked. "How would this increase the allocation?" Mullen explained that the formulas were elaborate and complicated, but the most that could be expected would be $3 or $4, maybe $5 million per year. This money is negligible compared to the $182 million per year now being collected by the Turnpike. Since the Turnpike has heavy traffic, it has heavy maintenance costs. To shift the Turnpike to the state government, without keeping the toll structure, would be extremely expensive. The lost money would have to come from someplace. Connecticut was able to replace its lost money by a whopping nine-cent-per-gallon tax increase. Whether the New Jersey legislature has the political will to do the same remains to be seen.

The New Jersey Turnpike is different from the Connecticut Turnpike in that a larger part of its heavy volume is made up of out-of-state motorists. It is the corridor: they cannot avoid it. When these people stop on the Turnpike to buy gasoline, they pay a state gasoline tax that goes to maintain other New Jersey roads. The maintenance of the Turnpike has already been paid for in their toll. In other words, the current arrangement benefits New Jersey residents by shifting much of highway maintenance cost to nonresidents. (Source was a telephone interview with Russell Mullen, New Jersey Department of Transportation, Trenton, June 30, 1988.)

13 *New York Times,* July 31, 1979, p. 51.
14 Lester R. Brown, Christopher Flavin, and Colin Norman, *Running on Empty: The Future of the Automobile in an Oil-Short World* (New York, Norton, 1979), pp. 80–83.
15 Ibid., p. 91.
16 Roger Ebert, *Roger Ebert's Movie Home Companion* (New York, 1989), pp. 534–535.
17 *New York Daily News,* July 26, 1979, p. 10.
18 *Newark Star-Ledger,* May 1, 1988, p. 12.
19 Brown et al., *Running on Empty,* pp. 64–69.
20 Richard P. Brennan, "The Automobile's Endangered Future," *Futurist* (October 1979): 323.
21 Isaac Asimov, "Isaac Asimov Designs Turnpike 2000," *New Jersey Monthly* 2, no. 6 (April 1978): 56.

Index